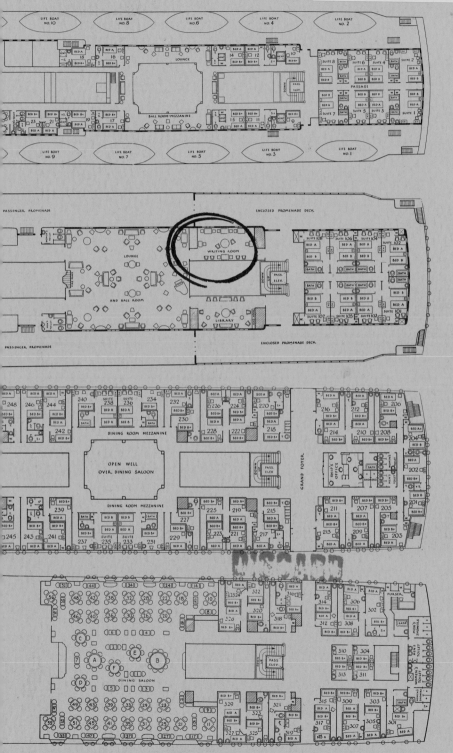

THE
MORRO CASTLE

HAL BURTON

THE VIKING PRESS   NEW YORK

First published in 1973 by The Viking Press, Inc.
625 Madison Avenue, New York, N.Y. 10022

Published simultaneously in Canada by
The Macmillan Company of Canada Limited

SBN 670-48960-3

Library of Congress catalog card number: 72-91826

Printed in U.S.A.

to Frank O. Braynard
of the South Street Seaport Museum
Master marine historian

ACKNOWLEDGMENTS

First, to the scores of survivors, many of them quoted in this book, whom I interviewed. While they were experiencing the *Morro Castle* disaster, as a newspaperman I was alternately covering the story for the New York *Daily News* and writing the accounts of other reporters assigned to its various phases. Like them, I have a vivid memory of the whole tragedy.

While it would be possible simply to quote from interviews given at the time by these survivors, it has to be remembered that these were obtained in a moment of extreme stress, while they were still in shock. The passage of time may have obliterated some memories, but those that remain represent the gist of the whole experience.

I have tried to confine myself to *factual* evidence. So many rumors and suspicions surrounded the disaster that some of them have inevitably been seized upon as fact. I have explained what *could* have happened—that the *Morro Castle* fire *might* have been arson, that revenge *might* have been a motive, but that positive, viable proof does not exist. The story itself is sufficiently enthralling without seizing on the obvious but unprovable villain, Radio Operator Rogers.

I owe thanks to the following persons, not mentioned in the body of this book, who helped me trace down survivors or establish that they were dead: Mrs. Helen Lund, Marine Engineers' Benefit Association; Bernard Raskin, National Maritime Union; Jerry Capp, Masters, Mates and Pilots Union; Joseph P. Glynn,

American Radio Association; Patrick O'Keefe, Veteran Wireless Operators' Association; Joseph Mezzara, Sandy Hook Pilots; Colonel George Amodeo, New Jersey Air National Guard; Sergeant Leo Coakley, Historian, New Jersey State Police.

Also Floyd Barger, executive editor, and Joseph McCarthy, chief librarian, New York *Daily News;* Sydney T. Gruson, senior vice president, and Robert Medina, chief librarian, *The New York Times,* for throwing open their immense files of clippings and photos, and Barry Facter, of the Bayonne (New Jersey) *Times,* who covered the several trials of Radio Operator Rogers; as well as Thomas Tighe, general manager of the Asbury Park (New Jersey) *Press* and John Notman, general manager of the Trenton (New Jersey) *Times.*

My gratitude as well to Thomas Gallagher, author of the first *Morro Castle* book, *Fire at Sea* (Rinehart, 1959) and to Simon & Schuster, publishers of Isobel Leighton's *The Aspirin Age,* which included a chapter on the disaster written by the late William McFee, an authority on maritime matters.

Hal Burton

CONTENTS

(*Illustrations follow p. 86*)

THE *MORRO CASTLE*

1

THE HAVANA FERRYBOATS

The New York harbor pilots, who wait at anchor off Sandy Hook, New Jersey, to guide every ship into port, called them "the Havana ferryboats." The term was affectionate, not pejorative. These were no blunt-nosed workhorses like the ferries from Staten Island to Manhattan, butting their way across the upper harbor day and night. They were glistening cruise liners 508 feet long, sister ships named *Morro Castle* and *Oriente*. With their shiny white hulls and sharply raked twin black funnels, they were the fastest and most modern boats plying between New York and Cuba in the 1930s.

The pilots used to say, "You can practically set your watch by the *Morro* and the *Oriente*." Around 5:00 A.M. eastern standard time, generally at three-day intervals, one ship or the other would come steaming past Scotland Lightship, four miles off the point of Sandy Hook, close to the anchorage of the pilot boat. A pilot would climb down a ladder into a waiting motor yawl, the *Morro* or *Oriente* would reduce speed. As the yawl drew alongside, a hatch at water level on the liner would slide open. The pilot would step aboard, ride an elevator to the navigating deck, shake hands with the captain, and then take command for the last fifteen miles up the narrow harbor channel. As sleepy passengers began to awaken, the ship's motors would pulse once more, driving her toward the Statue of Liberty and the downtown skyscrapers.

No ships on the East Coast worked so hard or so efficiently. Out of 365 days a year, the *Morro* and the *Oriente* rarely remained in port a total of more than 25 days, and then only for necessary repairs and inspections. Excluding a few longer cruises, the *Morro* loomed over the horizon at Scotland Lightship every Saturday morning. She made a brief pause at Quarantine,

3

where the Verrazano–Narrows Bridge now spans the lower harbor, taking aboard Immigration and Customs inspectors. But by 8:00 A.M. on the dot she was docked at the foot of Wall Street.

Yawning passengers strolled down the gangplank, not at all surprised to be arriving on schedule. Puffing tugs pushed barges alongside. Cranes unloaded a typical cargo: leaf tobacco, Cuban cigars, cotton bags, pineapples, grapefruit, and cattle hides. By 2:00 P.M. a new group of passengers was boarding; at 3:30 P.M. bon voyage parties were cut short by the call, "All ashore that's going ashore." The lines holding the ship to the pier were cast off, and other lines were made fast to waiting tugs fore and aft. With a long, bellowing blast that ricocheted between the skyscraper walls, the ship was pulled backward into the East River and righted on her course down the harbor at exactly 4:00 P.M. The tugs were dismissed at Quarantine, the pilot was dropped off Scotland Light, the dunes of Sandy Hook receded in the distance, and the *Morro* was on her way back to Cuba. It was routine and reassuring. The *Morro* and the *Oriente* were far from the biggest ships to make New York home port, but they were among the most affable. As a young reporter for the New York *Daily News,* I met them more than once at Quarantine to interview distinguished passengers, or possibly a movie actress perched smiling on the rail for the benefit of the press photographers. There was something relaxed about these two boats . . . or so it seemed at the time. Perhaps it was the polished welcome of the skippers, or perhaps the tanned relaxation of the passengers. These were most definitely pleasure ships.

On the night of Friday, September 7, 1934, chased by a storm of near-hurricane force, the *Morro Castle* was completing her 174th round-trip cruise, homeward bound past the Delaware capes. Rain squalls and gusts of wind buffeted the wheelhouse, where Chief Officer William F. Warms could barely make out the lighthouse at Cape May, with its two long and two short flashes at regular intervals. It was 7:30 P.M. In the grand ballroom, two decks high, passengers were seated for the Captain's Dinner, a last-night fixture on every cruise, enlivened by balloons, paper hats, and the strains of "Auld Lang Syne." However, Captain Robert R. Wilmott was not presiding at his table. He had died suddenly in his stateroom on the top deck. Chief Warms, exhausted after twenty hours on duty, stunned by his responsibilities, became the new captain of the *Morro Castle.*

The death of a liner's captain at sea was, in those more innocent days, like the death of a dictator. The shipping unions were weak, jobs were scanty, and the captain was an absolute ruler of his ship. A few minutes before seven thirty Cruise Director Smith had been summoned, without explanation, to the captain's quarters. A few minutes later Smith stepped up to the bandstand, silenced the orchestra, and told the passengers, "We have sad news." He canceled the party, but told the passengers, "You are welcome to entertain yourselves." Some passengers, made seasick by the roll of the boat, went promptly to bed. Others organized small parties in their staterooms. A few stayed up long enough to smell smoke trickling from a locker in the writing room, At 2:56 A.M. an officer opened the locker door and found the interior a seething mass of flames. He pulled a fire alarm nearby, setting bells clanging all over the ship. By 3:00 A.M. the midsection of the *Morro Castle* was an inferno. Half-clothed passengers, cut off from the lifeboats, fled to the after end of the ship. Most of the crew fled to the forward end. By 3:30 A.M. one of the safest ships in the American merchant marine was powerless, sheeted in flames, at anchor three miles off Sea Girt, New Jersey. Passengers leaped from the stern into a swirling sea. Crew members escaped from the bow in lifeboats. Of 318 passengers, 86 were lost, or 29 per cent of the total aboard. Of 231 crew members 49 were lost, or only 18 per cent of the total aboard.[1] The disparity was startling.

––·– ––·–

How did it happen? Why did it happen? To understand the reasons, it is essential to understand the times. The *Morro Castle* was born during the great American boom and died during the great American Depression. She and all those aboard on her final cruise were products of an era that began with financial euphoria and ended with financial ruin for millions of people.

In 1928, when the *Morro Castle* story began, it was still America the bountiful. Calvin Coolidge as President of the United States and Herbert Hoover as Secretary of Commerce were riding the crest of the biggest boom in history. On the New York Stock Exchange prices never stopped climbing. "The sky's the limit," happy brokers told their customers. Everyone from the corner barber to the bank president was in the market, paying only 10 to 20 per cent down for stocks, a procedure known as buying on margin. Even dour Andrew W. Mellon, who as Secretary of the Treasury seemed the very portrait of financial conservatism, had grudgingly admitted that prosperity was here to stay.

[1] Figures from U.S. Coast Guard official report.

New York City, the fortress of American capitalism, was bursting with free spenders. In the theater and nightclub district around Times Square, the streets blazed with light, and speakeasy hostess Texas Guinan greeted her customers with the cry, "Hello, sucker!" Down on Wall Street, home of the Stock Exchange, new skyscrapers dwarfed the Gothic tower of the Woolworth Building, at sixty stories long the tallest office building in the world. From its observation deck sightseers watched the white wakes of great liners furrowing the waters of New York harbor. At piers up and down the East and Hudson rivers, they could see ships of all sizes loading or discharging cargo. On the East Side, along Park Avenue, apartment buildings for the rich were going up at a feverish rate. Using New York as a measuring stick, America seemed to have a boundless future.

There was one flaw in this perfect image, but balanced against national prosperity it was a hairline flaw. The American merchant marine was close to bankruptcy. A fleet of a thousand ships that ferried troops and munitions to Europe during World War I had shrunk to a handful of ocean liners and rusty freighters. Shippers preferred the cheaper rates and more regular service of the foreign flag lines—British, German, French, Japanese, or Scandinavian. In passenger service the United States Lines still operated the mammoth *Leviathan,* biggest liner in the world, as well as the sleek *United States,* one of a distinguished family to carry the flag. Both rarely left the harbor with a full passenger list. American sailors, underpaid and surly, did not reflect the cheer or glamour to be found on ships like England's *Mauretania* or the smart French liners.

In Congress, though not in the country at large, the state of the merchant marine caused some mild disquiet. Members from coastal ports were under pressure from shipping interests for money to build more modern ships. Some from inland states felt a touch of frustration, remembering America's great past as a shipping nation. For in the middle 1800s Yankee clippers with billowing sails were the speed queens of the sea. In the early 1900s President Theodore Roosevelt brought the Navy to such size and strength that it became known as "The Great White Fleet" and sailed around the world to proclaim America's new role as a maritime power. By 1928 this fleet matched in size the British Navy, formerly unchallenged. On the surface, its admirals exuded confidence, but in private they were expressing concern to Congress and the President. A powerful Navy could not function without sufficient supply ships. To carry troops, there must be new liners fast enough to outrun lurking submarines.

Congress responded in the early spring of 1928. A Merchant Marine Act was voted, known as the Jones-White bill in tribute to its sponsors. A construction fund of $250 million was authorized. American companies could borrow 75 per cent of the cost of a ship and pay it back over twenty years at a nominal interest rate of 3 per cent. To assure safety and reliability, the plans for every ship had to be approved by the Navy. Passenger liners had to be designed for quick conversion to troop transports. To keep the merchant marine healthy, postal subsidies were increased for ships that carried the mails. Airmail service was still ten years distant.

Of all the shipping lines in the United States, the one most badly in need of new liners was the New York and Cuba Mail Steamship Company, also called the Ward Line, which had been carrying mail, passengers, and cargo to and from Cuba since 1840. Its venerable flagships, the *Orizaba* and the *Mohawk*, took seventy-two hours to wallow 1168 miles down the East Coast from a pier at the foot of Wall Street to a wharf in the harbor of Havana. Fast, modern liners like the *Mauretania* and *Europa* and older but roomier ships like the Cunarders *Caronia* and *Carmania* cut deeply into the cruise profits of the Ward Line. The Havana trip, once a restful excursion for sedate couples and men with business interests in Cuba, suddenly turned into a "whoopee cruise," a nonstop drinking party lasting from five to nine days. The price was incredibly cheap—$65 to $75 with two nights ashore in a Havana hotel, less than $100 for a longer stay.

At such bargain rates, almost anybody could afford the trip. It was tailor-made for the "jazz generation," in loud revolt against the proprieties. Young stenographers, secretaries, telephone operators, and salesgirls poured aboard the cruise ships. They scandalized the conventional by smoking cigarettes in public and wearing skirts that ended a little above the kneecap, a brevity considered almost indecent. Aboard ship they could be sure of finding single young men to dance the Charleston with them, romance them on the moonlit decks, and squire them to Havana bars, nightclubs, and beaches. Havana with its wide streets, palm trees, and glistening white buildings was the most wide-open city in the Western Hemisphere. Who from home would know what these liberated young couples were up to, and who would care? Certainly not the tolerant Cubans.

A cruise to Cuba or perhaps Bermuda permitted escape from the clammy hand of the prohibition law. Back in the States bootleg liquor was adulterated and sometimes poisonous. Drinking had to be done furtively, except in speakeasies, but there was always the chance of a raid by prohibition agents.

In a dry America joy was scarcely unrestrained. By contrast, on a whoopee cruise, the ship's bars opened just three miles offshore, the territorial limits of the United States. Bonded liquor was only 25 cents a shot. Most passengers stayed up until the 3:00 A.M. closing time before staggering off to bed. In the morning they awoke, bleary-eyed, to the breakfast bugle at 7:30 A.M. If possible, the trip back from Havana was even more bibulous than the trip down. Rum in Havana was only four dollars a gallon, but could not legally be brought into the United States. The last night before docking in New York, many people simply stayed up all night to finish the last drop. In fairness, there were also quieter passengers aboard—older couples who enjoyed the sea and ignored the noise, sport fishermen who had angled for huge marlin and tuna off the Cuban coast, and a regular contingent of Cuban and American businessmen. Now and then there were sedate excursions by social clubs from East Coast cities, whose members drank prudently and retired quietly to bed.

All this trade was lifeblood to the Ward Line, which was part of a conglomerate of shipping companies. The parent company was the Atlantic, Gulf and West Indies Steamship Lines, whose stock was one of the few not selling at a premium on the Stock Exchange. The conglomerate also included the Clyde-Mallory Line, plying to Miami, Charleston, Jacksonville, and Galveston; the Southern Steamship Company, between Philadelphia and Houston; the Porto Rico Line, from New York to Porto Rico and Santo Domingo, and the Santo Domingo Line. Their ships primarily carried cargo. They could wait a bit for new ships, but the financially pressed Ward Line could not. Long before the Merchant Marine Act became law, it was apparent that some form of government financing would be provided. Atlantic, Gulf and West Indies forehandedly commissioned the distinguished naval architect, Theodore E. Ferris, to design twin cruise and cargo ships, sisters down to the last detail. One was to be named the *Morro Castle*, after the stone fortress and lighthouse that guards the entrance to Havana harbor. The other was to be christened the *Oriente*, after a Cuban province.

Among naval architects tall, reserved Theodore Ferris seemed most certain to satisfy the joint requirements of the Navy and the shipping line. His firm had already designed 1800 boats, including hundreds of freighters hastened into action during World War I. He was given carte blanche to provide the maximum in speed, safety, efficient cargo handling, and luxurious accommodations. Each ship was to carry 489 passengers in first and tourist class, as well as 240 crew members and officers. Speed meant money to the Ward Line. Mail subsidies from the United States and Cuban governments could amount to $750,-000 a year if Ferris succeeded in reducing the time of the trip each way from seventy-two hours to sixty hours. He did succeed. Speed meant a faster arrival and more time ashore for the whoopee cruisers. Transatlantic liners vied for the "blue riband" to fly from the foremast as evidence of the quickest trip from New York to England and France. There was no "blue riband" on the Havana run, but cruise passengers took pride in riding on the fastest ships on the East Coast.

Safety was another requisite, though it meant more to the Navy and the Ward Line than it did to the customers. Who could conceive of trouble on a trip running so closely parallel to the American shoreline? For almost the entire distance, Ward liners traveled not more than from five to nine miles from the coast, close enough so that passengers in their deck chairs could see the surf on the beaches during the day and read the sparkling flashes of lighthouses and lightships all the way from Sandy Hook, at the entrance of New York harbor, past the brilliantly illuminated hotels of Miami Beach. Less than ninety miles of open water had to be crossed from Key West before Ward Line ships, a little after dawn, slid silently past the Morro Castle and then slowly up to the company pier in downtown Havana. On this crowded waterway, where ships by the dozen from the Gulf of Mexico, the Caribbean, and Latin America moved parallel, with wireless and Coast Guard stations at regular intervals, what could possibly go wrong?

Theodore Ferris was not this casual about it all. The "unsinkable" *Titanic* had struck an iceberg and gone to the bottom sixteen years earlier because her bulkheads were not watertight. On the *Morro Castle* there were nine watertight bulkheads with automatic doors. Because fires at sea were common, Ferris took special precautions. Tubes to transmit the smell of smoke connected all fifteen cargo holds with the navigating center of the ship. Automatic foam extinguishing systems were installed in the holds and the engine room. Electric sensor systems, illuminating a panel in the wheelhouse, would spotlight a fire in the 217 staterooms, the ship's offices, or the crew's quarters. There were automatic doors the full width of the ship at 130-foot intervals to close off fires, as well as additional automatic doors in the public areas.

There was one significant omission. No fire detectors were installed in such places as the lounge and ballroom, the writing room, the library, the deck veranda tearoom, or the dining room. From 7:00 A.M. until late at night, there were passengers in these areas. Watchmen "clocked in" regularly at a dozen checkpoints. There were forty-two hydrants along five decks, thousands of feet of fire hose, and more than one hundred individual fire extinguishers. A dozen lifeboats, holding 826 persons, could be lowered to the water by a touch on a lever. A dozen life rafts, eighteen life buoys, and 850 life preservers brought the total rescue capacity to 1918, nearly four times the maximum possible number of passengers and crew.

Ferris, confident that he had designed two superliners, in every respect the safest afloat, completed his plans in record time. In mid-autumn 1928 the United States Shipping Board granted a loan of $3,422,181 for construction of the *Morro Castle* and a similar amount for the *Oriente*. Including the company's investment, the total cost of the sister ships was estimated at $9 million. Herbert Hoover, in one of his last statements as Secretary of Commerce, expressed modest satisfaction that the rebuilding of the merchant marine was at last under way.

In January 1929 the work whistle at the yards of the Newport News (Virginia) Shipbuilding and Drydock Corporation let out a long blast, the signal for workers to return to their jobs after months of joblessness. Welders and riveters, engineers and steamfitters—all the hundreds of men required to build two big ships—trooped into the yards and in parallel drydocks began to create the gaunt steel skeletons of the *Morro Castle* and the *Oriente*.

"It was a great day and a proud day," recalls John P. Comstock, then a young employee of the company and subsequently its chief naval architect. "The whole town was cheering." The two senior captains of the Ward Line took up temporary residence in Newport News. They lived with the building crews every step of the way, memorizing every detail of construction. Thin, peremptory Joseph E. Jones was to be skipper of the *Morro Castle* until the *Oriente* was ready to sail. Then he would exchange commands with Robert R. Wilmott, a mild and fatherly ex-Englishman who had been with the line for twenty-six years. Wilmott never forgot his days in Newport News. Regular passengers on the *Morro Castle,* guests at the captain's table, grew bored by his reminiscences. One of them asked him:

"Captain, what in the world will you do if you ever have to leave the ship?"

"In that case," said Wilmott, roaring with laughter, "I'll take her with me."

Robert J. Smith, the cruise director, overheard the exchange as he passed the table. He still remembers, with a shudder, that humorous prophecy.

The *Morro Castle* and *Oriente* were half-sheathed with steel plating, and cranes were lowering their modern turboelectric engines into place when the stock market collapsed. It was "Black Thursday," October 29, 1929. Before the end of the year $15 billion in stock values had been lost. The Depression had begun, but even in early 1930 its full impact had not been felt. It was still possible to hope, and in this atmosphere of forced optimism the *Morro Castle* was launched. A special train from New York, making stops for dignitaries at Philadelphia and Washington, pulled into Newport News, carrying three hundred shipping men and government officials. Among the latter was the older brother of the FBI's J. Edgar Hoover, Dickerson N. Hoover, who was Inspector General of the Steamboat Inspection Service. Slightly more than four and a half years later, he would be feeling his way through the burned and blackened hulk of the *Morro Castle,* trying to fathom what had happened. On this gala day he was merely part of the backdrop to the official sponsor, an immensely excited sixteen-year-old named Ruth Eleanor Mooney. Her father, Franklin D. Mooney, was president of the Atlantic, Gulf and West Indies Steamship Lines.

It was a raw day, with a temperature of 44 degrees. Overnight the thermometer had dropped below 32 degrees, freezing the grease on the ways. Ruth Mooney [2] remembers exactly what she was wearing: "A black and rust-colored dress reaching down below the calf, and a heavy brown silk coat." Exactly at noon she swung a bottle against the prow of the ship, secretly worrying whether the bottle would break. "It would have been bad luck otherwise," she says. "That was an old seafaring tradition." The bottle did break, in a shower of golden spray. Even though it was still the prohibition era, she strongly suspects that the

[2] Now Mrs. Thurston H. Smith of Long Island.

bottle held champagne. "It certainly foamed like champagne."

Hesitantly at first, and then gathering speed, the *Morro Castle* slid backward down the ways and surged out into deep water. To the sound of ship whistles, factory sirens, and workmen cheering the boat they had built, America's newest and fastest liner was well and truly launched. On May 15, 1930, the *Oriente* was to follow. The *Morro* lived up to all expectations. On August 8, 1930, she developed a speed of just under 21 knots in her trial run. Just fifteen days later she was to make her maiden voyage. Weeks beforehand, every stateroom had been booked, though August was normally a time of light travel to Cuba. When the *Morro* tied up at Pier 13 East River on August 20, a thousand admission cards for those who wanted to inspect the ship were exhausted by noontime. The morning after she finally departed for Cuba—carrying, among others, Warden and Mrs. Lewis E. Lawes of Sing Sing Prison—the New York *Herald Tribune* headlined, "New $5 Million Ward Liner Is Expected to Set Speed Record," and she did. She covered the 1168 southbound miles in fifty-eight hours forty minutes and the northbound leg in fifty-eight hours.

Another newspaper, the Brooklyn *Eagle,* said: "*Morro Castle* is Ward Line's Defi to Cunarders *Caronia* and *Carmania,*" and quoted maritime experts as saying she was by far the finest and most luxurious ship built in the United States for the foreign trade. "The interior of the ship," said the *Eagle,* "suggests the spaciousness of a transatlantic liner. At night, lanterns will illuminate the white outlines of the ship while an orchestra plays for dancing in a realistic moonlight glow."

The arrival in Havana was more spectacular than the departure from New York. Captain Jones, driving his vessel at top speed, reached Morro Castle Lighthouse at 2:37 A.M. and had to anchor until Customs opened. The ship docked at 7:45 A.M. to the salutes of harbor craft and the cheers of a crowd lining the harbor quays. As each woman came off, she was handed a bouquet of flowers; each man was given a box of Havana cigars. At noon President-Dictator Gerardo Machado was host aboard ship to the entire diplomatic corps. It was a far bigger day for Havana than the maiden sailing had been for blasé New York. Cuban newspapers affectionately recalled the first *Morro Castle,* since scrapped, which had made her maiden voyage to Havana in 1900. Passengers, ashore on this trip for four days, took guided tours to the beaches and nightclubs, the bars and the inner city, the Presidential Palace and the parks.

A few of them, perhaps, flipped through a fifty-page anniversary brochure issued by the Atlantic, Gulf and West Indies Line, hardly noticing a brief paragraph on page 11: "During its years of continuous service, the Ward Line has lost but two ships, and it has never lost a passenger."

2
HOW HAPPY A SHIP?

The last cruise of the *Morro Castle* took place in 1934, the second worst year of the Depression. Some 11,340,000 men and women were jobless in the United States. Yet there still were people who could afford a trip to Cuba, and among them were 138 members of the Concordia Singing Society, mainly German-Americans from Brooklyn. In earlier years they had chartered trains to Niagara Falls and to the Chicago World's Fair during the Labor Day weekend, but this time they had chosen a ship. As the *Morro* pulled out into the East River, the men of the society massed along the rails of B Deck, just behind the veranda tearoom, and joined in the solemn strains of "Nacht des Herrn" ("Night of the Lord"), a traditional farewell to friends and relatives waving good-bye from the pier. These were stable, comparatively prosperous couples, most of them middle-aged or older, but there were youngsters among them, too. Herman Torborg, a former New York State senator, had brought his fifteen-year-old nephew, John Torborg, and his eighteen-year-old niece, Ruth Torborg.

"I remember how cheerful it all seemed and how beautiful the ship was, all white and spotless," Ruth Torborg recalls. Once unpacked and settled in their staterooms, the brother and sister embarked on an awestruck tour. An elevator, one of two aboard the ship, took them to A Deck, the sun deck. Above and forward of them they could see Captain Wilmott in his white uniform and gold-braided cap standing on one of the wings, looking downriver as the pilot, inside the wheelhouse, directed the course of the ship along the channel. Inside, passing deluxe bedrooms, they came out on a balcony overlooking the first-class lounge and ballroom, paneled in white-painted mahogany. One flight down, using a staircase that wound around the elevator, they came into the first-class smoking room, with a dome of leaded glass overhead. Every public room was richly trimmed with rare

14

wood or plywood paneling, and each was of a different period—Italian Renaissance in the first-class smoking room, Empire design in the library and writing room. In the deck ballroom, with its great casements opening to a view of the ocean, the architect had outdone himself. The orchestra platform was a copy of a Viking warcraft, with a sea horse for a figurehead, rising above a series of banked war shields. In all, there were five passenger decks, topped by the bridge deck, two decks for cargo, and an engine room that extended through four decks amidship, housing the boilers and turbogenerators that drove the *Morro*'s twin propellers. With a breadth of nearly 71 feet and a draft of 29 feet, she was a steady ship, one that could sail safely through any storm.

The young Torborgs, like all the other passengers, could not visit the working sections of the ship. Their contacts were with the stewards, the pursers, the cruise directors, and the waiters, who exuded cheerfulness because cheerfulness meant bigger tips. The men in dungarees who worked belowdecks in the engine room or along the decks were silent and anonymous, but they were not happy. The pay, even for the Depression, was minimal.

Colin Houston, a young Scottish immigrant, remembers that his wage was $10 a week—"and I sent six dollars of that to my mother." Houston was an able-bodied seaman. Steward Sirl Boggetti, whose father was chief steward of the Ward Line, recalls his wage as $45 a month. Chief Warms, now dead, was paid $185 a month, according to the recollection of his surviving son, Donald Warms.

"The food," says Houston, "was abominable. I can remember one seaman carrying a plate of rotten fried eggs up to the bridge deck and shoving the plate in Captain Wilmott's face." Says Boggetti, now retired, "The chef was allotted eighty-seven cents per person per day to feed the crew and passengers. If you look at the menu, you can figure how much was left over after the passengers had been fed." In its September 1934 issue, published just a few days before the *Morro Castle* burst into flames, the *Marine News* printed one of the ship's menus. For breakfast, the passengers were offered a choice of five juices, eight kinds of fruit, ten hot and cold cereals, four fish or meat dishes, eggs in five styles, five omelets, five pastries, and a choice of six beverages.

Dinner was even more Lucullan—fruit cocktail, a choice of three soups, red snapper, a choice of entrées ranging from lobster Newburg to roast beef and roast turkey, five vegetables, two salads, eight desserts, and after-dinner coffee in the smoking room. Meanwhile, belowdecks, the crewmen were dining on what they cynically called "slops." In July 1934 a young junior radio operator named George I. Alagna could stand it no longer. Enlisting support from another junior operator, William Borow, he concocted a plan. Just before the *Morro Castle* was ready to sail from Wall Street, Alagna and Borow walked off the ship. Under the maritime laws, each ship was required to have three radio operators, one for each eight-hour shift. The operators were hired and assigned by the Radiomarine Corporation, predecessor to the Radio Corporation of America. There was no time to bring in new men. Alagna and Borow stalked into the office of Henry E. Cabaud, executive vice president of the line, to demand better working conditions and better food.

"I was just twenty-seven years old and a young radical," Alagna recalled recently. "I can remember Cabaud banging on his desk and spluttering, 'I ought to have you arrested. You're holding up the United States mails!' But we stood our ground until he agreed to give us better food and relieve us of a few nasty chores no radio operator ought to be required to undertake, such as polishing brass in our spare time. The *Morro Castle* sailed two hours late that day, and Captain Wilmott never forgave me. The food got better for a little while, by the way, but in the end it was just as bad as it ever had been."

The recruitment of the crew was casual, to say the least. Seamen in those days were issued lifeboat certificates, attesting ability to handle a boat in an emergency, as well as able seaman's certificates, stating that they had served for three years on ships. Neither document carried a picture. There was no way to know whether the man hired was the man to whom the certificate belonged. In fact, these little pieces of paper were sold by sailors outside the Seamen's Church Institute to men who wanted to ship out. Some were foreigners, unable to speak, read, or write English. (As it later was made clear, the shipping master of the Ward Line, Angelo Vlaco, could neither read nor write English, though he could make out the words "lifeboat certificate" and "able seaman.") And if a man had a past criminal record, neither certificate indicated it. Joseph Curran, now president of the National Maritime Union, was a young "A.B.," or able-bodied seaman, in the early 1930s. He remembers applying for a job on one of the Ward Line ships. "No wonder the *Morro Castle* was a mess," he says. "They just lined us all up on the pier, glanced at our papers, and said 'You, you, and you.' No questioning, nothing."

Yet, mixed in among the crew and junior officers there were college students or college graduates from solid families, taking a year or a summer off to see a new corner of the world. Bow Lookout Robert Beresford had just graduated from Yale and was preparing to go on to law school. Quartermaster Louis Fleischman had put in two years at the University of Illinois before his family ran out of money. Thomas S. Torressen, Jr., third assistant purser, was the son of the marine superintendent of the Ward Line. William W. Tripp, a cadet engineer, was about to start his second year at Massachusetts Institute of Technology. Among the junior officers, Assistant Cruise Director Cluthe was a Columbia University graduate, and the parents of Cruise Director Smith owned two large hotels in Atlantic City.

Andrew Furuseth, at the time president of the International Seamen's Union, affiliated with the American Federation of Labor, said firmly that many seamen aboard the *Morro Castle* had paid high prices for their jobs. They earned a handsome profit smuggling narcotics into the United States. Those more ethical seamen who relied on their wages faced an unending grind of work. The ship was in shore at New York only eight hours. Seamen who wanted to visit families or friends away from New York had to sign off the ship and then sign on again when she came back into port. The result, on some cruises, was a turnover of personnel as high as 50 per cent. There was not, and could not be, any sense of solidarity among the belowdeck crew, any sense of responsibility in an emergency, or even any fully shared knowledge of the English language, so essential in the event of a disaster. During the two days the ship was docked in Cuba many of the bored, exhausted crewmen simply drank themselves into insensibility. "The vessel was so wholly and absolutely undermanned," said Furuseth, "that she could not be kept up except under conditions that did not give any consideration to safety at all."

Among the officers, there was understandably no turnover. The pay was niggardly, except in the case of Captain Wilmott, but they counted themselves lucky to have a job at all. Every one of them, from Chief Warms down to Fourth Officer Hansen, was licensed to operate a ship of any tonnage anywhere in the world. There simply were not that many American ships afloat.

Qualified skippers had to sign on for whatever rating was available. They had no other trade but the sea.

The regulations of the United States Steamboat Inspection Service required that on each voyage there should be fire drills, with crews reporting to their fire stations, and that the lifeboats, at least on one side, should be dropped to the water and rowed a half hour by crew members. In each stateroom signs were posted advising passengers to which boat they should report. The fire drills were held, although not with such regularity, but the passengers were not required to attend. Cruise Director Smith, when Captain Jones was commanding the *Morro,* asked why the regulations were not more strictly enforced. "Mr. Smith," said Jones, "you're safer on this ship than you are crossing Times Square."

Smith asked the question later of Captain Wilmott. "I wanted to have a fire drill to keep the passengers interested," Smith said. "It might take up to an hour. I thought the passengers would be interested in standing by their boats while the crew ran around with the fire hoses and showed how well the ship could be protected."

"No," said Wilmott. "The New York office doesn't want the passengers unduly disturbed. I don't want the men to run around and excite them."

Clarence Monroe, who was a wiper in the engine room, said recently, "The drills were a joke. We just went to our posts and stood around for a while, and even the stewards didn't come out. They were excused so they could wait on the passengers."

Smith, who has for years been cruise director for the Holland-America Line, snorted, "I'd like to see that sort of slackness on our line. Any passenger who failed to report to his boat would be called up before the captain."

The slackness could not be blamed on Chief Warms. He had once had his license suspended for thirty days for failing to enforce fire drills on a Ward Line freighter he commanded. Often he had stalked through the belowdecks crew quarters on the *Morro Castle,* beating on doors and sometimes kicking them in to rout out crewmen who had not responded to the alarm bell.

Along with the slackness, there was an element of tension. Wilmott considered Radio Operator Alagna "a Communist," and made no secret of his mistrust. The Chief Radio Operator, George W. Rogers, monstrously fat and six feet two inches tall, also fell under the captain's suspicion. "Mr. Smith," he said to the cruise director one day as Rogers walked past, "that is a very bad, bad man." Chief Warms, dour and sallow, stayed to himself and rarely ate in the ship's dining room, which earned him a reputation as a loner. Wilmott once asked an executive of the Ward Line to take Warms off the ship because "he don't know his mind from one minute to another." The captain himself was under a strain. Overweight (he was a prodigious eater), he had suffered a series of small heart attacks, two of them aboard ship. The *Morro Castle*'s Chief Surgeon, Dr. DeWitt Van Zile, told Fourth Officer Howard H. Hansen, "The skipper's not in good health at all." Wilmott himself told a friend he suspected somebody had poisoned a fish dinner that made him violently ill.

If this were not enough to transform Wilmott from a cheery father figure into a querulous old man in his late fifties, a series of incidents aboard ship added to his worries. It was a standing joke among the younger ship's officers that Chinese were being hidden in the holds and smuggled into the United States. There was a strict immigration quota against Chinese in the 1930s, but soon they moved along an underground railroad route that included a stop in Cuba. "Let's go down to Chinatown," one officer would say to another. So on each return trip from Havana, Captain Willmott checked every hold. Once he did find a dozen Chinese. He changed the ship's course and put them ashore at Santiago, in eastern Cuba.

The log of the *Morro Castle* on Cruise 169 southbound and Cruise 170 northbound—the last in the possession of the Ward Line—revealed the standard routine aboard ship. With Captain Jones in command, and 125 bags of mail, the *Morro Castle* departed New York at 2:30 P.M. Saturday, August 4. Jones personally unlocked the mail room three times to make sure no thefts had taken place. At 4:30 P.M. on Sunday, August 5, off Diamond Shoals Lightship, below Cape Hatteras, the watertight doors in the hold were opened and closed, and the boat came to a full stop for a fire and boat drill. The ship's two motor lifeboats were operated for five minutes each. Wilmott, concluding a short vacation, took command on the return trip. He twice searched the ship for contraband and stowaways, finding none.

Cuba itself had been in turmoil under Dictator Machado. His political enemies fled to escape assassination. One of them, General Julio Herrera, paid crewmen a bribe of $5000 to secrete him in the *Morro*'s wine cellar while Machado's soldiers searched the ship. He emerged when the *Morro* was well at sea, and received political asylum in the United States. Machado himself was overthrown and fled the country in March 1933, but the turmoil continued. Wilmott went on vacation in November 1933, and Captain Jones assumed temporary command. On November 11 he had no sooner arrived in Havana than Ambassador Sumner Welles came aboard. "Don't let the passengers go ashore," he ordered. "Unload your cargo and get out of port as fast as you can." At 4:15 P.M., as the *Morro* backed away from her pier, government gunboats in the harbor exchanged machine-gun fire with rebels ashore. The bridge was dotted with bullet marks; passengers snapped photos of the gunboats until ordered below-decks. Just as the gangplank was going up, two former Cuban Army officers leaped aboard. They had escaped Cubana Prison, one of them still in his pajamas. To drown out the sound of firing, the ship's band played "Happy Days Are Here Again."

The *Morro*'s wildest experience took place in September. A storm blew up as the ship passed the Florida Keys. Winds reached 100 miles an hour. The radio antenna was blown away. Wilmott, in command, for forty-eight hours had to look above the bridge to see the tops of the waves. The running lights went out. The 140 passengers, their staterooms flooded, slept on the main ballroom floor. One woman prayed for eighteen hours. When the ship's orchestra was laid low by seasickness, Gwendolyn Taylor, a crippled stenographer, played jazz on the piano and led the passengers in song as the ship hove to off Cape Hatteras, unable to move against the storm. "The *Morro* behaved beautifully," said Wilmott when he brought her in to New York. "She proved how seaworthy she is."

A year later Wilmott had lost this sense of confidence. He had become suspicious, even crotchety. Wild rumors circulated among the officers. The scuttlebutt was that Wilmott was frightened of Chief Radio Operator Rogers and intended to have him fired the moment the *Morro Castle* completed her 174th voyage. Rogers later told another version. Just after leaving Havana on September 5, he said, Wilmott called him to his office and asked: "What is the matter with your second radio operator, Alagna? I think the man is crazy. Second Officer Freeman was tuning in the radio compass. Alagna sent him a message telling him not to use the radio compass so damn much and to stop tuning in music on it. I want that man removed in New York. Another thing, I want you to take the key to the emergency radio room and keep it in your pocket. Don't leave it where Alagna can get at it. I don't trust him. He is vengeful. Before we left Havana, he said there were ways of getting even with the ship."

The story grew more and more curious, and Captain Wilmott's

suspicions grew more and more alarming. On the morning of September 7 Wilmott called Rogers to his office. He had heard that two bottles, one containing acid and the other "stink-bomb" liquid, had been brought aboard. His next visitor was Chief Warms. "He was worried that something would happen," said Warms. "He was afraid Alagna would harm him, and he was going to keep his door locked. He told me to keep an eye on Alagna." Finally the captain summoned Fourth Officer Howard H. Hansen. Now a retired Navy lieutenant commander, he remembers the conversation. "A bottle of acid and a bottle of stink-bomb fluid have been found," Wilmott said. "I've had a report that Alagna threatened to get even with the company by sprinkling the fluid in the dining room and lounge on the night before we reach New York. Then the boat would smell so badly that passengers could not come aboard for the next voyage." Hansen, puzzled, asked, "Why don't you lock him up?"—the same question Chief Warms had asked earlier.

"No," said Wilmott, "that won't be necessary. The bottles have been thrown overboard." To simple ship's officers like Warms and Hansen, the whole sequence of suspicions seemed baffling. Though Wilmott had become steadily more nervous, in every crisis he was calmly in command. In fact, when a small fire had been discovered two weeks earlier, on August 24, in one of the holds, he had simply attributed it to a carelessly dropped cigarette and delayed a report on the incident until he next reached New York. It crossed Fourth Officer Hansen's mind that "the old man" was badly upset, so badly upset that he shunned the Captain's Dinner that evening—something he had rarely if ever done before. Wilmott loved to talk, as he loved to eat, and his table was always the last in the dining room to be emptied.

At 6:30 P.M. a steward delivered the captain's dinner to his stateroom. Whatever his emotional state, his appetite was unchanged. There was a huge slab of steak, a mound of vegetables, and a slice of fresh casaba melon. "I can remember thinking, boy, how I'd like to have a meal like that!" says Hansen. A few minutes later the phone rang in Purser Robert Tolman's office where Tolman, Van Zile, and Smith were having a drink. "Van," said the captain's voice. "I'm having a little stomach trouble. Would you make up an enema and bring it up to me?" The request was not unusual. A continuous diet of *Morro Castle* food affected all the officers from time to time.

Van Zile disappeared, and Smith went to his table in the dining room. He had barely taken a bite of melon before a steward whispered in his ear, "Your presence is requested on the bridge." There he found Warms, Van Zile, Hansen, and a group of seamen standing outside the captain's door. "The old man's dead," they told Smith. "Can't I go in and pay my last respects?" he asked. "No," said Warms, "he looks awful. His face is all blue." A congested face is almost always a sure sign of a heart attack. Warms, stopping by for a brief chat, had found the half-dressed captain dead, tumbled head first into his bathtub. Dr. Van Zile had injected a heart stimulant, but it was too late. There were three distinguished doctors aboard the ship that night, Dr. Charles S. Cochrane, Dr. Theodore Vosseler, and Dr. Gouverneur Morris Phelps, all of them heads of departments in New York City hospitals. Called in as consultants, they gave a unanimous verdict. "There could be no doubt of a heart attack," Dr. Phelps told his son later. "It was a perfectly obvious case," Dr. Vosseler said to friends years afterward.

But suspicions die hard aboard ship. Howard Hansen still insists: "I think somebody gave the captain a Mickey Finn." A Mickey Finn is a violent purgative and sometimes contains knockout drops. Certainly Wilmott had made enemies aboard ship. When an engineer complained to him that he had lost all his wages in a gambling game belowdecks, one complete with a roulette wheel, Wilmott stormed down and personally threw the paraphernalia overboard. His attitude toward the smuggling of dope and aliens was stern and unbending. On one cruise he discovered a huge cache of Cuban rum at the bottom of an elevator shaft. On arrival in port he notified the Treasury Department, and for weeks after that agents in dungarees roamed the ship, masquerading as crew members, searching for the smugglers.

Purser Tolman, on the bridge with other officers, turned to Warms for instructions. "Notify the home office," said Warms. "Tell everyone I'm in command now and they're to obey my orders." Tolman wrote out a radiogram: "Wilmott deceased 7:45 P.M. Acknowledge. Warms." Later, after a request for more details from the Ward Line office, he sent another: "Confirming message from Warms stop Wilmott deceased acute indigestion and heart attack seven forty-five this evening stop All papers for entry in order. Tolman."

Whatever the suspicions about the captain, death put an end to them all. Every officer advanced one grade. Warms, so accustomed to taking orders from above, became master of the ship. Second Officer Ivan Freeman became Acting First Officer. Third

Officer Clarence Hackney became Acting Second Officer. Howard Hansen moved up to Acting Third Officer. All, to one degree or another, were facing jobs they were only partially familiar with. Down in the purser's office, where Smith, Tolman, and Van Zile had gathered again, there was speculation that another captain would take over from Warms when the ship reached port. Dr. Van Zile put an end to it by raising his glass in a toast. "Here's to death," he said. "Which one of us will be next?"

3

FIRE IN THE NIGHT

To the officers of the *Morro Castle*, the death of Captain Wilmott was like the death of a father figure. Most of them thought of him as a nice old man, at times a bit too fussy, who ran an unusually tight operation. From him, all important commands had emanated; by him, even the most trivial decisions were made. He delegated almost no authority. Fourth Officer Hansen said recently, "Warms never did anything on his own. All he did was to relay the master's orders." In earlier years Warms had been a Long Island friend and neighbor of Captain Wilmott, but later he had moved to New Jersey. On duty, he was a cipher, self-effacing, lacking the presence and decisiveness generally associated with the second in command of an ocean liner.

Now he was himself the master, though few passengers had ever seen or met him, and fewer cared what kind of man was in charge of their destiny. Some of the older people aboard later recalled a sense of solemnity and a vague unease. Most of the younger people, those under thirty-five, had only a sense of letdown, a feeling of disappointment that so lively a cruise was ending so grimly. Without music, toasts, and dancing it was a long last night at sea. The girls in their long evening dresses, the men in their dinner jackets, bow ties, and starched shirt fronts, were all dressed up with no place to go.

One of the younger people, Agnes Prince,[1] read something ominous into the captain's death: "A corpse somewhere over our heads, a ship without a captain, and the boat rolling as a storm followed us up the coast. It was an eerie sensation." Agnes was more sensitive to these nuances than her shipmates. She was a newspaperwoman, the society editor of the Pottstown, Pennsylvania, *Mercury*. She also had a keen eye for the temperaments of the passengers. "There were a lot of quiet people aboard," she said

[1] Now Mrs. Abraham Margolies of Coatesville, Pennsylvania.

24

recently, "but there also were a fair number of swingers, single men and women out for a good time. They simply took the party to their staterooms."

Others clustered in the lounge, ordering setups to mix with their Cuban rum. John Torborg recalls seeing a woman in a low-cut evening gown stagger up the grand staircase and fall flat on her face. Steward Sirl Boggetti remembers hearing a report, passed on to Warms on the bridge, that six young women—too drunk to walk—had to be carried to bed by other stewards. "There was always a certain amount of heavy drinking the last night out," he says, "and the story could very well have been true."

Assistant Cruise Director Cluthe, who had preceded Smith, serving as Acting Cruise Director of the *Morro Castle*, says: "I believe it possible that maybe even a dozen girls were carried drunk into their cabins. There was a strange mixture of people on these cruises—a lot of respectable older people, middle-aged people, a lot of distinguished Cubans, and some distinguished Americans. But also there were a number of girls, young secretaries and clerks, who were away from home for the first time, and some of them would go wild. On a good many cruises, when we got close to sailing time, we would check in the passengers at the gangplank. Often some girls were missing. It was easy to figure what had happened. Whenever we docked at Havana, there would always be a group of Cuban gigolos in their white suits offering to show the girls the town. We knew what hotels these gigolos used; we'd send cars around, rout the girls out, and bring them back to the boat." Cruise Director Smith, it should be noted, indignantly denies that any such promiscuity occurred. Both he and Cluthe were on this last voyage.

The two days and nights in Havana preceding the sailing of the *Morro Castle* had been hectic. Agnes Prince's sister Ruth,[2] then twenty-eight, recalls being warned not to go anywhere alone; stewards were being provided as escorts. On the tours passengers were escorted through town in a cavalcade of open cars. They saw armed soldiers in doorways, soldiers on the roofs of public buildings, and security guards at the pier, where a bloody longshoremen's strike had dragged on for months. Troops surrounded the domed marble capitol and the gleaming Presidential Palace. Machine guns chattered in the night, and a twelve o'clock curfew was strictly enforced.

[2] Now Mrs. Irving Coleman of Allentown, Pennsylvania.

Gouverneur Morris Phelps, Jr., accompanying his father and stepmother on the return trip, remembers being arrested the night of September 4 because he overstayed the curfew. "A bomb went off next door to the police station while they were questioning me," he says, "and while everyone was rushing around, I simply walked out the door and back to the ship."

Havana had lived with tension for years. Ruth Mooney recently recalled a visit to the city in 1933 with her father and mother, at about the time Machado was overthrown: "I was looking out a window of our suite in the Hotel Nacional when two cars came by, driving parallel. The men in one car shot everyone in the other car. My mother pulled me back, drew the curtains, and said, 'You didn't see anything.' I protested that I most certainly had seen a shooting. She repeated, 'You didn't see anything.' I realize now, nearly forty years later, that it wasn't safe to talk about some of the things you did see in Havana."

Frank Dittman, Jr., [3] then sixteen years old, had been vacationing with a schoolmate on a southern Mexican plantation. He came into Havana by freighter from Vera Cruz in late August 1934, on the way back to classes at the Taft School in Watertown, Connecticut. "I'd shot a lot of game down there," he says, "and I had a shotgun as well as a big collection of shells mounted on a board." His cousin, George Pierce, manager for the Otis Elevator Company in Havana, came aboard the freighter to meet him. "The first thing he asked me," recalls Dittman, "was whether I had any firearms or ammunition. I showed him my collection of shells. 'My God,' he said, 'you've got to get rid of these. If they catch you, you'll be thrown into prison and you'll never get out.' I had to leave everything behind."

Most *Morro Castle* passengers considered themselves immune from the troubles of Havana and thought they were guaranteed against harm by the simple fact of American citizenship. The soldiers, the bombs, and the gunfire gave their visit a spice of danger, as well as something exciting to tell their friends back home. Isolated by language and customs, they had no understanding of the terror felt by native Cubans, no sense of the blood lust that convulsed the island, no knowledge of the firing squads that mowed down opponents of the regime.

Almost all passengers went on two standard motor trips, the City Tour and the Night Tour. On the daylight City Tour, driving down broad streets fringed by palm trees, they visited his-

[3] Now a probation officer in Nassau County, Long Island.

toric churches, the capitol, the Presidential Palace, and finally the white marble monument to the battleship *Maine,* topped by a huge, bronze American eagle. (Sunk mysteriously in Havana harbor in 1898, the *Maine* had provided the spark that set off the Spanish-American War and made Cuba a republic.) On the Night Tour they went to an arena to watch the national game of jai alai, stopped for drinks downtown at Sloppy Joe's, a tourist rendezvous, visited a nightclub, and placed a few cautious bets at the gambling tables in the Casino. It was all new and strange and very foreign to them.

"I remember it as a lovely experience," says Mrs. Emil Lampe, who at the age of eighty-eight has forgotten very few details of the cruise. "We drove out after dark to the Sans Souci, an open-air nightclub on the beach. It was all colored lights and a marimba band, and Cuban girls dancing the rumba in their long dresses." Mrs. Lampe's late husband, Emil, was one of two sponsors of the Concordia Singing Society excursion.

Ruth Torborg remembers best her visit to Sloppy Joe's. She had her first taste of alcohol there, fresh pineapple juice laced with rum. "At my age, it made me feel very devilish and very grown-up," she says. "Of course I saw all the soldiers with guns scattered around the city, but I just felt they were there to protect all of us."

Among the passengers was Frank Loveland, an officer of the Massachusetts Corrections Commission, who subsequently became Assistant Commissioner of Federal Prisons. Loveland and his wife, Nathene, were on their honeymoon. They found the atmosphere of Havana too hectic and too menacing. Though they had planned to stay two weeks, two days were enough, so they decided to return with the *Morro Castle.* Havana was a last-minute choice for the Lovelands. They had been invited to England, but at the last moment their host was called to South Africa on business.

"Havana looked fine at first glance," Loveland recalls. "It was outwardly a lovely tropical city, but entirely too much was going on to make us feel secure.

"We sensed a feeling of tension. There were rumors of an imminent revolution, and lots of sounds of shooting after dark. When we went on the Night Tour, our car was searched three times by soldiers. It was scarcely the tranquil place we had envisioned, so we decided to finish our honeymoon in New York."

Thomas Cannon, Jr., at the time a banker but now Collector

of Taxes in Livingston, New Jersey, had been invited on the cruise by a friend, a junior officer on the ship, whose name he no longer remembers. He left Mrs. Cannon at home because she disliked the sea. "Fortunately for her," he adds wryly, "considering what happened to me." Cannon recalls feeling a sense of release when the *Morro Castle* cast off her moorings at 6:00 P.M., September 5, and soon left the sun-flooded city sinking in the distance.

That night the waters were calm, the stars were out, the six-man orchestra was playing jazz tunes in the ballroom, but Captain Wilmott was not there to mingle with the passengers. Nor had he come down to dinner. He was secluded in his cabin, prey to suspicions that his ship might be sabotaged, urging his officers to be unusually watchful. The once garrulous, gregarious master had scarcely been seen by the passengers during the entire trip southward, according to Boggetti, who served the captain's table. "We stewards were all asking each other, 'What's the matter with the old man?' " Boggetti says. "He loved to socialize, and here he was behaving like a hermit."

Cruise Director Smith, who had no time for speculation, was busy organizing the standard shipboard entertainments—the horse race, at twenty-five cents a bet, in which wooden horses moved along a slotted board; deck tennis under lights; and later a movie in the ballroom. The band moved out to the deck ballroom, playing under blue and green bulbs that flicked on and off. Young singles who had struck up acquaintances on shipboard paired off in remote corners of the deck. Most passengers, tired from long hours in Havana, were in bed by midnight. Only a few stayed up long enough to catch sight, in the distance, of the blinking lights marking the shoals off Florida. With its twin engines pulsing quietly, the *Morro Castle* cleared the deep waters of the Gulf of Mexico and slid back onto the Continental Shelf, eight miles offshore. Smith, who collected a seventy-five-cent commission from each three-dollar ticket sold for the Havana tours, found that he had made a two-hundred-dollar profit. He handed over that sum, in bills, to Purser Robert Tolman, who locked them in a heavy steel box and slid them into the ship's safe. Tolman had charge of all the ship's funds, as well as the mails.

The next afternoon, September 6, a bank of clouds began to mass on the southern horizon, but the wind blew straight and true from the tropics, hastening the *Morro Castle* toward New York. With this following wind and at her service speed of 21 knots, the ship might have reached Ambrose Light long before her scheduled arrival time, forcing her to lie-to off the entrance to New York harbor until the shore crew came on duty at the pier. Surviving officers and crew members do not remember exactly when, but at some point off the Carolinas Captain Wilmott ordered the running speed lowered, either to 17.7 or 18.8 knots. The exact speed is in dispute. There were already first signs of an oncoming storm that night. The *Morro Castle* began a slow roll, a steady roll. With a length just over 500 feet, she was small enough to be "a little tender," in shipping parlance, more sensitive to wind and waves than the big transatlantic liners almost twice as long and broad. There was just enough motion to make some passengers a little queasy. Crew members noted a number of empty chairs in the dining saloon that night.

The next morning, by breakfast time, the clouds thickened and the wind changed, blowing lightly from the east. It was the first evidence of a developing northeaster, a storm generated by a low-pressure area in the tropics, building up force some three hundred miles east-southeast of Jacksonville, Florida. Northeasters whirl as they move up the Atlantic coast. Winds shift from south to east to northeast, finally reaching gale strength. Light rain beaded the windows of the wheelhouse, where Captain Wilmott was watching the progress of the storm. Crew members working in the open donned yellow oilskins. This sort of weather is usual along the Atlantic coast in September and October—hurricane weather, the sailors call it. Robert Beresford, [4] lookout on the bow, remembers how unconcerned his fellow crewmen seemed to be. "After all," he says, "they had been through far worse weather."

As the dull gray day wore on, the intensity of the storm deepened, and more passengers took to their berths. Israel Rudberg, an electrical appliance salesman from Shenandoah, Pennsylvania, says, "She was pitching pretty hard by the time we all came down for the Captain's Dinner. It was sort of a glum last night for what was billed as a sunny tropical cruise." By this time the *Morro Castle* was passing off Delaware Breakwater and the wind was blowing from the east at a steady eight miles per hour. There were higher winds ahead, fourteen miles per hour off Atlantic City. Intermittent rain, sometimes heavy, was beating down. In the dining saloon, at 7:45 P.M., there was an air of anticipation. Cruise Director Smith and the stewards had tied

[4] Now a Common Pleas Court judge in San Jose, California.

together clusters of balloons, to be released at the end of dinner. The orchestra was on the bandstand. Just at that moment a steward leaned down beside the cruise director at his table and whispered, "Don't change expression, but the old man's dead." Within five minutes Smith had made the announcement, and the party was over. Passengers drifted silently from the room.

Such was the isolation of the radio officers from the rest of the ship's personnel that Second Operator George Alagna came off duty at 9:00 P.M. without even hearing of the captain's death. He does remember feeling the growing force of the storm, the pitch and heave of the ship as she moved northward, and the sting of the rain when he moved from the wireless room into his adjoining bunkroom. Twenty minutes later he was awakened to be told, "The captain's dead." Alagna, after hearing the news, turned over and went back to sleep. In the captain's cabin, a few steps down from the wheelhouse, Second Steward James Pond [5] was laying out Wilmott's body on a bed, composing the limbs and then drawing a blanket over the contorted face.

"It was something I didn't mind doing," says Pond, now in his seventies. "I had done it before on other ships when somebody died at sea. Besides, I liked the captain. He was a nice man —I suspect a little henpecked at home—and I'd traveled with him on a hundred cruises."

In the wheelhouse, just forward of the cabin, Acting Captain Warms was checking the compass, the lights on shore, and the fathometer, which registered the depth of water beneath the ship's keel. As he told his son years later, he was nearly dead from exhaustion, for he had been on duty the better part of thirty hours. The senior officers of the *Morro Castle* enjoyed no eight-hour day.

Two decks below the bridge, in the lounge and ballroom, the smoking room and the deck veranda tearoom, passengers played bridge, strolled on and off a 150-foot section of B Deck protected from the rain and wind by a roof and windows, or drank the liquor nearly all of them had bought in Havana. Some remained aloof from the late night parties. The loners included Edward M. Kendall, of Babylon, Long Island, New York. A moneyed sportsman, he had been angling for marlin off Cuba with the Phelpses. Kendall earlier had been a big-game hunter in the Canadian Rockies, and he had spent a year on a chartered yacht diving for sunken treasure off Tahiti. "The *Morro* was quite an impressive boat, the first cruise liner I'd ever been aboard,"

[5] Subsequently chief steward of the Moore-McCormack Lines.

Kendall recalls. "She was glistening, varnished, ornate, with fancy drapes. But the crew struck me as a low class of roustabouts, and the passengers were a mixed bag. We didn't socialize with them because they weren't our kind of people. I had a few drinks and went to bed early in my cabin on C Deck."

Kendall's judgment was a bit sweeping. The *Morro Castle* was a microcosm of America. The passenger list included such socially acceptable couples as the Right Reverend and Mrs. Hiram Hulse (he was Episcopal Bishop of Cuba); Mr. and Mrs. George Whitlock (he was president of the First National Bank of New York); Dr. and Mrs. Phelps and their son, and Mr. and Mrs. Edward Brady and their daughter Nancy of Philadelphia (he was president of the United Gas Improvement Corporation). There were others, like Senora Renee Mendez Capote, daughter of a former vice president of Cuba, and the German Consul General stationed in Havana. But then there were many waiters, bitter about low pay and stingy tipping, sodden from a drunken shore leave, and some crewmen culled from the dregs of the waterfront. Every facet of Depression America was represented on that cruise of the *Morro Castle*.

Like Kendall, Dr. and Mrs. Phelps also went to bed early that night. They had been married only a short time. Phelps's first wife, mother of Gouverneur, Jr., had died. He had married a younger woman, the former Katharine Brower. They had a quiet after-dinner drink, paced the deck, and then went below to their stateroom, close to one shared by Kendall and the younger Phelps. "But," Dr. Phelps told his son later, "we couldn't get to sleep until about one A.M. because there was so much running around and partying going on."

Gouverneur ("Guvvy"), Jr., stayed up, wandering idly through the public rooms, occasionally stopping for a chat. Finally he organized a game of bridge with Walter E. Byrne, a student at Amherst College, and two other casual acquaintances. They played for a few hours in the smoking room, just a hundred feet down the deck from the writing room and library. "We were really just killing time," says Phelps. He was a lively twenty-seven-year-old, an employee of Morgan, Davis & Co., stockbrokers, and still single. As the bridge game broke up about 1:00 A.M. ship's time (2:00 A.M. eastern daylight time ashore), he continued to meander through the public rooms.

Like Ruth Torborg and five of her friends from the Concordia Society, he was reluctant to call it a night. Ruth had bought a nineteen-dollar green velvet dress from the Frances Shop in the East New York-City Line section of Brooklyn. In the 1930s that area was solidly German-American. The streets were lined with brownstone houses, each with its own gate and polished brass stair railings leading up to the front door. These were people who could afford a cruise and afford to dress for it. Nineteen dollars, however, was a high price in Depression days, and Ruth was determined to get some use from her purchase. "All of us, boys and girls, were pretty noisy," she says, "and the girls were terribly giggly, but we were sober. In our Concordia Society the notion of a high old time was to drink a bottle of beer and start singing. At one point we said to each other, 'We'd better quiet down.' We had planned in advance to pack our bags very early in the morning."

In the lounge, just off the writing room, one of her friends saw a group of passengers amusing themselves by throwing lighted cigarettes into a wastebasket. One cigarette missed the mark and started a tiny, smoldering fire in a rug. When this was reported to watchman Arthur Bagley, sitting just off the lounge, he hurried out and gave the amateur arsonists a blistering rebuke. Bagley's rounds took him through the writing room, but there he saw nothing amiss. The room was empty. In one corner was a vast locker in which 150 blankets had been stored. These had been taken off berths at the beginning of the summer and were not to be replaced until the weather grew colder. Some of them, perhaps all, had been cleaned commercially with the compounds in use in the 1930s, which included flammable dry-cleaning fluids. Chief Cruise Director Smith recalls complaints from the stewardesses aboard that they had to clean blankets, and assumes they used other flammable compounds, such as kerosene. A Yale lock kept the doors closed. Second Steward Pond is still certain he had to use a key to open it. Steward Daniel Campbell told a court of inquiry later that the lock was never closed.

The restless nighttime life of the *Morro Castle* continued as the ship moved northward, at 1:55 A.M. passing five miles east of Barnegat Lighthouse, a little north of Altantic City. Through sheets of rain, those in the wheelhouse could watch the blink of the light, shining brilliant for ten seconds, then darkened for ten seconds. Over the whine of 24-mile winds in the rigging they could hear the blasting sound of the lighthouse's Tryfon horn warning ships off the shoals. In the radio room, where Third Radio Operator Charles Maki was on duty, the airwaves were jammed with the whine of wireless messages from other ships.

Transmissions from the twin Radiomarine towers at Tuckerton, New Jersey, only a few miles away, came in with a roar. Another Radiomarine station, WIM at Chatham on Cape Cod, added a more distant voice. There were nearby signals of ships moving northward on the same shipping lane—the plodding old freighter *City of Savannah,* quickly outdistanced by the faster *Morro Castle;* the brand-new 600-foot freighter *Andrea Luckenbach,* which matched her in speed; the rakish white *Monarch of Bermuda,* well out ahead on a return trip from the British colony; the Dollar liner *President Cleveland,* and lesser ships scattered down the coast like minnows. It was a routine night at sea in the radio room. Coffee bubbled gently on an electric hot plate, the rain pelted down on the metal roof, and at one-minute intervals the foghorn bellowed. Passengers had been hearing that mournful sound since late afternoon when the storm began to make up.

On the bridge Quartermasters Samuel (Red) Hoffman and Louis Fleischman were alternating at the wheel, following the navigating orders of Acting Captain Warms. The wind had built up to 34 land miles an hour—an implacable, persistent wall of air pushing against the *Morro Castle* as she butted her way up the coast. On a much smaller United Fruit Company freighter Richard Berry [6] remembers looking across at the brilliantly lit cruise ship and saying to himself, "I wish I was on that boat instead of this old tub." Chief Engineer Arthur Farr [7] of the *Luckenbach* recalls that his own ship, with twelve million board feet of lumber from Oregon—the largest cargo of its type ever carried up to that time—overtook and then fell behind the *Morro Castle* several times earlier in the night. "She was a lovely sight, a really handsome ship," he says.

At about 2:15 A.M. Paul Arneth, [8] a member of the Concordia group, tired of cabin-hopping from one party to another. He went down to his stateroom on C Deck just below and started to undress. He had taken off the jacket of a white suit he had bought in Havana and had stripped off his shirt. Then he realized that his roommate, George Ridderhoff, an older Brooklyn businessman, was not in his berth. "Gee," he said to himself,

[6] Now a vice president of the United Fruit Company.
[7] Now an iron company executive in Portland, Oregon.
[8] Now a wholesale meat dealer in New York City.

"I'd better find Mr. Ridderhoff. He has to get some sleep." As Arneth recalls it now, he threw on a bathrobe, climbed the stairs to B Deck by the aft staircase, and looked for Ridderhoff at the bar in the smoking room. The bar was closed, so he wandered into the main lounge, where Steward Daniel Campbell was serving setups to a party of four late-stayers. "I smelled smoke," Arneth says. "Very pungent smoke and very distinct. I called the steward over and said to him quietly, so at not to create a panic, 'Hey, I smell smoke.' He said, 'All right, let's find out.' The smell intensified as we walked down a short corridor, past a fire-alarm box, and into the room. On the inner wall of that room there was a big closet or locker. You could see the smoke pouring out of the cracks in the twin doors. The steward opened the doors, and the whole interior was a mass of flames. I ran back to the fire-alarm box, broke the glass, and pulled the lever inside. I guess the alarm registered on the bridge, if not all over the ship. The steward grabbed a fire extinguisher from the wall and squirted it on the flames. Members of the crew started to rush in and out; a few minutes later they dragged in a fire hose. There was no pressure. Only a trickle of water came out."

Arneth was torn. His fiancée, Ruth Fabel, was on the deck below, and he could not find Ridderhoff. The fire had already spread to the lounge, so he went forward, hoping, somehow, that Ridderhoff might be there. As he hesitated, he was caught up in a stampeding mob of crewmen rushing for the boat deck and was swept along with them.

Other passengers have a different memory of the fire. Ruth Torborg remembers, "Our little group decided we'd all go to our rooms and pack; then we'd come back to the lounge and wait for dawn. We were poking along through the lounge, toward the writing room, leaning against the furniture, saying, should we do this or that, sort of aimless. Then I saw a man in pajamas and bathrobe turning in a fire alarm. I said, 'Hey, you can't do that.' He said, 'There is a fire, you know,' and then we could see the smoke rolling down the corridor. We kept saying to one another, 'No need to get excited,' and we went back through the lounge toward the stern and out onto the open deck." John A. Kempf, a New York fireman in his late twenties, testified later at a hearing that he thought he had smelled smoke as early as 12:45 A.M. Kempf, now retired, lives the life of a recluse in Greeley, Pennsylvania, and flatly refuses to talk to anyone about the fire.

Just off the veranda café Second Steward Pond was adding up

the food and beverage accounts, which he would turn over to the purser before the ship reached port. In a little cubicle next to him, he remembers, watchmen Bagley and Jerry Dunn were having a cup of coffee. Just as Pond totted up the last figures, the phone rang. Sighing heavily, Pond picked it up. Someone forward wanted a pot of coffee. Sighing, he put a cup and saucer and a thermos jug of coffee on a tray and started out the door. Just then the phone rang a second time. It was Henry Stamm, the switchboard operator. "Campbell reports a fire in the writing room," he said. "Get everybody up!" Pond slammed the tray down on his desk and started forward at a dead run. "I thought I was going fast," he says, "but an officer passed me on the way, going so fast I saw only his back. When I got to the writing room, there were already crewmen fighting a fire in the locker, but they weren't getting anywhere. The whole interior was one red glow, and the paneling overhead in the writing room and lounge was ablaze. I know it was a little before three A.M., because I looked at my wristwatch."

Pond continued forward, hammering on the doors of eight suites and shouting. "Get up! There's a fire!" Then an odd impulse seized him. He had bought a canary—black, like all Cuban canaries—as a souvenir of the trip while in Havana. Battling against a tide of crewmen who were coming up the crew's staircase, he made his way to his quarters, seized the birdcage, and then was carried back up to the boat deck by another surging mob of sailors. Silhouetted against the flames, he opened the door of the cage and watched as the bird flew to freedom through clouds of smoke and rain.

At about 2:40 A.M., Steward Campbell [9] began to wonder whether the two couples in the lounge would ever go to bed, and tried to figure some tactful way to get them to leave. "It's only quarter to three," one man said. "That's ship's time," said Campbell. "It's actually quarter to four, shore time. We'll be picking up the pilot pretty soon." Campbell desperately wanted the lounge cleared. He had to clean the room before the ship docked so he would have a full eight hours of free time ashore before the ship sailed again. When Arneth reported the fire, he walked with him into the writing room. "There was a concealed locker," he said later, "and I looked and saw the smoke coming from that concealed locker. I opened the door, and what I once knew

[9] He is now dead, but Pond attended his funeral. His account of the event is taken from the record of two subsequent federal investigations.

as a locker was just one mass of flames from top to bottom and from one side to the other. It was completely gutted."

Gouverneur Phelps, Jr., says, "I started being aware of smoke some time toward three in the morning. I went into the writing room. There was a steward there with a fire extinguisher. 'There's a small fire smoldering in the paneling,' he said, 'and I'm trying to put it out.' He added, 'I called them once before and they told me, if it gets any worse, let us know. Then I called again, and the wiring was out, and now I can't get through.'"

Phelps is not a superstitious man, but he remembers a thought that crossed his mind. While the *Morro Castle* was tied up in Havana, he had fished from one of the lower decks and hauled in half a dozen tarpon. Later in the day, after many black looks from the crew, he learned of the old sailors' tale that anyone who catches fish from a passenger ship or freighter is encouraging a disaster.

4

GÖTTERDÄMMERUNG

It must have seemed to William F. Warms, who at that time had been master of the *Morro Castle* for just a little more than eight hours, as if the Furies had descended on the ship. First, his captain had died; next, he took command in hurricane weather, heading straight into winds of unpredictable velocity; and now, at 2:50 A.M., he had a fire on his hands. How bad a fire it was he did not yet know, but between three and five precious minutes had already been wasted while stewards engaged in a futile struggle to put it out. Everything went wrong that night, he recalled later.[1]

A minute or two before 2:50 A.M. night watchman Arthur J. Pender observed "what I first thought was steam but which I later found was smoke was coming from a ventilator on the hurricane deck, what I thought was a cargo ventilator." Without notifying the bridge, he went in search of the fire. He never got as deep as the cargo holds, for on his way down he found not one but two fires: the first in the writing room; a second one, puzzlingly separate, across a corridor in the library. He snatched the nearest fire extinguisher and joined the two watchmen and Steward Campbell. Perhaps only sixty seconds might have been gained had he notified the bridge, but every second was crucial that night.

On the bridge, according to Warms's subsequent recollection, night watchman Harold Foersch reported to Warms and Acting Second Officer Clarence Hackney: "Captain, I see and smell a little smoke." "Where?" Warms asked. Foersch said, "That little ventilator on the port side, near number one stack." The vent was an air intake that led into the writing room and down to C Deck

---

[1] Warms died in 1953, but many times before that he had recounted the story of the fire to his son, Donald, now an Asbury Park, New Jersey, insurance man. This account includes some of his testimony at the federal hearings but in most aspects has been supplied by the junior Warms.

and the foyer on D Deck near the purser's office. Warms set out on a dead run for the officers' staterooms, a few steps down and perhaps fifty feet astern on the boat deck, shouting for Acting First Officer Ivan Freeman and Acting Third Officer Hansen, both off duty and asleep.

"Clarence and Ivan," he ordered Hackney and Freeman, "grab fire extinguishers, get on down there, and put that fire out. Look in the passageway on A Deck, then in the writing room, and go all the way down to D Deck if you have to."

Just a second after both men left on the run, watchman Dunn, panting and wild-eyed, grabbed him by the lapels and said, "We have a bad fire down there." In less than three minutes, at 2:53 A.M., Hackney was back on the bridge, gasping, "It's pretty bad. We'd better get water on it."

Warms could see smoke billowing out of open portholes on the sun deck, where the grand ballroom/lounge mezzanine formed a railed passageway around the ballroom itself, two decks deep.

"Break out the hose, and I'll get men for you," Warms said to Hackney. He turned to able seaman Joseph Welch. "Wake up the bos'n and crew and tell them to get to their fire stations. Hurry!"

Welch clattered down the crew's staircase to the forecastle bunkrooms on D Deck, where a few lights were burning dimly, and shook bos'n Harry Urbich by the shoulder. "Get up!" he said. "The ship's on fire!"

Urbich mumbled a few words and turned away from Welch, fast asleep. Welch could smell the reek of Cuban rum and told Warms later, "The man was dead drunk." His shouts had awakened the deck crew, and the men in their underclothes stampeded toward their fire stations in the forward end of the ship without anyone to command them. By now most but not all of the phone system was out, as Freeman discovered. He ran five decks down to the engine room to order maximum pressure on the fire hose lines and then ran back five decks to the bridge.

Warms, ignorant of the vast speed of the fire—by now the whole ballroom was ablaze and flames were shooting down the corridors aft—continued on course directly into the wind. "She's bad," Freeman had told him. "We'd better turn her inshore, toward the beach." Warms's answer was: "We are not going yet. We can hold her."

At 2:55 A.M., over a phone line still in working order, Warms called the engine room to ask: "Is there a fire down there?" The exact time was logged by Cadet Engineer Tripp. He passed the phone to Third Engineer Arthur Stamper. "No," said Stamper, "but a little smoke is coming in." That smoke, increasing in density, was being pumped through the ship by the mechanical ventilating system.

At the back of the wheelhouse Quartermaster Louis Fleischman was standing beside the twenty-seven-panel Derby fire extinguishing system. Warms glanced at it as he put down the phone. The panels gave him a reassuring message. Since the system did not cover the public rooms but only the staterooms, he verified that the fire was still confined to the general area of the ballroom/lounge and writing room. But one minute later, at 2:56 A.M., lights began to flash all over the board, blinking on first at the top and then spreading down toward the bottom in a cluster of fiery droplets.

"My God!" said Warms. "The whole thing's going."

According to the information coming over the Derby system, every stateroom on the ship was either aflame or hot enough to activate the alarm panels. At 2:56 A.M. Warms yanked a fire alarm lever and bells began to ring all over the ship, a muffled, scarcely audible ring, as many passengers later described the sound. At 2:57 he pulled an overhead cord. Loud above the sound of the wind and waves was the hoarse bellow of the *Morro Castle*'s whistle, a short and a long blast, the call to stand by boats. At 3:00 A.M. exactly, as Warms told his son, he gave the signal, "Stand by," and at the same moment called to Hoffman, "Left wheel."

The *Morro*, still traveling at 17.7 knots, according to Warms's recollection, heeled over three degrees and the ship swung from north almost to the west. Passengers were thus being brought closer to shore. The wind, instead of blowing from front to rear, began to blow across the ship, leaving the stern area reasonably free of flames. But the ship had already traveled north against the gale for ten minutes as winds fanned the fires below.

A few seconds before 3:00 A.M., there was a tremendous explosion. The ship's Lyle gun, which could fire a breeches buoy to another ship so that passengers could be evacuated, was stored over the writing room, and under it one hundred pounds of powder, the propelling agent.

"The Lyle gun is what really blew it," Howard Hansen says. "It just spread the fire. The explosion smashed all the windows in that area and let the wind in. Not to overlook the fact that crewmen were breaking windows on the boat deck and sun deck to try to get to passengers in the forward suites."

Hansen was asleep in his bunk when Warms woke him up by pulling on his feet. Barefoot, in only his white officer's pants, he rushed down to the fire. "But all the hose stations on the promenade deck were out of order," he says, "and we lost minutes bringing down three hoses from the boat deck, two levels above us. One month before the fire, a leaky hydrant on the promenade deck spread a film of water over the deck. A woman slipped, broke her ankle, and sued the company for twenty-five thousand dollars. The captain told the mates, 'You get a Stillson wrench and put the caps on those hydrants so nobody can get 'em off.' They capped so many hydrants that only three worked on the boat deck and eight on the promenade deck—and none of those latter hydrants was anywhere near the fire. There was just no pressure on the ones we were using.

"After the Lyle gun went off, I said to Freeman, 'We've got to stop this ship. This fire is all out of control.'"

Hansen rushed back to the bridge, but here his story totally contradicts that of Warms. "'We have to stop her,'" he says he told the captain. He quotes Warms as answering, "No, no. We'll make it to Quarantine." If Hansen's memory is accurate and Warms said that, it was an indication of the frenzy that had seized Warms, just as it had seized the whole ship. For Quarantine, well into New York harbor, was still three to four hours distant.

At approximately 3:10 A.M. (no one logged the exact time) the electric wiring had burned through and the ship was in darkness—the smoke below so thick, according to Hansen, that "you couldn't see two feet in front of you."

Bow Watchman Beresford, standing on a wing of the bridge, could see the red glow of the flames on the tossing waves, could watch people struggling to force their bodies through eighteen-inch portholes, and could hear their screams, "My God! My God! I'm burning to death!"

Warms at that moment turned to Quartermaster Hoffman and told him to swing the ship still farther left.

"She will not hold," Hoffman told him. The gyrocompass, the electric steering apparatus, and the standby hydraulic system all had burned out. There was an emergency steering system on the stern, which took six men to operate, and it could have been reached. It was still possible to scramble down the crew's stairway to the engine room and then to reach the stern through two six-foot-high tunnels in which the propeller shafts ran. Warms did not order this to be done.

The ship's turbines were still turning over, and the engine room crew was still on duty, but the *Morro Castle* now had no working rudder. For a moment she drifted helplessly. Warms did the only possible thing left to him. At 3:10.5 A.M., according to the engine room log kept and saved by Cadet Tripp, he ordered slow speed ahead. At 3:13 he began to steer the ship by its motors. Rushing out on the bridge, into the storm, he ordered full speed ahead on the starboard engine, stop on the port engine. In the minutes that followed, he ran from one wing of the bridge to the other, calculating the ship's course, trying to keep her zigzagging closer to shore. At the same time, he was bellowing orders to the crew, trying to stop them from breaking more windows, and directing that the lifeboats be lowered on their davits to a point level with the boat deck, in preparation for "Abandon ship."

At 3:21 A.M. the signal came down to the engine room, "Stop all engines." Warms and Hansen each have a story about the issuance of this order. According to Warms, the fire was so fierce that the engine room crew had to be evacuated, and he issued the appropriate order. Hansen, some thirty-six years later, has another version. "I committed mutiny," he says simply. "When Warms told me, 'We'll make it to Quarantine,' I said to him, 'You damned fool, that's forty miles away! We've got to stop this ship. We won't last that long.'

"I hit him under the right eye, he knocked against the fathometer (which measures the depth of water under the ship's keel), and he fell to the deck. Freeman came running in. 'Where's Warms?' he asked. 'The bastard's on the deck,' I said. Warms got to his feet. He had a bruised right eye. 'What are you fixing to do?' Freeman asked him. 'Drop the hook,' Warms said, and he yelled out the order for the anchor to be lowered."

Beresford and another sailor by this time were standing by the levers that released the anchor. "They kept yelling, 'Drop the anchor!' " Beresford recalls, "but neither one of us knew how to do it. Finally one of the officers came up and released the levers." The anchor went down with a rattle, its four heavy hooks seizing the sandy bottom at a depth of 12 fathoms (72 feet). Then there was one long blast of the whistle, the signal for "Abandon ship."

"I have never seen such total confusion," says Beresford.

"Everybody in the crew was running all over the place. It was like a village volunteer fire department trying to put out a fire in a skyscraper."

The last moments of life for the *Morro Castle* are best described by George Alagna.[2] "At 2:56 A.M. the lights went on in my cabin," he says. "I woke up choking from smoke. I could hear people running, and then a scream, 'We cannot control the fire. The pressure is gone.' I ran into our sleeping quarters and woke Rogers. He was sleeping soundly, and it was hard work to rouse him. He was a big bear of a man. He got out of bed grunting, pulled on his pants and shoes, and the two of us ran into the wireless room." They were followed by Third Operator Maki, who was on duty. Alagna remembers the exact time. It was 3:00 A.M. and he was due back on duty at 4:00 A.M. ship's time.

The first man in the wireless room. Alagna discovered that the power to the wireless set was gone. A small bulb, kept burning when the electrical supply from the ship's generators was working correctly, had gone out. Alagna tried a fresh bulb, but still there was no power. He switched on the emergency battery system just as Rogers lumbered in, sat down in his chair, and adjusted the wireless to the "distress" frequency. But he still had no orders from the bridge to send a distress message.

"Rogers told me," says Alagna, " 'George, go to the bridge and see what orders the mate has to give.' I went forward, but I couldn't get Warms to pay any attention to me. He was saying, 'Is it real, or am I dreaming? Is it real, or am I dreaming?' Flames were shooting out from the center portion of the ship, and the smoke made me gag. There were even yellow flames in the passageway between the mates' quarters and the wireless room.

"I ran back fifty feet to the wireless room, and Rogers looked up at me. 'What about the distress signal?' he asked. I remember answering, 'They've all gone crazy up there on the bridge, and I can't get any cooperation.' It was exactly 3:10 A.M."

Some minutes earlier, on the *Andrea Luckenbach*, Radio Operator George Silverman took a radio bearing on shore stations and climbed to the bridge to report it. Silverman later[3] estimated the time at 2:53 A.M. "There seems to be a ship on fire,"

---

[2] Now president of a technical school in California.

[3] In conversation with fellow members of the Veteran Radio Operators' Association.

the second mate said to him. "I saw it, too," Silverman said later. "The captain told me to call WSC, the station at Tuckerton, and find out if he knew of any ship afire."

Chief Engineer Farr, in a stateroom across from the wireless room, was a light sleeper. He woke to the whine of Silverman's message. A wireless buff, he could read the Morse code. "Haven't heard of any," WSC replied. Farr rolled over and went back to sleep—a brief sleep. The time element is but one of many unresolved questions relating to the last moments of the *Morro Castle*. According to testimony by Rogers, it was 3:13 A.M. when the chief operator said to Alagna, "They're asking about a fire, but we have no orders." It could have been just after 3:00 A.M. when the chief operator and his first assistant tumbled into the wireless room. By then, in the midst of panic, smoke, and flames, they had ceased to keep the ship's wireless log. Both operators had wrapped wet towels around their heads and over their noses and mouths to keep out the smoke. "We looked like a couple of Bedouins," says Alagna.

At 3:15 A.M., as they knew, the silent period would begin. This period, still observed on ships of all nations, lasts for three minutes every half hour around the clock so that ships can stand by to receive emergency messages. It was a direct outgrowth of the *Titanic* disaster, when the radio operator of "the world's safest ship" refused to stop sending commercial messages and receive a warning that the *Titanic* was heading straight into a huge field of icebergs and ice floes.

Alagna, sitting beside Rogers, consulted his wristwatch, the clock on the wall having stopped. "At three fifteen exactly," says Alagna, "I told him, 'Now,' and Rogers began to transmit. He had no orders, so instead of an SOS he sent a CQ, which means, 'Stand by for important message.' "

The little vibrator on the transmitting set chattered back and forth as Rogers signaled, "CQ-CQ-KGOV," the "KGOV" being the call letters of the *Morro Castle*. Tuckerton broke in: "KGOV, wait three minutes."

"They just assumed the *Morro Castle* couldn't be in trouble," says Alagna. "They must have figured we wanted to supplement the information from the *Luckenbach*. But Rogers replied, 'No, ORX, KGOV,' the 'ORX' indicating an emergency."

Rogers turned to Alagna and said, "WSC asks me to stop sending." Alagna answered, "Stop, nothing. It's an emergency." Again he dashed forward, feeling the heat of the deck through the soles of his shoes, and clambered to the bridge. This time he took his wireless operator's hat. "I wasn't sure Warms could recognize me without it."

In the wheelhouse Quartermaster Hoffman was frantically turning an unresponsive wheel, and Warms seemed even more deeply sunk in his daze. "He didn't seem to recognize me at all," says Alagna, "but I finally got his attention when I asked, 'Captain, what about Mr. Wilmott's body? Shouldn't we put it in one of the boats?' He came to, for just a second, but then he started on a dead run, hollering, 'Abbott! Abbott! Damn it, where are you, Chief?' I followed him around a corner of the wheelhouse, and there was Abbott, in full white uniform, cowering against the far side, out of the wind. He was wringing his hands, and saying, 'What shall we do? What shall we do?' Warms shouted, 'Where's the water pressure?' Abbott's answer was, 'It's too late now. A hundred hoses couldn't hold this fire.' "

Abbott was right. The three pumps serving the fire hose system had a capacity of 1300 gallons a minute, but only six of them could be supplied with the maximum pressure of thirty pounds at one time. That was one of the fatal flaws of the safety system aboard the *Morro Castle*. The ship had been designed with forty-two hydrants, but it had been designed on the assumption that only a few of them would have to operate at one time. By this moment crew members had opened every working hydrant (the exact number was never established) and pressure had dropped below one-fourth of normal.

Alagna by now was a frantic young man. He snatched at Warms's sleeve and demanded: "Do you want the chief operator to stand by for an emergency signal?"

"He said, 'All right,' " Alagna remembers, "and I went back with the message. Just minutes later I went forward a third time."

By now the composition floor in the radio room was so blistering hot that Rogers had to put his feet up on the rungs of his chair. When Alagna returned to the bridge, he was desperate.

"Captain," he screamed, "Rogers is dying in there! We can't hold out much longer. It's unbearable."

Warms muttered, "I can't help it. I can't do anything." He was a shattered man, drooping in his white uniform.

"A ship has sighted us," Alagna said. "How about some orders?"

Warms looked at him dully. "Can you send an SOS?" he asked.

"Yes!" Alagna panted.

"Then send it," said Warms.

"But what's our position?" asked Alagna.

"Twenty miles south of Scotland Light," said Warms. "About eight miles off the coast." Actually, he was only between three and four miles offshore.

The SOS order was given at exactly 3:18 A.M. ship's time. A precious eighteen minutes had been wasted since the gravity of the fire became known. As he felt his way toward the radio shack, Alagna lost his way in the swirling smoke and flames. He crawled down to B Deck and crossed to the leeward side. He remembers seeing a man and woman standing there, just clear of the fire. The man's arm was around the woman's waist: "They were just looking out toward the lights on shore, perfectly at ease." [4] Somehow—he doesn't know exactly how—Alagna made his way up one deck and with the assistance of a crewman ("who accused me of not having the intelligence of a cadet") found his way through blistering paint and popping, overheated rivets to Rogers' side once more. He burst through the door and shouted, "Send the SOS! We're twenty miles south of Scotland Light." At 3:23 A.M. the message went out.

The message was received, loud and clear and complete, aboard the nearby *Luckenbach*. Her skipper, Captain Harry (Sam) Hill, ordered a left turn toward the *Morro Castle* and full speed ahead. "We could do a maximum twenty knots," recalls Arthur Farr, "and we shot out of our position like a racehorse out of the starting gate."

On other ships the message was broken by static. The intense heat generated by the *Morro Castle* affected her signals. On the *Monarch of Bermuda*, it was received as, "About twenty miles south of . . ." There were some garbled words, and then ". . . otland." To all these other ships the message was meaningless.

Just as Rogers finished keying the SOS, the batteries in the *Morro Castle's* wireless room exploded, filling the transmitting shack with sulphuric acid gas and covering the floor with boiling battery fluid. Within a minute or two the emergency generator conked out. Calmly, oblivious to heat, acid, and fumes, Rogers made his way to the far side of the room and by feel alone reconnected a wire that had melted loose. At 3:24 A.M. he sent his last message: "CQ, SOS, de [from] KGOV. Twenty miles south of Scotland Light. Cannot work much longer. Fire directly under radio room, need assistance immediately."

[4] Later he learned this calm couple was Dr. and Mrs. Theodore Vosseler of Brooklyn.

In the bland words of an official log, operators at WIM, on a Cape Cod sandspit nearly 250 miles to the north, logged the sequence of events:

3:15 AM EST   Silent period.

3:16 KGOV calls CQ and WSG [Tuckerton] and stops. WSG tells KGOV to QRX [be silent] 3 mins. KGOV waits a couple of seconds and resumes calling CQ and says "QRX may have emergency call."

3:24   SOS SOS SOS de KGOV, "SS *Morro Castle* afire 20 miles south of ? ? ? LV [light vessel]." Lost the name of the LV as KGOV signals dropped out and note broke up and couldn't read the word. Hear nothing after this from KGOV. WSC called him immediately and said, "? ? ? position?" Then the *Monarch of Bermuda* called KGOV and asked repeat of position. Several other ships call KGOV but missed their calls. Hear no more from KGOV here. Word was passed it was "Scotland LV."

3:35 WFCQ [*City of Savannah*] and other calling KGOV but he has not opened up since his SOS. Apparently the fire has put his radio out of commission.

3:45   Silent period all quiet here nil heard here from KGOV since his SOS call.

Rogers, still at his post, was done in. He laid his head down over his transmitter, which by now was dead. "He seemed almost asleep," says Alagna. "He muttered something about going back to the bridge for further orders. I knew both of us would die if we stayed there. I shook him and said, 'Chief, don't you want to see your wife again? The whole place is on fire, and there's nothing more we can do. Skipper says we're to abandon ship. Hurry!'" Arm in arm, the two men staggered forward, with flames licking their backs.

Just then a quixotic impulse seized Acting Captain Warms. Despite the almost unbearable heat, he ran down the stairs to Wilmott's cabin, battered at the door with his fists, and then realized it had swollen shut. Weeping, his feet blistered, he retreated down a steel ladder three levels to the forecastle deck. It was not until later that he realized he had shattered the knuckles of his right hand while trying to rescue his captain's body.

Alagna and Rogers shuffled forward, the former carrying the 250-pound weight of the chief operator, and found themselves at the top of the ladder. The abandoned wheelhouse was an incandescent ball of flame, and out of the choking smoke behind them other flames shot out. Down on the forecastle deck, Alagna recalls, he could make out Warms and a cluster of officers and crewmen, far enough forward to be safe from the fire. As for Third Operator Maki,[5] it subsequently transpired, he had left the ship on one of the first lifeboats to be launched.

As for the late Captain Wilmott, he had fulfilled his careless prediction. He had taken his ship with him.

[5] Deceased in 1953.

5

"ABANDON SHIP!"

There was no order, logic, or reason in the *Morro Castle*'s last half hour of viable life. Her end was in the same frantic tempo as the beginning of the Depression, the day of the 1929 Wall Street crash. In each case, events raced forward relentlessly. There were human panic, noise, and confusion, and then the disaster was complete. But only money values perished on Black Thursday. Human beings perished off Sea Girt on the morning of September 8, 1934, and with them another fragment of the American dream, a trusting faith in the skill of American shipbuilders and the competence of American merchant mariners.

That morning the *Morro Castle*'s officers were frenzied, the crew was divided between the panic-stricken and the dutiful, and the mood of the passengers moved from sleepy confusion to absolute terror. Cut off by the fire amidships, passengers stampeded to the stern. Crew members, except perhaps for a few who tried to fight the flames, stampeded to the forward boat deck. Only Captain Warms on the bridge and Cadet Engineer Tripp in the engine room kept accurate logs of events. But these only began to explain what happened after Warms pulled the fire alarm at 2:56 A.M. To this date, the stories told by living survivors conflict in important respects.

Amid this fiery horror, Chief Engineer Abbott [1] should have been the calmest officer aboard. He was the only four-striper remaining after Wilmott's death. The rank symbolized his past service in command of Ward Line ships. Instead, by the evidence, he was the most panic-stricken. Whether his appropriate station was at the lifeboats, supervising the evacuation of passengers and crew, or whether it was at the engine room five decks down, he failed on both counts. The fire alarm woke him

[1] Now dead.

from sleep in the cabin he shared on the bridge deck with First Engineer Anthony Bujia.[2] Bujia jumped from his bunk, hauled on his one-piece "boiler suit," and sprinted barefoot down the crew's companionway to a platform just above the engines, from which the machinery of the ship was operated.

Abbott, moving slowly, put on his full-dress whites and gold-braided white cap. Across the peak of the cap the words "Chief Engineer" were embroidered in gold. Whether or not this delay was justifiable will forever remain one of the unanswered questions of the disaster. By putting on working clothes and going directly to the engine room, he might have given his engine room crew of forty-seven men the leadership they badly needed in this crisis. He might have drawn on them to man the stern rudder so that the *Morro Castle* could continue to steer a true course. By dressing in whites, he did make himself highly visible, a symbol of assurance to passengers and crewmen on the upper decks . . . except that he had no assurance himself.

Over a phone line from his cabin, Abbott rang up Bujia to ask, "How are things down there?" Bujia answered, "There's some smoke, but no flames are coming in." The ship's automatic ventilating system was drawing the smoke from above into the engine room. Bujia later conceded that he should have closed the vents, "but that wasn't until some time afterward, and by then it was too late."

In leisurely fashion Abbott puttered down toward the engine room, taking the port companionway to A Deck, where disorganized crewmen were unrolling hose, attaching it to the hydrants, and then turning on the water. Just a trickle came out of the nozzles. "Open the valves!" Abbott shouted. The crew shouted back, "They're open as far as they'll go." Almost musing, he continued down to C Deck forward where he met three panic-stricken women. He flung open the door to the crew's companionway and said, "Go up to the boat deck and wait there." This was a means of escape that other passengers, barred by flame, could not use. A steel shell surrounded the companionway from C Deck to an opening in A Deck just below the bridge, and thus no fire could get in.

On the D Deck landing of the companionway he met Bujia, who was on the way up. "Is that you, Mr. Bujia?" he asked, coughing in the dense smoke. "What are you doing, and where are you going?"

2 Reconstructed from Abbott's later testimony and conversations by Bujia, also dead, with his wife, Celia.

"To the bridge. I called you through the telephone and speaking tube and got no answer."

"How is everything below?"

"Good, but we can't stand it much longer."

"Keep the men going," said Abbott. "Don't let anyone leave. Keep them working. Keep the engines going. Don't shut down the turbines until we are driven out."

Coughing and wheezing, Abbott turned back up the companionway to the bridge deck while Bujia went back to his post on the engine room platform. Abbott was not a young man (he was fifty-seven), and surviving crewmen describe him as flabby. The events of the night had numbed him. He used to boast that he knew every rivet in the ship, and now all that knowledge was useless. As he cowered in a corner outside the wheelhouse, those who saw him said he seemed to have given up all hope. Not so the crewmen just below him on A Deck. They were throwing deck chairs and life rings overboard—everything loose that might float and might support a passenger in the water.

When the alarm rang, Able Seaman Clarence Monroe was sleeping in his quarters off the boiler room. "I didn't even hear it," he said, "but a cadet woke me up. I was all packed and ready to take a week off for my brother's wedding. I put on a pair of dungarees and climbed up the companionway to the bridge deck. My fire station was on the port side, but it was already ablaze. We tried to fight the fire with the hoses, but all of a sudden there was no more pressure. Flaming strips of paint were peeling off the superstructure and being blown aft by the wind. That's what made the fire so bad. We were always painting that ship—I guess the idea was to keep the crew busy—and the layers of paint must have been inches thick.

"I could see people jumping, back near the stern, and the ship was still under way. We lowered the forward three boats level with the boat deck. I can remember seeing Abbott jumping back and forth, trying to figure out which boat was going to be lowered first so he could get in. He finally picked No. 1 boat, and he kept hollering, 'Lower away! Lower away!' Lifeboats 7 and 9 came down next. I got in No. 9. We went down on orders of Hackney, and then the whistle blew for 'Abandon ship.' "

Colin (Scotty) Houston, an engine room wiper, was off duty and asleep on the same deck as Monroe, but in another compartment. "I tried to get up the starboard side," he recalls, "but it was just impossible. I finally did get up on the port side on the boat deck. The whole sea was red, and a big cloud of smoke was trailing over the water beyond the stern of the ship. I helped break some windows so we could get passengers out of their staterooms, but of course I didn't realize that what I thought was an act of mercy was also letting the wind into the superstructure and spreading the fire still more. I could hear Hackney yelling, 'Get them boats over! Get 'em off!' One or two of them got hung up on the davits, and they had to chop the cables with axes to let them down. I could see Abbott in No. 3 boat, and he was hollering, 'Lower away!' But then one of the cables got fouled and he hopped out and into No. 1." Abbott was panic-stricken, but at least he had orders to back him up. Warms, realizing there was nothing more the chief engineer could do and sensing his condition, had told him, "Go ahead. Get in a boat."

Purser Robert G. Tolman [3] had moved from his quarters on C Deck behind the ship's office to a suite on A Deck so he would be near the bridge to handle any messages occasioned by Captain Wilmott's death; he took with him Assistant Purser Russell Duvinage. "The only escape," Tolman said later, "was by the crew's stairs. The grand foyer outside my office was full of flames. I burst into my stateroom in pajamas and put on my uniform jacket and trousers. All I could see was flame, and all I could hear was bells and whistles. There was fire in the elevator shaft, and the flames were sucking down the staircase. [Others described the flames as "tumbling down," fed by layers of varnish.] About five minutes later Bob Smith came bounding out of his bedroom, yelling, 'Why didn't you wake me before?' Then the fire got so bad we had to run aft; we couldn't get forward any more."

In the engine room, when the command, "Stop all engines," was followed by "Abandon ship!" there was a wild scramble as crewmen battled each other to be first up the iron companionway steps. From the grating platform above, First Engineer Bujia called down to Third Engineer Arthur Stamper: "Secure the boilers and shut down. Let the fire pumps keep running, and get out." Then Bujia himself fled up the companionway to the boat deck. He hesitated there, beside Boat No. 7.

"Someone grabbed me," he later told his wife, "and yelled, 'Are you going, or do you want to die here like a rat?'" Bujia hopped in as the boat slid smoothly down its cables and landed with a *plop* in the sea.

Paul Arneth, after turning in the fire alarm, had gone forward for the second time to look for his fiancée, Ruth. "I was

[3] His testimony, combined with conversations with Robert Smith.

caught in a mob of crewmen rushing for the boat deck," he says, "and when I got there just about all I could see was crew. The only exception was a gray-haired man wearing only his pajama tops. Later I found it was Dr. Cochrane. The two of us, the only passengers around, jumped into No. 1 boat with Abbott. I never saw a man so panic-stricken."

Boat No. 1 was motor powered. Arneth recalls that one of the sailors (it was Quartermaster Fleischman) shouted, "Try to start that motor!" He also remember that Abbott said, "Don't start it. There are sparks coming from the ship." As Boat No. 1, propelled by a northeast wind, swept down the length of the *Morro Castle*, Abbott spoke again. According to Arneth, he said, "Let's try to hold on by the stern. We might pick up someone." According to Seaman Fred Walther, Abbott said, "We can't do a thing. We might as well head for shore." The lifeboat, with Arneth and seven sailors taking oars, swept through bobbing heads and imploring cries and pitched toward the shore.

Assistant Cruise Director Cluthe, meanwhile, had spent hours in Purser Tolman's cabin discussing the captain's death. About 2:00 A.M. ship's time, he recalls, he went to his stateroom off the grand foyer. He spent a few moments changing the gilt buttons and epaulets on his uniform to a clean uniform, and then lay down to sleep. The night had been a little too exciting for this young man, and sleep did not come easily. He turned on the light over his bunk in Room 318 and began to study a Spanish-English textbook given him by a friend in Havana. "I don't know what time it was," he says, "but there was a knock on my door and obviously all hell had broken loose outside. There was the sound of whistles and bells and people running—even a bugler. He was one of the stewards who woke everyone up for breakfast on the cruise by blowing reveille on his bugle.

"I reported to my duty station on the bridge, and then I thought about Bob Smith. I rushed down to his room, and it was so smoky I couldn't see my hand in front of me. I dragged him out, laid him on the floor, and he came to and put on his white uniform. When we got outside, the elevator shaft was in flames, and so was the staircase. All the passageways had four to eight inches of water running down them. I could see that the only safe way out for the passengers was aft, so both Bob and I kept urging people in that direction."

Robert Smith, after two drinks in the purser's office, had gone to bed a little after midnight. "I was awakened," he said, "by my assistant breaking in and yelling, 'Bob, for God's sake, get up.

Half the ship's on fire.' I got up and put on my white uniform pants, coat, and cap, and walked out into the lobby, and they had hoses on the fire coming down the stairs and the elevator shaft. That was sometime after three A.M. I had slept for almost an hour while they were working outside my door."

Smith, who also believes the captain was given a Mickey Finn to induce a heart attack, is puzzled by his own sound sleep. "I was never that heavy a sleeper," he says. "I think I must have been slipped a sleeping powder or something, though I can't imagine why, for all the men with whom I was drinking were already up and around. Maybe I got a drink that was made for someone else." For nearly half an hour, Smith estimates, he was running up and down the passageways on C Deck beating on doors to awaken passengers. "But to this day," he says, "I couldn't tell how many of the people I was trying to get up actually got up. I couldn't stop to check."

Howard Hansen, making his way astern, suddenly confronted Van Zile, the ship's doctor, on the afterdeck. "Hanse," said Van Zile, "it's time to go."

"No," said Hansen. "I'll stay. You go if you want to."

"Well," said Van Zile, "I've got to have a drink first." He rushed back to his cabin and came out with a jug of rum.

"He took a long swig out of a gallon jug," says Hansen. "Then he put it down on the deck, threw on a life belt, and jumped overboard. He jumped feet first. I suppose those blocks of heavy cork inside the life preserver came up and hit him in the chin, for I saw blood gush from his face, and then he turned over, face down, and floated away."

6

"JUMP OR BURN!"

Between 3:00 A.M. and 5:00 A.M., medical experts say, are the hours of deepest sleep. It was just about 3:00 A.M. ship's time (4:00 A.M shore time) when pandemonium took command of the *Morro Castle*—bells ringing faintly in some staterooms, loudly in others; stewards banging on metal serving trays or battering on doors, and above all this noise the commanding voice of the ship's whistle, calling, "Attention! Attention!" How many passengers were sodden with drink or simply sodden with sleep will never be known. It was enough that they woke to the most frightening experience of their lives. Some fled naked down the corridors to the stern, pursued by smoke and flame; some were in their nightclothes. A few, prisoners of habit, dressed themselves carefully as if they were about to walk down the gangplank. There were women who put on their rings, brushed their hair, slipped into dresses and coats, and emerged on the lurching deck carrying their handbags.

Flames were sweeping unhindered down the corridors of B and C decks, rolling down staircases thick with many layers of varnish, licking out open portholes in the ballroom and dining room. No fire doors had been closed. The Ward Line had dispensed with automatic doors; they had to be shut manually. Though Warms, on the bridge, had ordered, "Shut them doors!" the mate who received the command never passed it on. Possibly he was wise. The fire had gained such headway by the time passengers were awakened that closing the doors could have trapped scores of them in the flames. The plywood paneling in the public rooms, six layers of kiln-dried wood glued together with an outer veneer of precious wood, was feeding the fire and sending out gusts of choking smoke, black and oily. All the elegant decor of this magnificent cruise ship was being consumed—the Italian Renaissance paneling of the smoking room; the imitation Louis XVI trim of the library with its panels

54

painted in the style of Watteau; the mural of Perseus rescuing Andromeda on the ceiling of the dining room. Heat, surging through the steel superstructure, made the decks almost unbearable to stand on. Marine glue that held the planking in place began to ooze out stickily; oakum, used for calking, gave off a stifling odor. The ship was still moving head-on into the storm, which swept tongues of flame and billows of smoke back through the fog and rain toward the stern. Now darkness was beginning to give way to the first wan light of day on the horizon, and at intervals the storm wrack lifted to reveal lights ashore, the lights of Sea Girt, Belmar, and Spring Lake, where people still slept soundly, unconscious of tragedy a few miles distant.

Each survivor of the *Morro Castle* has a different memory, depending on where his or her stateroom was located and how far the fire had progressed in that area. Lillian Davidson [1] was on C Deck not far from the open stern. A registered nurse at Columbia Presbyterian Hospital in New York, she was accustomed to emergencies, and her account is unemotional. "It was just about three A.M., and I was sleeping blissfully," she says, "when there came a battering on my door. It was Dr. and Mrs. Paul Giannini of Brooklyn. They had been very kind to me and my roommate, Martha Bradbury, [2] who was also a nurse at Presbyterian. 'Get up, girls,' the doctor called. 'Don't bother to put on your dresses. Just put on your life preservers.'

"We came out in our nightclothes, barefooted. I remember seeing Bob Smith, the cruise director, helping passengers to the stern. Behind us was nothing but smoke, nauseating smoke, and an occasional lick of flame. I could hear the ship's whistle blasting away. Somebody ordered us up a companionway to B Deck, but the smoke was so terrible, so choking, that we came down again to C Deck. The people were all jammed together in the stern in semidarkness, and I can remember the heat of the fire coming up from the deck. I really don't know whether the ship was still under way—there was such pandemonium. Great sheets of flaming paint were peeling off the superstructure and whipping past us, carried by the wind. There were women whose hair was aflame as they beat at it with their hands. I said to Martha, 'We'll have to jump.' She said, 'But I have so much to lose!' For some reason I had a calm faith that I'd make it to shore. I remember saying, 'I have nothing to lose. It's either jump or burn.'"

[1] Now Mrs. Perry Lockwood, Fort Myers, Florida.
[2] Now Mrs. Martha Valentine of Long Island.

Lillian Davidson climbed up on the rail, pushed out as she leaped, to clear the ship, and dropped 27 feet 6 inches into the waves on the starboard side. "Martha jumped just afterward," she recalls, "but the high seas separated us. I paddled around for a while alongside the boat, but then I heard somebody say she might capsize, so I struck out for shore. It was daylight by then, but the same wind that blew toward shore set off a tide rip that held me outside the breakers. I counted the windows on the cottages and hotels in Spring Lake over and over again, just to keep alert. I had lots of company in the water, but they were all dead, lying face down, still floating in their life preservers. I'd probably gone overboard a little before three thirty A.M. ship's time, but as the hours passed, I didn't have the strength to get in. I could swim, but not for such a long session. Then a plane came boring through the storm and circled me three times to show that I'd been recognized."

Mr. and Mrs. Robert O. Meissner of Brookyn, members of the Concordia Society, survived the disaster to die normal deaths years later, but they left their children a legacy. A few days after they were rescued, each of them sat down and wrote out an account of their experiences, which constitutes perhaps the most coherent record of the fire. Wrote Mrs. Meissner:

Being a very light sleeper, I was awakened at three o'clock by hundreds of sparks passing by our stateroom, No. 314 on D Deck (forward of the dining saloon). I immediately woke Rob, my husband. He looked out the porthole and said, "My God, hurry and dress, the ship is on fire." I was panic-stricken and hysterical, crying and trembling. He forced me to put on a few clothes and put life preservers on each of us. We opened our door and found the whole place flooded. Water was over our shoes, with charred pieces of wood floating around. No one woke us. We heard no whistles or fire bells. When we reached the corridor upstairs, jammed with frightened people crying and pushing toward the deck, all the lights went out. Some people on deck were crying and shivering in their nightclothes; some were jumping into the dark, angry water. Only a few had life preservers. The round ones with the ship's name on them were locked on the bulkheads.

The engines were going full blast, and the wind fanned the flames into a fury. We could scarcely breathe. Some of the crew held sheets under the fire hoses and tore them into strips so we could breathe into them. The rails were burning now, and the decks. We went below one deck, choking and coughing. The center of the ship was a mass of flame. The doors from the stern to the interior of the ship looked as if they were ready to burst open and burn us all alive. The officers and crew, except for two Negroes, did not come to the rear where people were screaming and drowning. One of the few people I did recognize on deck was Mrs. Julia Rueda, a Cuban woman living in New York. She'd been seasick, and I'd taken care of her two little boys, Dickie, age three, and Benito, age seven. Tears were streaming down her face as she begged: "Please help me with my babies. Take Dickie, my baby, and try to save him." She made me promise not to let go of him. She jumped off with Benny. He was crying, jumping up and down, saying, "I can't breathe. I can't breathe," and when she lifted him to the rail, he said, "Don't push me over." Mrs. Rueda jumped off with him. Somebody threw over a line with a life ring attached for Dickie, but when he went overboard into the water he fell right past it.

It was either burn alive or jump into the ocean. So, afraid as I was, I chose the water and slid down a hawser. I couldn't stop myself and went way down under the water. I came up screaming and grabbed the rope again, and then my husband swam up and helped me hold on until somebody could rescue us.

Both Meissners were fully dressed. Mrs. Meissner even had on her waffle-weave spring coat. Meissner put on his business suit and black shoes. As a parting act, he jammed a new gray fedora hat on his head. It had been given him as a going-away present by a son-in-law, Robert Durland. Mr. Meissner wrote:

There was panic in the corridors on B Deck. We had to go up there because the dining saloon was a mass of flames. I yelled at them, "Be quiet! Go slow!" There were about two hundred people on the afterdeck, men in BVDs, women in nightgowns, but by then very little panic. I told my wife not to jump until I told her to. I made her get down near the deck where there was more fresh air. By then we had moved down to C Deck. The ship was still going. Her propellers were churning up the water in great shape.

Nevertheless, people did jump, and no doubt were dragged under. We kept moving half an hour when the engines stopped after having fanned the flames all through the boat. We saw a ship five miles away [actually the *Andrea Luckenbach*] and I quieted the people by saying help was near, but that ship never came near us. A daylight never looked prettier to me than that one. Some men told jokes, and there was even a group singing "Hail, Hail, the Gang's All Here." When I saw my wife go down the hawser, I jumped and landed close to her. I knew then we were going to be rescued. This was a sad ending to wonderful trip. I don't think anyone on the boat could say or would say different.

Lillian Davidson and the Meissners were among the lucky ones. The *Morro Castle* life preservers were filled with heavy blocks of cork, sewed into compartments. Acting Third Officer Hansen, who by now had found his way through smoke and flames to the stern, says: "Those poor passengers didn't know how to handle life preservers. A lot of them held their hands at their sides. When they hit the water, the cork blocks slammed up under their chins and knocked them out so that they drowned, or fractured their necks so they died instantly. Then there were others who held their hands over their heads. They just simply slipped through their life preservers, and a good many of them drowned right there alongside the boat."

Luck also accompanied Eleanor Friend [3] and her roommate Augusta Tusrin.[4] "Our cabin on C Deck was practically at the stern," Miss Friend remembers. "I'm a very light sleeper, and when the commotion began, I went out on deck, apparently just as the fire alarm was turned in. I could hear the noise, but I assumed it would soon be over. There was one very nice officer there [Robert Smith] who was reassuring the passengers as they came out, then all of a sudden there were waves of flame and smoke. I went back to the stateroom and put on my tweed coat over my nightgown. As the flames came out, they swept from one side of the ship to the other, so I jumped—one of the first. A group of us got together and made a circle, singing and talking to keep up our spirits. Among them was Augusta, but then I lost her.

"Though I had a life preserver, I was getting tired, but still I swam around until I found Augusta again. For a long time I held her head out of water by her hair, but then she drifted away from me again."

Augusta Tusrin has a more sardonic memory. "The rich people got it in that fire," she says, "the people in the luxury cabins up on A and B decks. We were lucky that we couldn't afford such luxurious accommodations. Both of us, I guess, woke about the same time. By the time we were out on deck, the ship was on sort of a zigzag course but still moving. Then the fumes and odor hit us and we could see the whole center of the ship with flames shooting up and blowing back toward us."

[3] Now of Glens Falls, New York.
[4] Now Mrs. Herman Shapiro of Forest Hills, New York.

The scene in the water, lit luridly by the fire, was as grim as a scene from Dante's *Inferno*, as Augusta Tusrin describes it: "There were people screaming for help, tossed to and fro by the waves. There were bodies floating face down. People without life preservers were swimming from body to body, untying the preservers and putting them on themselves. People were hanging on to us, including a dishwasher from the galley. The waves would lift us high in the air and then drop us down into the troughs, where all we could see was a wall of water on either side. It was then that I fainted, and if it hadn't been for Eleanor I most certainly would have died."

Six girls from the Concordia Society excursion jumped almost simultaneously. Among them were Elsie Suhr,[5] Ruth Fabel, and Charlotte [6] and Ethel Behr. "We all held hands," says Miss Suhr, "after lingering on C Deck until the heat and smoke were too much for us. There was a priest there, and as I remember he said, 'Will all Catholics come over here, and we'll say a Hail Mary.' Someone in our group got very angry and yelled, 'What's the matter with the Protestants?' and we all started to say the Lord's Prayer together. There was very little panic on that deck, but believe me, I was scared. It was so crowded and so dark you couldn't see anything, and you didn't know who was on deck. But after we jumped, I felt more sure of myself. I remember giving the side of the ship a push to get away from her. The propellers must have stopped, but there was still a suction. After a while one of the girls began to cry and to say she couldn't go on. I said to her, 'What's the matter with you? Hang on!' She did hang on, and we sang and talked for hours, waiting for rescue."

Ruth Fabel, part of this group, woke up choking and gasping. "At first I thought it must be somebody smoking a cigarette outside my door," she says, "but it was too thick for that. I woke my roommate, Mary Gilmore, and said, 'We'd better get up and dress and put on our life preservers.' There was really panic in the corridors, people pushing and shoving, and I lost Mary almost at once. The decks were so hot my feet hurt, and the ship was still in motion. But I could see the lights onshore, and that gave me confidence. People were just showering down into the water, and a lot of them simply fell right through their life preservers. I was supposed to jump with Elsie Suhr, but I wouldn't. She was heavier than I was, and she'd have pulled me down. Anyway,

[5] Now of Lakewood, New Jersey.
[6] Now of White Plains, New York.

being dreadfully afraid of the water, I was scared to jump. I had wet rags over my nose, but I still couldn't breathe. The next thing I knew, somebody threw over a rope and I saw Mr. [George] Ridderhoff, a family friend. 'Where's Paul?' I asked. 'Nobody knows where anyone is,' he said. 'Now be a good girl and slide down.' I let go of the rope when I hit the water, but I didn't know there was no boat there. The propellers must still have been moving, for I saw several people sucked toward the ship. I paddled as hard as I could and got away. I saw two or three young fellows, and eventually all of us got together, and I felt sure we'd be saved."

Elsie Suhr's memory of a Catholic priest on C Deck was correct. Father Raymond A. Egan [7] of St. Mary's Church in the Bronx, New York, ordained for only fifteen months, was aboard on a vacation trip. He appeared on deck with Switchboard Operator Henry Stamm. Standing several rungs up on a steel ladder, he recited a number of rosaries and heard the stammered confessions of those seeking absolution. He brought a small space of quiet and reassurance to a scene of panic. With the flames crackling behind him, as Stamm dabbed at his burned face with a wet cloth, he moved firmly through the prayers—the Apostles' Creed, an Our Father, three Hail Marys, the Gloria, a sequence of exhortations, and a general absolution. One crewman later told a colleague [8] that he said seventeen rosaries. With his hands and feet burned, Father Egan was one of the last off the stern.

In the vortex of all this frenzy, there were those who were calm beyond belief. Mr. and Mrs. George Whitlock [9] were far forward on B Deck in Suite 108, one of the more luxurious staterooms. Whitlock was president of the First National City Bank of New York, returning with his wife from a business visit to the bank's branch in Havana. She was crippled by a leg injury and barely able to walk. Whitlock tenderly guided her down the promenade deck through smoke and fire, and then down to C Deck, where nearly all passengers had congregated. With the help of crewmen, he put a life jacket on her, rigged a "bos'n's chair," with loops of rope fitted around her body, and lowered her to the water, where she disengaged herself and swam safely away. Whitlock, however, stayed on deck, urging—and

---

[7] Who died in 1957.

[8] Monsignor Jeremiah Nemecek, still a pastor in the Bronx.

[9] As they told the story to their daughter-in-law, Mrs. George Whitlock, Jr., of Garden City, Long Island.

sometimes shoving—people overboard. He was one of the last to leave the stern of the *Morro Castle*.

Evelyn Hendrix [10] had boarded the ship with her friends and neighbors, Agnes and Ruth Prince. "They lived just a few squares away from me in Pottstown, Pennsylvania," she says. "We all had jobs, and we all had the same vacation time. When we decided to go on a cruise, we called Wanamaker's, in Philadelphia, and asked what was available and at what price. They recommended the Ward Line highly, and that's how we found ourselves on the *Morro Castle*. I really don't remember who my roommate was; all I remember is that she got to the stateroom first and took the lower bunk so that I had to sleep on the shelf above her. The next thing I knew, there was a steward banging at the door, yelling, 'Fire! Fire! Get up!' I had my clothing all laid out for disembarkation in the morning, so I grabbed a brown plaid suit and rushed out on deck. The ship was still moving and I could see lights ashore. I kept wondering why the ship was driving straight up the coast instead of turning toward the shoreline. I jumped, I guess, at about three thirty A.M. ship's time. That was when my watch stopped.

"There were three boys on deck we three girls had dated. They thought it was all a joke, but when it got really hot and smoky, we all jumped, one after the another, and then in the water we stuck together."

Agnes Prince, with a newspaperwoman's alertness to oddities, remembers that the number thirteen figured in the cruise from beginning to end. The ship sailed from Pier 13 East River, the Prince sisters shared stateroom 313, and their hotel room in Havana was No. 13. "It must have been a lucky number," she concludes, "or we wouldn't be here today." Ruth Prince was the first to smell smoke. She woke her sister and then called Operator Stamm on the telephone. "Is there a fire aboard?" she demanded. "A slight fire," said Stamm. "Nothing serious." The smoke thickened in seconds. Both girls knew where their life belts were, underneath the berths, and both knew their life stations. They dressed hastily and went out into the corridor. A group of young men came toward them. "There's a fire, you know," said Agnes. "Oh, you're kidding!" said the young men, but just then a burst of flames swept down a corridor of C Deck, where their stateroom was located.

"It was, purely and simply, pandemonium," says Agnes. "The lights went out, and I can remember a sailor grabbing me

[10] Now Mrs. John Mengel of West Leesport, Pennsylvania.

roughly and shoving me toward the stern. We simply followed the mob, and climbed up to C Deck. I can remember the sight of the priest giving absolution to kneeling people, and I kept thinking, 'This can't possibly be happening to me.'"

Ruth picks up the story: "I have never seen such confused, frightened people in my life," she says. "There were women with their hair still in curlers, men with no clothes, everybody pushing and shoving and confused. We climbed from D Deck to C and because our lifeboat stations were on B Deck we continued up. The whole place was in flames, with the boats hanging at crazy angles. Below us, we could see a few boats that had gotten away, with people in them, but they didn't stay around. Either the crew was panicky or there weren't enough men to handle the oars in that fierce wind. I kept thinking, Oh, here we are, about to be burned to death like rats. So then we went back down to C Deck. The ship was shifting and heaving under the force of the gale, and the wind was howling through the rigging— screaming, I might better say. Pieces kept tumbling off the superstructure. Agnes and I went overboard before the ship stopped, but we pushed out far enough to get away from the propellers."

There were gallant people as well as cravens, Agnes Prince remembers—a handsome young man who gave his life preserver to an elderly man, saying, "You need this more than I do. . . ." Cruise Director Smith, the one responsible person in this collection of mad and frustrated crewmen and passengers, joking: "You've nothing to worry about, girls. We're going to put this fire out. You're as safe here as at 42nd and Broadway. A boat will be along any minute to pick you up." In the water the Prince girls became part of another group that sought security in numbers, that clustered together, that helped one another, that joked and sang and predicted an early rescue. Yet all the time, says Ruth, there was silent witness to the magnitude of the disaster, bodies that floated alongside them and that they ignored.

The Lovelands, Frank and Nathene, can still remember the utter panic on the stern of C Deck. "I awoke to a noise that sounded as if somebody were playing shuffleboard over my head," Mrs. Loveland says. "I opened the door and saw flames, but I still thought it was something localized. I said to my husband, 'Something doesn't sound right to me,' and he said, 'Oh, it's just people on the deck above. Let's go back to sleep.' Then when I saw the flames I slipped on a gingham dress and was about to start out the door when Frank ordered me to put on my underpants. I obeyed him, quite meekly, and we started out together. We came out on a deck full of smoke and flame. We had to keep climbing until we reached C Deck. It was full of noise and singing. People were chanting hymns, others with life preservers were asking us for help—and we had forgotten our own life preservers! We had the calm of shock. We felt perfectly hopeless, to go in that ocean in the dark without much chance of being saved. I wasn't so worried about myself; I could swim well, and I had my life-saving certificate. I hit the water, and then I couldn't find Frank. I swam out into the middle of a lot of people, and I was the only one without a life preserver. I tried to rest on someone's life preserver while treading water, and two men shoved me off. There wasn't much chivalry out in that dark and tossing ocean.

"Yet I learned something from one woman I had despised while on board. I could hardly look at her in the dining room, she was so loud and demanding, with such bad manners. In the term of the day, you'd call her a floozy. Yet she was the noblest person there. After I took a life preserver off a corpse, we swam together. When we got cold we could hold our bodies close, and one would tread water while the other rested. We swam to one lifeboat, and they turned us away: 'No room, full up.' I felt like Alice in Wonderland: 'No room, no room.' That was not my feeling. A few minutes earlier I saw a baby floating in the water, still alive. I held that child in my arms until its face turned blue and I knew it was dead, and then I let it float away into that maelstrom of wind-whipped waves."

"Naturally, we didn't think of life preservers," says Frank Loveland. "Another two minutes and our cabin would have been sealed off by flames. I wasn't worried about my wife, for she was an excellent swimmer. Myself, I could barely swim ten to fifteen yards. There was one little child on the deck with its mother, and neither had life preservers. At the very stern a purser in uniform was standing, wearing a life preserver and holding a bag of papers or money—I don't know which, and I don't know who he was. I said to him, 'Why not give your life preserver to that woman with a child?' He simply looked at me and remained silent. By then the ship had anchored and Nathene had jumped. I stuck as long as I could. When I did jump, I was caught by a flagpole sticking out from the stern, and jammed in the angle between the pole and the ship. I just stayed. I knew that if I went in the water I'd be dead, so I just took the smoke. People were sliding down ropes hanging over the stern. They'd start down, burn their fingers and palms, and then drop into the water like ripe apples. I could reach over and help the people on the ropes, so I forgot my own trouble. One little child was lowered by his mother; then I tied a rope around her and helped to lower her. My shoulders were burned from the roasting heat, but finally I saw a lifeboat out beyond me. I dropped in, and they picked me up."

Nathene Loveland was a long time forgetting the *Morro Castle*. Her weight dropped from 124 pounds to 96 pounds, and for months she suffered from terrible nightmares.

7

THE LAST AGONY

It was in keeping with the unutterable confusion aboard the *Morro Castle* that the one officer in uniform visible to the passengers on C Deck was not a seafaring man at all. It was also, possibly, the salvation of many, jammed on the after-deck in a space only twenty feet long and fifty feet wide. For Cruise Director Smith was the only officer they knew, saw regularly, and therefore trusted in this moment of horror. He was their liaison with the captain. Tall and genial, at this moment he exuded confidence. The ship was still plunging straight into the storm when he appeared on deck. "Don't jump!" he shouted. "You'll be chewed up by the propellers. Just wait, and there'll be boats along." Most passengers, accepting this both as an order and as a promise, stood fast. Of the few who ignored him, nearly all were sucked into the propellers or dashed against the steel-plated side of the *Morro Castle*, which was still moving at close to full speed. As the babbling and wailing rose to a crescendo, Smith shouted, "Silence, please! I am waiting for orders from the bridge." It was quiet for a moment, but as tongues of flame licked toward the stern, the noise began again. He heard a man bawling, "Jump! The ship is going to blow up!" This man, he is quite certain, was John Kempf, the New York fireman. "He acted and sounded like an officer," says Smith, "and some people believed him."

"The ship is not going to blow up!" Smith bellowed, and then paused. Through the soles of his blistering feet, he could sense that the *Morro Castle* had stopped. From deep in the trough of a wave, a man cried to him, "Smith, for God's sake, send us a boat!" At that exact moment, as he was framing a reply, he felt a light tap on his arm. An elderly woman, dressed even to white gloves and coat, with a glistening leather handbag under her arm, was peering up at him. "Mr. Smith," she said, "please save me." Wordlessly, he took off his life preserver and tied it around her. "God bless you," she said, and walked to the rail. "I then saw several of our own lifeboats going past us with only a handful of people aboard," says Smith. "But they didn't stop to pick up anyone. They disappeared in the smoke that lay low on the waves, trailing out perhaps three hundred feet behind the ship."

It was then that Smith realized that the *Morro Castle* was doomed. "I knew we had to jump pretty soon, because we were all being badly burned," he recalls. "If we didn't jump, we'd be incinerated. A whole group of passengers went overboard in a rush, and I helped some of them. The crew had put hawsers overboard by then, but most of the people were too far away from them and too frightened to use them. It was so hot on C Deck that I could hear the glass popping in the portholes and the flames crackling just a few feet behind me. I heard one man screaming, 'Jump! Jump! I'm being burned! Jump!' as he danced nude against a background of flame with his hair on fire. With that, a human torch, he jumped overboard."

Some fifty passengers still lingered, torn between the known terror of fire and the unknown terror of the sea. "Come on!" yelled Smith. "We'll go down to D Deck." Only a handful followed him, for suddenly flames barred the steel stairway leading to the lower deck. The rest turned to Purser Robert Tolman, dressed only in his uniform pants. Tolman, though senior in rank to Smith, had succumbed to a sort of wordless despair. He did not take command. He had helped the stewards rip apart wet bed sheets and handed them to the passengers to put over their mouths and noses so they could filter out the heavy, acrid smoke. When he found one man wearing two life preservers, "I took one away and gave it to a lady myself." Finally, when C Deck became unbearable, he clung to the rail, stood on a fishplate—a tiny projection between decks—and helped pass the rest of the passengers down to Steward Boggetti on D, a little more than nineteen feet above the water.

Acting Third Officer Hansen, who had found his way safely to the stern through a rabbit warren of staircases and passageways not yet afire, was equally helpless in the face of a disaster he could not even comprehend. Acting First Officer Freeman had made the same trip a few moments earlier—a trip too complicated for the terrorized passengers, who were unwilling to move a step toward the flaming center of the liner. Freeman came back to the bridge and told Hansen: "The stern's full of passengers. See what you can do to get 'em overboard." By then, recalls Hansen, "The lifeboats were burning on their davits. I found my way back to the tourist lounge. I helped the crew throw overboard settees, tables, boxes, and anything else that might float. Eventually I jumped myself. The ship was a goner. There simply was nothing else I could do."

Assistant Cruise Director Cluthe remembers the nightmare aspects of the fire. "We had an awful time waking the passengers," he says. "We had to ram the doors with our shoulders in some cases to get them out—some of them drunk, some of them half drunk, and some of them stupefied by sleep. Imagine their confusion, not knowing what was going on: people running around screaming, water running down the corridors, flames crackling and whistles blowing. A good many of them were young Cubans who were going north to school. It wasn't possible to give them reservations until the *Morro Castle* had sailed from New York and we could see what was available. So you might have a mother and father forward and two daughters aft. That led to terrible confusion in the passageways as families tried to find each other.

"I came out on C Deck, where I found Bob Smith. It was a tiny deck, and people were jammed in as they would be on a New York subway train. There were two wooden doors, one on each side of the main part of the ship, and in each door was a glass porthole about an inch thick. That fire was so hot that the glass melted and trickled down over the doors. We were really fighting for our lives. People went down the mooring lines and hung like a lot of flies, one atop another. Others were sitting on the railings, and a number of them jumped over before the ship lost way. I was fearful of the suction, and screamed, 'No, don't do it!' It was cruel, seeing people so petrified, and we never knew when the doors were going to go.

"There was still pressure in the water system, so I snatched up a hose and played it on the doors. I got so exhausted, so cold —in the middle of that heat from the fire—that I could hardly control myself. I just had on an undershirt and my white pants, no insignia of rank. When you aren't trained in these things, it is very hard to know what to do. All I had in my mind was to get these poor souls off the ship.

"I don't blame those who got away in the lifeboats. People later called them cowards, but I don't agree. There weren't enough trained oarsmen aboard, and it was just about impossible to handle those big, heavy boats. So when almost everyone had gone, I went overboard. I had no life preserver, but I bumped into a woman's corpse with a life preserver hanging on one arm. I was too weak to put it on. I just lay on it."

Down in the engine room, where Third Engineer Arthur Stamper was in command, the fourteen-man crew departed a moment after "Stop all engines" clanged out on the bell that responded to the ship's telegraph system. The departure was calm, most of the men contended. There was disagreement on this detail, however. It was a hysterical flight, said Oiler Antonio Giorgio after he was rescued—men grabbing at each other's legs, pulling each other down, crowding up the winding steel ladders and the crew's companionway toward the passenger decks. After officials of the Ward Line talked to him ashore, he retracted his whole story. Other crewmen said they were told: "If you're good to the company, the company will be good to you." At a time when jobs were almost impossible to find, that was promise enough to close men's mouths.

At about 3:32 A.M. ship's time First Engineer Bujia appeared on the deck above the operating platform and called to Stamper: "Shut everything down but the feed pump and the fire pump and get out." Virtually by feel, because his flashlight gave out only a dim glow amid the smoke, Stamper pushed buttons and pulled switches until the main motors fell silent, but the turbines still were running. These could explode from overheating, for the oil supply lines were to be turned off. As he groped his way into the lower engine room, he collided with Junior Engineer Lewis Wright. "Shut off the fires and turn off the oil," he ordered, and then crawled between the twin turbines to lower the bars that served as switches. His work was not yet done. Peering at the gauges in the dim illumination of his flashlight, he set maximum pressure on the fire pump and the steam valves. This assured that water would continue to flow to the hydrants as long as any pressure remained in the boilers.

"When we stopped the turbines," he said later, "we hollered to see if there was anyone left, and when no one answered, we took our chances and jumped." They could not use the same escape route as the crew. Cadet Engineer Tripp had tried. He came back into the engine room gagging and vomiting. "Too much smoke," he gasped, and then fumbled his way into the starboard propeller shaft tunnel, which led all the way to the rear of the ship. This, a few minutes later, was the route of escape for Stamper and Wright. Within this six-foot-high tunnel, as they moved toward the stern, they breathed fresh air. Eventually, using a crew's companionway, they stumbled out on D

Deck. Grimy as he was, Stamper in uniform was a visible token of command. Marjorie Budlong, daughter of an oil company executive, recalled him later as a calming presence.

"The ship can't blow up," he assured questioners. "We've shut off the oil valves. Don't jump until you have to. The lifeboats ought to be along soon." He turned to a group of fully clothed women and said, "You don't need all those clothes. They'll pull you under. Just wear your slips." Obediently, woman after woman followed his orders. As the women on C Deck had done, they piled their bags, girdles, coats, and shoes neatly on the deck. One passenger, Mrs. James F. Kennedy, had inadvertently anticipated his instructions. She came on deck in a bathing suit. "There was so much commotion and so much smoke I was sure we would have to swim," she told the newspapers later, "so I dressed for swimming."

Edward J. Brady, a Philadelphia corporation executive, had been sick. The Bradys took the trip so he could recuperate. He jumped a moment after his wife, but the waves separated them. He died in the water. Their daughter, Nancy, and Mrs. Brady survived.

Though Ruth Torborg and her fifteen-year-old brother, John, were at opposite ends of the ship when the fire broke out, coincidence brought them together on D Deck. "I was sitting on a stanchion," says John Torborg, "with my Uncle Herman standing alongside. I said to Uncle Herman, 'Gee, I wonder where Ruthie is?' With that there was a voice in back of me saying, 'Is that you, Jack?' and there she was. We stayed on D Deck until it was a quarter of six or so. Somewhere we got a life preserver, and I gave it to Ruthie. There wasn't much panic, except at one point when the ship must have swung into the wind and the smoke blew back. People yelled, 'Jump, jump!' But when the ship turned again and the smoke wasn't so bad, everyone calmed down. Someone led people in prayer; there was a little bit of singing, but not much. There was a fellow named Smith who was there, the cruise director. He and another fellow said to go from the stern along the side to get to the front part of the boat, but nobody wanted to budge."

John, now in his fifties, seems to have remembered every detail. "By quarter of six," he says, "there were other boats about —the *Monarch of Bermuda*, the *Savannah*, and the *Luckenbach*, and I think the *President Cleveland*. About then Ruthie went over the side. Ruthie was a heavy girl. She started down on the hawser, but couldn't hold her own weight, and down she went.

I was at the rail watching her. I saw a piece of cork from the life belt, another piece, and then up came Ruthie. She waved to me, then she struck out for one of the lifeboats from the rescue ships, and we saw her picked up. Now there weren't more than twenty-five people back there. I saw a crewman come out of one of the doors. He was wearing a sort of jump suit [uniform for the engine crew] and his suit was smoldering. He threw over a deck chair, and then over he went and held onto the deck chair in the water.

"It was raining, and it was cold, mostly, I suppose, because we had been so hot on that deck. There were four of us left: My Uncle Herman, myself, Mr. [William F.] Price, a retired New York City policeman, and George Ridderhoff. I didn't have a life belt, but Uncle Herman did. He said he would go over first, then I could go over and hang onto him with the life belt. We could see the *Monarch* not too far away, maybe one hundred and fifty feet. My uncle went down the hawser and swung himself free and began to paddle away. He looked very dignified, because he always swam the breast stroke. Mr. Price said to me, 'Go ahead, your uncle is waiting for you,' so I went down. I was so cold when I touched that water that I went up the rope about five feet and then dropped into the water. I passed Uncle Herman and went right to a lifeboat from the *Monarch,* and they pulled me in. Then they got Uncle Herman and then Mr. Ridderhoff and then Mr. Price. Mr. Price's wife had a bad heart condition, and this was a rest vacation for her. He wouldn't let us leave without her, so we tied a rope under her arms and she went down the hawser. The minute she touched the water, she died, so we pulled her body into the boat, too."

There had been a dramatic moment as Mrs. Price was being lowered. A lifeboat swept past, directly under her, just as a passenger leaped for the rail, intending to jump into the boat. Price pulled a pistol and leveled it at the man. "If you jump," he said, "you are a dead man." From this real story, perhaps, grew a more melodramatic one. Lewis Perrine, sixteen, a student at Staunton Military Academy in Virginia and a young man with a lively imagination, later told reporters that he saw Acting Captain Warms shoot and kill a crew member, a looter. Warms with some anger denied the story; Perrine's aunt, Mrs. Howard C. Warren, said her nephew had imagined the whole thing; and Perrine himself later said he didn't actually see the shooting but had seen the body on the deck. One newspaper later reported that a body was washed ashore with a bullet hole in the head, but police and rescue crews on the New Jersey shore scouted the story, and the official list of the *Morro Castle* dead includes nobody dead from gunfire. It was, however, of a piece with the hysteria that had gripped those aboard the ship and shortly gripped newspaper readers and radio listeners in New York City and down the New Jersey shore. For when a ship so safe and so modern could become a flaming hulk, no story was too fanciful to be rejected: The disaster itself was almost beyond comprehension.

Thomas Cannon, Jr., and a friend were having a drink of champagne in their stateroom when the alarm bells went off. "The corridor was full of smoke," he recalls, "but we had never had a fire drill, and I didn't know where anything was. Fortunately, my friend said it looked serious and we found some life preservers. If we had been farther forward on the ship, we at least would have had a chance. We could have gotten to the forepeak. But we were aft on B Deck, and we had no chance, either jump or burn. Of course the crew came down in their uniforms and were the first ones over the railing, leaving men, women, and children. I suppose it was around six in the morning when I jumped, and I was in the water until noon that day. If I hadn't been so active all my life, I probably wouldn't have made it. We were trying to get to the *President Cleveland*, but we were wasting our time because they were trying to stay clear of the *Morro Castle*. Those waves were maddening! You either had to go over or under them. If you went under, by the time you had composed yourself, you were going the wrong way." Cannon came within a fraction of an inch of death. A knot on the back of his life preserver rubbed against his neck, and almost wore through his spinal cord before he was rescued.

Young Frank Dittman had nagging problems to face even before the fire began. His roommate, a stranger and years older, turned in drunk every night. "I was an idealistic young man," he recalls, "and I was disturbed I had to share a stateroom with this fellow. But I wouldn't have known there was a fire if he hadn't shaken me and said, 'Better get out of here—the boat's on fire.' I stuck my head out the porthole, and the sea was a vivid red. Looking up, I could see lifeboats aflame, hanging from the davits. 'Gee,' I thought to myself, 'I wonder how I'm going to dress if I have to swim.' I'd been on the swimming team at the Taft School, so I wasn't worried about making it to shore. I put on an undershirt, a pair of pants, and then a life jacket. My room was adjacent to the grand staircase on C Deck, and when

I went out, the crewmen were spraying water up the stairs. There was a tremendous amount of smoke and a stifling smell of pitch. 'What's the story? What do I do?' I asked one of the crewmen. His eyes were bloodshot from the smoke as he stared at me and said, 'Kid, do the best you can.'

"I went across the ship with a tight feeling in my belly, saying to myself, 'Gee, maybe I can help somebody.' When I got out on the afterdeck, the cruise director was there, leading people in songs. He was really magnificent. I went up to B Deck, but by then the flames were overwhelming. I saw some people forward, just behind a wall of flame, trying to get to the lifeboats. By that time B Deck was impossible. The smoke and flames were fantastic. Burning stuff was flying in the air, and the smoke was so unbelievably heavy one couldn't see or breathe. I looked over the rail, and the water seemed a mile away. People were crying that it was better to jump than to stand there and smother to death. But there was one sane, calm person. I stood next to an old lady who was joking, so unconcerned, and she smiled at me. That gave me courage. Next to her was standing a thirteen-year-old Cuban boy, and he was crying. They told me later his name was Raymond Lione.

" 'We can't stand here, can we?' he asked. 'No,' I said. 'Let's jump.' He asked, 'Will you kind of look after me?' I said, 'Sure, let's jump.' We went over hand in hand. I'd forgotten I had no life preserver; I gave it to a woman on deck who had none. We seemed to go down a mile under the water. I remember how surprisingly cold that water was, particularly because the Atlantic in September is at its warmest. The poor little boy was shivering, and then I found out he couldn't swim. I told him, 'Hang onto my shoulders and move your arms and legs.' As it started to get light, I found myself in a cluster of ten or twenty passengers. Someone suggested we form a circle and stay together. The little boy said to me, 'I don't think I'm going to make it,' and I could see he was blue with cold."

By now Dittman began to realize the dimensions of his nightmare. A woman screamed at him, "Help my friends! They're drowning!" Dutifully, he swam over to an unconscious woman and held her head up. After a while he could see no life. He peeled back her eyelids and then he knew that he was witnessing death. With no qualms, he took her life preserver and put it on the little boy. "The little fellow was almost unconscious, sort of whimpering," says Dittman. "I remembered that my mother had died when I was thirteen, and it was almost as though I were there. I began to feel terribly tired, and I knew I must have a life preserver of my own. A body came floating by face down. I had a brief struggle with conscience, a debate with myself, but I had the little fellow to take care of. I felt I couldn't hang onto him much longer, so I rolled over the body, untied the life preserver, and said to him, 'Gee, let's keep going.' By that time I could see all kinds of activity, people rushing up and down the beach, fishing boats circling around, and even a plane flying overhead with somebody in it pointing at me. I thought, 'Well, I'm going to make it.'"

Mrs. Emil Lampe thinks she may have been the "old lady" who smiled at Dittman, though she was actually only forty-six years old at the time. As she came out on deck with her husband, Emil, she was determined not to give way to panic. "I came out fully dressed," she says, "and I had my life preserver on. My husband and an officer threw me over the rail, and then my husband slid down a hawser, but I lost track of him. George Ridderhoff lit with a splash in the water beside me, and then he drifted away too. Somehow I got together with three friends, a girl named Dorothy Verfenstein, a girl named Mae Malone, and Mae's mother, Mrs. James Dillon. We all held hands, but pretty soon Mrs. Dillon became delirious. Then she smiled, her head slumped forward, and I could feel that her hands were cold. Mae kept saying, 'I hope Mother will wake up,' but I knew she never would. Just the same, I kept hold of one of her hands until a lifeboat picked us up." Lampe, who had drifted away, was pulled aboard another lifeboat. Like most of the men aboard the *Morro Castle*, he had bought himself a white summer suit in Cuba. By the time he finally was delivered ashore, the suit had shrunk so much that his arms and legs stuck out six inches.

Edward M. (Ted) Kendall, Harvard '02, was sound asleep in his C Deck stateroom when young Gouverneur Morris Phelps, Jr., bounded into it and said, "The ship's on fire. You'd better get up." Kendall put on an old pair of fishing pants, a khaki shirt, and a pair of shoes. Then, forehandedly, he slipped three ten-dollar bills into the watch pocket of the pants. "When I got out on deck," says Kendall, "I happened to see a big life ring with the name 'Morro Castle' on it and a long rope attached. I went out on the deck, where an officer in white uniform was yelling for quiet. The planking on the deck was roasting hot, and flames were shooting out the doors at the end of the superstructure. I thought, 'This won't do,' so I climbed over the rail to D Deck. There were several sailors huddled there, incoherent with terror.

One of them asked if he could have my life ring. I said, 'No, I may need it myself.' The smoke from the fire was black, gritty, strangling, like soft coal. 'I can't stand this,' I told myself. People were dropping past me from the upper deck, shrieking. A lot of them put their hands up and simply fell out of the life preservers. I wasn't worried about the waves; I used to swim in the surf at Southampton, Long Island, when it was so rough that lifeguards warned people off the beaches.

"So I plopped into the water, about twenty feet below, and struck away from the turmoil toward the lights on shore. About a quarter mile distant a big man with a life preserver grabbed me and said, 'Will you help me?' I gave him a crack and got away. There was a pelting cold rain, and I'd duck under the water to get warm. It really wasn't all that bad. About halfway to shore I heard a group of happy singers, a family. 'You seem happy here,' I said. 'Yeah, we're fine,' they said, and I continued on my way. Somehow I felt that if these people could be so confident, I had no cause to doubt that I'd make it."

8

THE CALMEST MEN

Those who have frequently witnessed death are calmest when they face it. In more than twenty-five years as a Protestant Episcopal clergyman, Hiram Hulse had read the last rites of his church over hundreds of the dying and had intoned the majestic funeral service from the Book of Common Prayer over still more hundreds of the dead. Now, after nearly ten years as Episcopal Bishop of Cuba, he faced death himself, and he faced it with the tranquil spirit of a man at peace with God. Bishop Hulse and his wife, asleep in a forward suite on B Deck, were on their way to the United States to attend a church convention. They awoke, choking in smoke, to a chorus of screams, the hammer of running feet, and the wild red glare of fire reflecting from the waves outside their porthole. The bishop knew how deep the peril was, but he concealed his knowledge. "Get up, dear," he said to Mrs. Hulse, "but be calm. We'll make it." [1] He dressed, hesitating a long moment over a trunk containing his clerical vestments and cross of office, but then reluctantly realized he could not take them with him. Dressed in civilian clothes, as a Protestant clergyman might be, he urged his wife to put a coat over her nightgown. Through passageways alternately fiery and smoky they made their way aft, down the companionways to C Deck, and finally to the crowded little afterdeck on D.

It was not, to the bishop's practical mind, a time for prayers, but a time for action. Quietly, with the help of stewards, he directed his wife over the side on a hawser. Halfway to the water, she blacked out and fell into the sea unconscious, but a sheet of smoke mercifully veiled her from her husband. Bishop Hulse waited until all women visible to him had gone over the side, and then went over himself. He felt the certainty of divine protection as he slid down the rope, searing the palms of his

[1] Told to William H. Rich, an American businessman in Havana.

75

hands from the friction. A moment later he, too, blacked out and tumbled into the water.

In Suite 1 on A Deck, where the most luxurious accommodations were located, Dr. Cochrane was awakened by pounding on his door. It was his friend and traveling companion, Dr. Vosseler. Gagging and coughing, he climbed out of bed in only the top of his lightweight pajamas. "I was crawling on my hands and knees trying to find the door," he said later,[2] "but then I remembered that there was an open window just above my bed." His deck, far above the water, was fitted with windows rather than portholes. "I climbed through, onto a narrow ledge high above the forecastle deck, and then hand over hand made my way across the forepart of the ship and out onto A Deck itself." As Chief of Surgery at a Brooklyn hospital, Cochrane was no stranger to emergencies. A tall, somewhat frosty man, he seemed to his patients to have ice water in his veins. At this moment, despite his outlandish costume, he was perfectly self-possessed, though just beyond him, on the seaward side of the ship, Chief Engineer Abbott was leaping between Lifeboat No. 1 and Lifeboat No. 3, screaming, "Lower away!"

Farther back on the deck, between other lifeboats and the superstructure, two men were playing a hose on the advancing flame. "My sister is in there," Cochrane told them, and pointed— he thought—to Suite 3, just behind his own. Deck Storekeeper William O'Sullivan seized a wrench and smashed the window. Acting First Officer Freeman gave him a heave and he lit inside the stateroom. He called out, "Is anybody here?" and when no answer came back, he felt through the room, fell over a trunk, and began to black out. A shout from Freeman brought him to. He fumbled his way to the window, stuck out his hands, and Freeman yanked him to the deck.

Despite all his outward calm, Dr. Cochrane had lost his sense of direction. He had sent O'Sullivan into Suite 5 instead of Suite 3, just vacated by Dr. and Mrs. Vosseler. His middle-aged spinster sister Catherine, unconscious from smoke, burned to death in her stateroom. With her vanished her diamond jewelry, never to be found. It became a legend among surviving members of the *Morro Castle* crew that she was carrying a million dollars in gems with her, but it was only a legend. No more than a modest claim for her missing jewelry was made by her brother.

Dr. Vosseler's self-possession was even more remarkable. When he heard the alarm and smelled the smoke, he opened his

[2] To Dr. Vosseler, who repeated his story to Harry W. Voege.

stateroom door. He walked about sixty feet toward the rear of the boat, toward the companionway. Then, like the careful yachtsman he was, he stepped out on deck in his pajamas to verify the direction of the wind, and thus the direction in which the flames were blowing. Thereafter, he threaded his way through shoving, cursing crewmen preparing to lower lifeboats, and back along the starboard deck to Suite 5 where his wife, a cripple, had already opened the window. Gently, he pulled her out, and they started forward. Smoke and flames were so thick that they lay for a moment in the scuppers, a drainage channel for water. "Go down to the foredeck," a passing steward told them. "You'll be safest there." Hand in hand, with Dr. Vosseler bracing his wife, they made their way down steel ladders to the forecastle deck, two levels and about twenty feet below. "I knew that was the right thing to do," he said later, "because I could see the wind blowing the fire toward the stern." George Alagna recalls their total calmness. "Boats were being lowered, the whistle was blowing, crewmen were shouting, and passengers were screaming for help," he says, "and they just stood there, looking out to sea, ignoring everything. The doctor had his arm around his wife's shoulders, and neither one was saying a word."

Vosseler's aplomb was matched by that of Dr. Phelps, Sr., under even more chaotic circumstances. He woke just as his son battered on their door, took one look out the porthole, and said to his wife, "Katy, it's a pretty bad fire. Better get up and put on your clothes." As if dressing to go ashore, Mrs. Phelps put on her dress and shoes while her husband slid into a pair of fishing pants. They were just starting out the door when Katharine Phelps had a thought. "Wait a minute, Guv," she said. "I've forgotten my pearls." She ducked into the stateroom and slipped a gleaming band of pearls around her neck. Next she put on her white gloves and camel's-hair polo coat, and at long last was ready to abandon ship. "At least," said a friend [3] years later, "Katy went like a lady."

Of all those aboard, the senior Phelps perhaps was least fearful of the sea and most aware of the peril of a fire at sea. He had been a yachtsman for years. He had raced in the North Sea against Kaiser Wilhelm II's *Meteor,* and for years he had piloted his own sailboat along the New Jersey shore. In 1904 he had been a young hospital interne when the excursion boat *General Slocum* burned in the East River off Hell Gate, killing 955 passengers, most of them children. Scores of victims had

[3] Miss Reba Kendall, daughter of Edward M. Kendall.

been brought into the municipal hospital where he was in training. The skipper of the *General Slocum* had kept his boat at full speed, fanning flames back over the passenger decks, in a desperate effort to reach shore. Now, as Dr. Phelps could sense, the skipper of the *Morro Castle* was doing exactly the same.

"This is going to be another *General Slocum* disaster," he told his wife and son as they emerged on the fantail of C Deck and into a jam-packed mob of passengers. "The fire is absolutely hopeless, and it's going to get steadily worse. Anyway, there's an onshore breeze that will carry us in if we go over the side, and besides I can recognize those lights ashore. We can't reach the lifeboats in all this flame. There are bound to be a lot of boats along to pick us up. We'll have to go over the stern." In this moment of total confusion Phelps, Sr., did not forget his obligations as a doctor. An officer, probably Robert Smith, touched him on the elbow. "We have a boy over here, and he's badly burned," he said. "Can you help him?" The boy was ten-year-old Braulio Saenz, one of three children of Mrs. Margaret Saenz, a Cuban living in New York. "Great strips of flesh had been burned off him," young Phelps recalls, "and he was weeping, '*Mi madre! Mi madre!*' When Father bent over him he cried, 'Don't touch me.' Just then all the lights went out, and the three of us moved over to the rail!" The boy died a moment later, unaware that his mother had already perished in the A Deck cabin from which two crew members had rescued him.

"There's no sense in staying any longer," Dr. Phelps told his wife after a cool re-estimate of the situation. "Katy, climb down the flagpole to where it joins the stern, and then drop into the water. I'll join you in a minute. And hurry! We don't want a lot of people jumping on top of us."

Katharine Phelps, whose stepson had given her his own life preserver, slid down the same flagpole from which Frank Loveland was to tumble a few minutes later. She gave way to one brief moment of panic when her arm jammed in the angle between the pole and the boat, just below D Deck. She felt a numbing pain in her trapped right elbow and called out, "I'm stuck!" Young Phelps and another man shinnied down the pole, lifted her loose, and let her drop into the water. A minute later Dr. Phelps jumped from the stern rail, almost into her arms. A blackened oar from one of the lifeboats drifted by. Phelps, Jr., saw them both seize it before they drifted out of sight in a pall of smoke.

The younger Phelps felt utter calmness now that he knew his

parents were safe for the moment—calmness, coupled with a hesitancy to leave even the doubtful security of shipboard. He was further buoyed by the assurance radiating from Robert Smith, who was calling out, "Don't jump. Don't jump. Surely help will come." So he waited, standing behind a metal cuddy cabin on the stern, a shelter for the lookout in rainy weather. On either side, sparks and smoke shot past him. Finally, a little after 5:00 A.M. ship's time, he went down a hawser on the stern, with molten metal showering down on him. As he hung just above the water, a familiar figure appeared on another hawser just five feet away. It was his Amherst friend, Walter Byrne. As the *Morro Castle* slowly rolled in the waves, he could see her dying. The whole amidships section blazed like a giant forge. Flames belched from the portholes. In one of them he could see a woman screaming, half in, half out. Not too much later the burned forepart of her body floated past him. Another woman floated by with just her hair visible. He pulled her head out of water, but when he saw she was dead, he let her go.

Phelps was too busy trying to survive to feel any emotion at this moment. As the *Morro Castle* dropped into the troughs of the waves, he was pushed beneath the water. It was happening every sixty to ninety seconds, and each time he had to hold his breath until the vast bulk of the ship lifted sluggishly higher. He had time only for a few gasping conversations with Walter Byrne, and always they were the same: "How are you?" "I'm fine." But as time went on he could feel the cold creeping into his bones. North Atlantic water, however warm, is not tropical water. There is always a slight chill in it.

Heroism, dogged courage, common sense, and surprisingly little cowardice marked those who jumped or slid down ropes from the afterdecks. The stewards, as a group, took care of their passengers with the same solicitousness they had earlier displayed in bringing them drinks, assigning them to deck chairs, and responding to whatever demands were made for special services. The waiters—on this ship a notably surly crew—mostly looked out for their own skins. The "black gang" from the engine room, totally isolated from the passengers by their duty stations deep down in the ship, went overboard without concern for anyone else, for, after all, these confused, milling people were strangers to them. The able-bodied seamen and the handful of officers who reached the stern concentrated to the last moment on manning the boats and containing the fire.

Headwaiter Charles Wright, who refused to consider himself

a hero, carried four-year-old Robert Lione on his back all the way to shore. He found his reward in the fact that the boy survived, and later came to a hospital to thank him. There was also a man, still living, who has been haunted ever since by an act of brute cowardice. He was snugly afloat in a life preserver when, as he describes it, "A heavyset man without a life preserver swam up to me, pleading: 'Can I hang on . . . just for a minute?' " He gave the man a shove. "All I could think," he says, "is that he might pull me down and then both of us would drown." The man floated away, flailing at the water. A moment later he dropped his head into the water. He was dead.

Some, however inwardly frightened, displayed only calm confidence. Mrs. John Holden of Cincinnati went over the rail with her husband. As she did so, she called to her sons John, seven, and Ruben, twelve. "Remember," she said, "if we're separated, we'll all meet at the Hotel Roosevelt in New York." The boys and their father made it to shore; their mother drowned. They next saw her in a temporary morgue on the New Jersey coastline. Israel Rudberg, the electrical appliance salesman, helped lower a lifeboat before the flames on the port side became too intense. He gave up when the boat jammed in the davits, tilting at an angle. As a seaman leaped forward with an ax to cut loose the cables, he felt his feet blistering. Scorching hot tar was oozing from the deck planking. Rudberg had jammed a roll of exposed film into the coat pocket of his pajamas. He went overboard with the exposed film, thinking, "Well, at least I'll have a memento of this." Miraculously, the film survived the salt water, but when he later had it developed he wished he hadn't. The photos were of four shipboard friends who drowned. He still remembers their faces, not their names.

Ethel and Gladys Knight, of Shrewsbury, Massachusetts, came out on the afterdeck together, just in time to meet Dr. S. Joseph Bregstein [4] of Brooklyn and nine-year-old Mervin Bregstein. The Knight sisters, both secretaries, had no doubt where their duty lay. Gladys took the hand of a young girl and jumped overboard with Bregstein. Ethel begged him to let her take his son, "for I'm a pretty good swimmer." In the cold, tossing vastness of the sea, she held him for hours, but finally was exhausted. Mervin drifted from her arms and was drowned. Both sisters survived, and so did Dr. Bregstein.[5] He later became president of the

[4] Who later talked to this reporter.

[5] No longer to be found. The medical societies of Greater New York do not list him as a member.

Morro Castle Survivors' Association, which until World War II conducted annual memorial services at Convention Pier in Asbury Park, New Jersey.

Sirl Boggetti, having put life preservers on a score of passengers, finally jumped himself. Like any other seaman, the thought of leaping into those heaving waters did not terrify him. "It didn't scare me at all," he says. "We often jumped into Havana harbor from the lower decks, just for fun. I was young, tough, and only twenty-eight, and I could have swum all the way to Bermuda." Boggetti struck out for a floating deck chair—he had given away his life preserver—and calmly waited for rescue.

Lifeboat No. 1, long before this time, had been seized by the wind and driven around the stern. It carried Chief Engineer Abbott, twenty-seven crew members, and exactly three passengers: Dr. Cochrane, Paul Arneth, and Senora Capote. Seaman Carl Pryor had pulled her from Suite 15 on the starboard side of A Deck. No. 1 was a motorboat. With this extra power she could have stayed close to the ship to pick up her full capacity of sixty-three persons. Why she failed to do so can be traced to Chief Engineer Abbott. The chief engineer, his lungs inflamed by smoke, had abandoned his responsibilities as the most experienced officer aboard the *Morro Castle*. He was, by all evidence, the mere shell of a man, shattered by circumstances over which he felt he had no control.

How Abbott reacted is one of the mysteries of this moment, sometime close to three fifteen in the morning, ship's time. Seaman Charles Angelo thought he heard the chief engineer tell the oarsmen, "Stay around. We may be able to help some people." Quartermaster Fleischman, also in the same boat, remembers shouting to a sailor, "Start that motor!" There was a pungent smell of gas. Seaman Charles Walter said later, "Abbott commanded, 'Don't do it. There are too many sparks coming from the ship.'" With that, driven by wind and waves, Lifeboat No. 1 swept toward the shore, driven by the wind. It was a humiliating moment for Abbott, an old salt, more than twenty-five years at sea, born and brought up in the tradition of the sea at Bucksport, Maine. In his panic he sensed that he had violated a tradition. As Dr. Cochrane glanced at him, he ripped off his epaulets and gold braid, muttering, "I'll go to jail for this." To Dr. Cochrane, this was simply one more talisman of the *Morro Castle* madness.

Motor Lifeboat No. 2 on the port side, the only one so powered, was never lowered to the water. Neither were oar-powered Boats 4, 6, 8, and 12 on the port side, every one of which was ablaze. A sailor, acting without orders from the bridge, did manage to lower Lifeboat No. 10. It left the ship with seven crewmen and three women, all friends: Anne Conroy, Flora La Roche, and Florence Roberts, of Providence, Rhode Island. There were not enough sailors to man all the oars. Boat No. 3, on the starboard side, left with one stewardess, First Engineer Bujia, and about a dozen seamen. In Boats 5, 9, and 11 the situation was identical. These six boats, with a capacity of 408 persons, carried only 85, and most of them were crew.

Time seemed to stand still during those fiery moments. Only the ship's officers kept an accurate log, and once the *Morro Castle* had anchored even they lost track. Some passengers had kept their watches on ship's time, some had set them ahead in anticipation of landing at the morning on shore time, an hour ahead. The discrepancies, even thirty-eight years later, have not been totally sorted out.

9

CHAOS ON
THE HIGH SEAS

To Captain Warms and the thirteen seamen huddled around him on the forepeak of the *Morro Castle*, it seemed a miracle that a ship already had sighted them. The ship was the *Andrea Luckenbach,* just seven miles away, steaming at top speed toward the *Morro Castle*'s point of anchorage. What they did not realize—and what it has taken thirty-eight years to bring to light—is that the captains of two other ships nearby had received and postponed action on the SOS. While the *Morro Castle*'s passengers floundered in waves ten to fifteen feet high, some dying of exhaustion or lacking the will to struggle on, the Furness liner *Monarch of Bermuda* was picking up her pilot and moving up Ambrose Channel toward New York harbor. The more sluggish freighter *City of Savannah,* not many miles distant from the *Morro Castle,* also continued to steam stolidly northward.

Aboard the *Monarch of Bermuda* Captain Albert R. Francis was in the wheelhouse, personally commanding his ship as it drove northward into the storm. Francis, a laconic Englishman, had joined the Furness Line thirty-two years earlier as a cabin boy. Those who knew him described him as a reserved, self-possessed, and deliberate man. At 3:23 A.M. he could scarcely have been more deliberate. That was the moment of the first SOS from the *Morro Castle,* received in garbled and undescipherable form. "See if they don't transmit again," he said to Radioman Sydney E. Jones. Between 3:26 and 3:28 A.M. a complete SOS was received, including the *Morro Castle*'s location. At 3:29 A.M. Radioman Jones notified the bridge. "Very well," said Captain Francis. That was all. The *Monarch* continued on her course. Captain Francis is now dead. Nobody knows why he did not immediately order his ship turned about—she was perhaps 20 miles north of the *Morro Castle.* There is only one possibility:

he must have assumed that the *Luckenbach* could handle the crisis. Yet SOS, by the unwritten law of the sea, is the one emergency signal that must be responded to by every ship within a reasonable steaming distance.

Radioman Jones, whose duty was simply to receive and pass on these messages, kept a laconic log of the whole event. At 3:34 A.M. he noted, "*Luckenbach* says approaching *Morro Castle,* expects to be there in half an hour." At 4:20 A.M., on orders of the captain, he sent the *Luckenbach* a query: "Are you in sight of the *Morro Castle* yet?" There was no answer. At 4:24 A.M., just one hour and one minute after the first SOS, Captain Francis finally bestirred himself and sent another message: "Am off Ambrose. Can I be of any assistance?" A terse "Yes. Hurry" came back from the *Luckenbach.* About this time, as Arthur Farr recalls, the *Luckenbach* was lowering four lifeboats, manned by thirty-five crewmen, about a thousand feet seaward of the incandescent *Morro Castle.* "She was one ball of flame amidships," Farr recalls. "We could see people jumping overboard, and there were hands thrusting pitifully out of some of the portholes."

Captain Francis now hurried. Drowsing passengers, in their berths, felt the *Monarch* heel over to the left as she made a great sweeping curve and started back to sea at a full 20 knots. From the bridge came a message to the *Luckenbach:* "Coming. Give exact location, please." A very few minutes before 5:40 A.M. this great white ship, with a plume of sea water curling from her bow, came charging southward, passing within 60 feet of the flaming ship on the shoreward side, so close she very nearly fouled the *Morro Castle*'s anchor chain. Captain Francis was handling her almost as if she were a motorboat. She made an immense curve around the stern of the *Morro Castle,* one that wakened every passenger still asleep, nearly flinging all of them from their berths, and then took up a position to the rear of the *Luckenbach,* parallel to the *Morro* but a little behind the *Luckenbach.* On one terse order from Francis, barked through a megaphone, "Away all boats!" eight lifeboats dropped down the davits and hit the water at the exact same moment.

The inexplicable sluggishness of Captain Francis has been verified by two young apprentice pilots, Si Haraldsen and Bill Baeszler.[1] They were awake and aboard the pilot boat *New York,* anchored near Ambrose Light. Waiting for other inbound ships, they saw the *Monarch of Bermuda* loom out of the fog.

[1] Now retired as senior pilots of the New York–New Jersey Harbor Pilots' Association.

The nearby pilot boat *Sandy Hook* drew alongside, the cruise liner slowed down, and Pilot Frank Miller climbed aboard. "What's wrong?" Baeszler asked his friend. Just then a signaling light aboard the *Sandy Hook* began to blink, laboriously spelling out the message: *"Morro Castle* afire twenty miles south of Scotland. Proceed to scene and assist." It was then between 4:00 A.M. and 5:00 A.M. ship's time, according to their recollection. The old *New York*, a coal-fired vessel built in 1897, with a buff stack and black hull, lost no time in moving south. William J. Walsh [2] remembers how she shuddered as the engine room crew poured on the steam pressure and the grimy firemen shoveled coal into her furnaces.

On the bridge of the *Savannah*, Captain John Henry Diehl received the 3:23 A.M. SOS complete. He was not too many miles distant from the *Morro Castle* but still out of sight. It was a quiet night on this clumsy ship, inbound from the Carolinas with assorted freight, and Chief Operator Harold Gauley [3] had decided to sneak down to the galley for a bite of food. Just then he heard the first SOS. Gauley phoned the bridge, told the captain, and put the earphones back on his head. To his bewilderment, the ship continued to throb steadily ahead at no increase in speed. When the second SOS came in, he phoned again. A few minutes later he felt the *Savannah* sluggishly change course. Possibly the time lost was not more than ten minutes, but that again was precious time to the burned, frightened, choking passengers and crew afloat in the towering waves. "I wonder what kind of wild goose chase they're sending us on this time," grumbled Captain Diehl, as he issued orders to make ready the lifeboats.

Both Diehl and Francis performed magnificently when they finally reached the *Morro Castle;* both were paid high tribute in the newspapers and at testimonial dinners; but neither ever admitted publicly they had taken their own sweet time in turning about. One authority on maritime disasters [4] suggests that too many needless SOS messages had been sent out during the 1930s, so that skippers were suspicious of them. And there had never before been a fire that burned with such speed, virtually destroying most of a ship, in Atlantic coastal waters. The vision

[2] Subsequently a pilot.
[3] As he told Pat O'Keefe, of the Veteran Wireless Operators' Association.
[4] Frank Braynard, secretary of the South Street Seaport Museum in New York City.

of the *Morro Castle* afire sobered them both. "Two huge towers of flame, horrible screaming," was the way Francis described it. "Unbelievable," said Diehl, who arrived on the scene a few minutes after the *Monarch of Bermuda.*

There was still another ship involved in the *Morro Castle* disaster. The Dollar liner *President Cleveland* arrived at approximately the same moment as the *Monarch.* The *Cleveland,* inbound to New York from Manila, had come up from a point 22 miles south at full speed. Here again indifference or confusion compounded the tragedy. Captain Robert Carey maneuvered his ship half a mile forward of the *Morro Castle.* By 6:20 A.M. the *Cleveland* was in position to lower a motorboat and two lifeboats that had been made ready for rescue. Carey, a beefy man, an old-timer in the trans-Pacific trade, simply stood on the bridge and stared. His officers were trained to obey their captain absolutely, but this long delay was too much for First Officer Dwight Randall. "For Christ sake!" he burst out. "We must do something!" At 7:08 A.M. Captain Carey roused himself from his musings and gave the order, "Lower boats." Randall took command of one lifeboat, Chief Officer James J. Henderson of the other. They made a complete circuit of the *Morro Castle* and saw nobody. By then many of the passengers had drifted far from the ship. At 8:00 A.M., after more musing, the inexplicable Captain Carey retrieved his lifeboats and turned his ship toward New York. At 8:00 A.M. there still were hundreds of people in the water, closer to shore. There was an ironic sequel to the captain's lethargic performance. All four of his subordinate officers asked to be transferred from the ship; all four were fired when the *President Cleveland* got back to San Francisco a week later.

——·—— ——·——

Whatever woes beset the *Morro Castle* that early morning, they were more than matched by the human and mechanical failures that beset the United States Coast Guard. Records recently uncovered reveal a small horror story. The Coast Guard radio station at Rockaway Inlet, New York, was being dismantled so that the Navy could receive and handle all radio transmissions. The intermediate frequency transmitter and receiver for commercial ships had already been moved to the Brooklyn Navy Yard. But it was not yet installed. So Rockaway received no SOS. Aboard the cutter *Tampa,* tied up at Pier 18 Staten Island, about thirty miles from the *Morro Castle,* a seaman in training as a radio operator could not copy or comprehend the high-speed distress transmission hammered out by Chief Radioman Rogers.

THE
MORRO CASTLE

Ruth E. Mooney (on platform), daughter of the president of Atlantic, Gulf, and West Indies Steamship Lines, swings a champagne bottle against the prow of luxury liner *Morro Castle* at her launching in Newport News, Virginia, on March 5, 1930. (*Photo:* United Press International)

Pushed into mid-Hudson by a tug, the *Morro Castle* begins her maiden voyage to Havana.

Inside this innocent-looking locker (at arrow) in the *Morro Castle*'s writing room began the fire that engulfed almost the whole ship in a matter of minutes. Passengers fled in their night-clothes; the flames and smoke forced them to jump overboard in the darkness.

Left: As surviving crewmen work frantically to saw through the anchor chain, a tiny boatload of other survivors pulls out from under the looming hulk of the vessel and is swept toward shore by gale winds. (*Photo:* Acme)

Rescue ships stand by the flaming cruise liner (center). In the fore-ground is the luxury liner *Monarch of Bermuda,* and in the background the freighter *City of Savannah.*

Lifeguards sprint into the breakers to pull survivors ashore at Spring Lake, New Jersey.
Below: The first lifeboat from the *Morro Castle* is swept ashore at Spring Lake.

Exhausted survivors are carried to a Spring Lake bathhouse.

First-aid squads from more than a dozen New Jersey shore communities assisted in resuscitating those overcome by smoke or exposure. Here an elderly woman is being treated.

Still dazed and in shock, two women who swam ashore from the ship wait for medical assistance at the first-aid building in Spring Lake.

Snapping all towlines, the *Morro Castle* drifted ashore a few hundred feet from Convention Hall in Asbury Park. Here thousands view her from the beach and boardwalk.

Above right: After the fire the once charming promenade deck of the liner is a mass of twisted metal, dotted by the skeletons of burned chairs.

Right: Three lifeboats that never got away. Burned on their davits, these boats that might have saved several scores of lives hang uselessly alongside an upper deck of the *Morro Castle.*

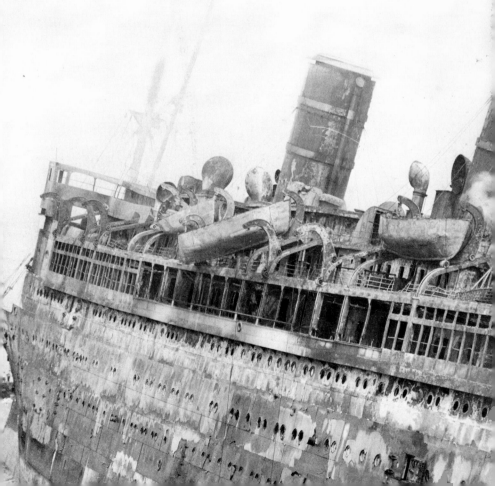

The "hero" of the
Morro Castle, Chief Radio
Operator George Rogers, and
his wife "read all about it"
in an edition of the
New York *Daily News*.

Unjustly suspected,
because he had led a radio
operators' strike aboard
the *Morro Castle*, Second
Radio Operator George Alagna
is arrested and handcuffed
as a material witness.
He was released, with
apologies, within a day.

Acting Captain William F.
Warms is sworn in to testify
before a hearing of the
United States Steamboat
Inspection Service.

Muted end. The burned-out
hulk of the *Morro Castle*
is towed to a shipyard at
Baltimore, Maryland, to be
converted into scrap metal.
The multimillion-dollar liner
was declared a total loss.

The cutter *Cahoone,* twenty-five miles farther out to sea, with two trainees on the radio desk, was equally at a loss. Two hundred miles away, in Boston harbor, a more experienced radioman jumped from his chair, ran to the bridge, and blurted to the commander: "Sir, the *Morro Castle* has sent out an SOS from south of Scotland Light!"

The *Cayuga,* which could be of no help at all, was the only Coast Guard ship to receive and decipher the transmission. Assuming, logically, that ships closer by had received the same message, the skipper of the *Cayuga* did not send it on. But fortunately there were Coast Guardsmen ashore who did act promptly. Surfman Stephen M. Wilson, on watch at the Shark Harbor Coast Guard station, was first to see the *Morro Castle* afire. "I saw her in a line right over the bell buoy off the inlet," he said later. "There couldn't be any question of mistaking her, as she was the only vessel in sight." Passing ships were routine to Surfman Wilson, whose duty it was to patrol three miles of beach every night. Fifteen minutes later his job was no longer routine. At first glance it looked to him as if the moon were coming up over the sea. It was no night for a moon, as Wilson knew from the rain beating on his oilskin hat and uniform. He looked more closely and a moment later saw a puff of flame. "I notified the skipper," he said, "but by the time we could get back to the lookout tower she was all ablaze." The skipper, a chief bos'n's mate, frantically rang up the neighboring station at Manasquan, five miles south.

"Yes, we know," said Manasquan, "and we're launching our powerboat." Manasquan had gotten the word from a Navy radio direction finder station in the same village. Now the Coast Guard telephone wires and the radio transmitters were alive with orders and messages. Mackay Radio at Rockland, Maine, and Sayville, Long Island; Radiomarine at Tuckerton, at New York, and at Chatham, Massachusetts, were all transmitting messages, hoping to reach the silent cutters so close by and so oblivious to the tragedy. Operator Eberhard Engelder [5] at Tuckerton phoned the Coast Guard in New York. Delay piled on delay in the confusion of the moment. It was after 4:00 A.M. when the *Tampa* got the message; it took her until 5:39 A.M. to round up her crew, some of whom were ashore. It was 8:00 A.M. before she reached the *Morro Castle.* Cursing operators, transmitting letter by letter, finally got through to the *Cahoone* at 4:00 A.M., but at a speed of 15 knots it took her until 7:55 A.M. to reach the *Morro Castle.*

[5] Now retired and living in Tuckerton, New Jersey.

At this moment, when fast ships were at a premium, the Coast Guard's finest and fastest ship, the 21-knot *Champlain,* was on a ceremonial mission more than a thousand miles to the north. To Ruth Bryan Owen, Ambassador to Denmark, a cruise home on this powerful boat was an agreeable conclusion to the state visit she had just paid to Greenland. When she disembarked in New York four days later, she was stunned by a wave of criticism from Republican members of Congress, one of whom pointed out that the speedy *Champlain* could have reached the *Morro Castle* more than an hour ahead of the slower, older *Tampa* and *Cahoone.*

At the scene, misunderstandings played havoc with the rescue work. By now the waters inshore from the *Morro Castle* were alive with fifteen Coast Guard patrol boats and surfboats, wallowing in seas so high that their crewmen could see only a few feet in any direction. Survivors, feebly waving for help, would sight a boat and then with bitter disappointment watch it drop into the trough of the waves and vanish from sight. Yet all this time the *Cahoone* and the *Tampa* were standing by the anchored *Morro Castle.* Captain T. C. Crapster,[6] heading a subsequent Coast Guard board of inquiry, bitterly summed up what happened: "Vessels standing by conveyed the impression that all passengers had been rescued. The *Monarch of Bermuda* was so busy handling press radio traffic (to and from New York newspapers) that the *Cahoone* could not break in. Had the *Morro Castle* or the *Monarch of Bermuda* given the *Cahoone* any information that lifeboats had gone ashore or that passengers had gone over the side, the *Cahoone* could have gone inshore to search, and some lives would have been saved. Instead, she stood by the *Morro Castle* until 9:30 A.M. She was then informed by the *Tampa* that there were people in the water off Spring Lake. When she was finally given orders to search, she could recover only bodies of the drowned." The bridge of the *Cahoone* was high enough so that her men could see above the waves. Many who died, unseen from the surfboats, might have lived had the *Cahoone* cruised on the shoreward side of the *Morro Castle.*

In this moment of crisis the men of the *Cahoone* made a belated and useless gesture. It was close to noon, and winds were gale force. The cutter lowered a nineteen-foot surfboat and six oarsmen. After only fifteen minutes in the sea, the oarsmen were done in. The boat was recalled after picking up two bodies. As the *Cahoone,* in utter futility, continued her patrol inshore, she

[6] From Coast Guard board of inquiry report.

saw not a living person—only more bodies, face down in the waves.

On and on went the litany of blunders. At Cape May, on the southern tip of New Jersey, the Coast Guard maintained an aerial station with two float planes. This station was not required to deal with distress signals, and in this moment of fiery crisis did not. Quartermaster Third Class Bryant Hill was handed the *Morro Castle*'s SOS a little after 3:30 A.M. Hill, feeling a stirring of concern, handed the message on to Acting Officer of the Day, Quartermaster Frank W. Hess. Hess yawned, put the message on a table beside his bed, and went back to sleep. He made no attempt to get in touch with the commanding officer of the base, who was at his home in Cape May village. The commanding officer finally did arrive at 8:30 A.M., took one look at the scudding storm clouds, and said, "It's too hazardous to fly." It was well after midday when he felt some stirrings of conscience. Tom Burley, announcer for the local radio station at Asbury Park, broke into a musical program broadcast from the city's Convention Pier to say: "It is a tremendous disaster. Bodies are coming ashore at Sea Girt, Shark River, Manasquan Beach, and Belmar." At that moment the young commander, Lieutenant Tom Burke, burst into the office of an ensign and said: "There's bad trouble off Sea Girt. Let's go!" Two planes, which also had wheels, wavered off the ground, rose into the storm, and battled their way northward some one hundred miles until the smoking *Morro Castle* lay beneath them. Without radio communication, they hovered over passengers waving weakly from the sea and helped to guide rescue boats to them. By 2:30 P.M. the storm had reached full gale speed of 60 miles an hour. As helpless as butterflies in a high wind, the two Coast Guard planes bounced through the sky and barely made it safely back to their station. The quartermaster, the acting officer of the day, and the commanding officer all were later reprimanded.

But this was part and parcel of the *Morro Castle* disaster, a compound of resolute men, most of them dungareed young Coast Guard recruits who had grown up along this coast and knew what their duty was; officialdom, confused at the start but later coldly effective; and those who did not know what to do or, knowing what to do, failed to do it.

At Point Pleasant Beach John P. Kennell had come down to launch his speedboat for a day of bluefishing when he heard the news of the *Morro Castle* fire on his car radio. A Coast Guard picket boat was drawn up on the beach, and sleeping in

it were two seamen. "They said they had orders from Bos'n's
Mate Lawrence Bowden not to take the boat out," Kennell said
later. "It was already nine in the morning. I told them there
were people in the water in need of help. They asked me if
I'd take the responsibility." Kennell did not hesitate. "Of course
I will," he said. "Then they told me they didn't have enough
crew. It ended with my going out with them, and we got seven,
all alive, and brought them ashore. The second time out, we met
Bowden. We were still inside the inlet. He called out through
a megaphone: 'What are you fellows doing out here in that
wind? Head her for Sandy Hook. You'll never get back in.' He
didn't see me, but I jumped up and called, 'What do you mean
by such orders? We've saved seven people already, and we may
save more.' The crew told me, 'We ain't afraid of the surf, but
we have a yellow-bellied captain.'" To a degree, the Coast
Guard's board of inquiry agreed. By its decision, Bowden was
barred from ever commanding any Coast Guard installation
again, and was demoted.

Commander Earl G. Rose, aboard the *Tampa,* was as much
in the dark as his colleagues aboard the *Cahoone.* "He had
simply been told," said the board of inquiry, "that the *Morro
Castle* was on fire and that they needed help. He knew nothing
of the extent of the fire. As he arrived on the scene, the commercial liners were leaving, and he saw no lifeboats or people
in the water. He naturally assumed that all the people except
those on the forecastle had been taken aboard the liners. He had
no way of knowing what was going on, onshore or along the
beach. It was not until 9:30 A.M. that he received his first information that there were any people in the water and that they
needed assistance." Resolute Skipper Rose, having passed the
news to the *Cahoone,* decided that the Coast Guard had a dual
duty: to save lives and to save property. He dedicated the
Tampa to the saving of the *Morro Castle* and the remnant of the
crew still aboard. At the same time he sent a stream of messages on the radio calling in all available Coast Guard boats to
pick up survivors. A Coast Guard statement later said: "We
concur in stressing the fact that it was the paramount duty
of the *Tampa* to see that the fourteen living survivors of the
Morro Castle were given assurance of safety while standing by
their vessel according to the best traditions of the sea."

So in the end it was the "pipsqueak fleet," as Coast Guardsmen called their little boats, that did much of the work of rescue.
At Manasquan, Picket Boat CG 2390 put to sea at 3:30 A.M.

The wind and sea were so wild in that narrow inlet that the oarsmen could not get CG 2390 across the bar. Chief Bos'n's Mate W. M. Rymers called them back and sent all his available men to Spring Lake, where a powerboat was put to sea. Out they came, from fourteen of the Coast Guard life-saving stations along the northern Jersey shore, each station five miles from the next one, boats bobbing and thrashing in the wind and waves, their lee rails dipping under water. They came from little resort and commercial fishing towns like Long Branch, Spring Lake, and Spermaceti Cove, Sea Girt and Barnegat and even Sandy Hook, far to the north. Without them, one hundred more people might have died. But they were not alone. There were commercial fishing boats like the *Diana* and the *Paramount,* cabin cruisers barely able to breast the waves, and the most incongruous sight of all, a rakish racing yawl owned by Dr. C. Malcom Gilman,[7] who lived nearby. Commercial radio stations kept up a continuous chatter of information as the day wore on. And as the news spread, as newspaper extras were being cried on the streets of New York, some strange osmosis gripped people in the New York–New Jersey area. Over narrow macadam roads, where the traffic backed up for miles, in cars that overheated and often stalled, a ribbon of humanity extended from the Pulaski Skyway in Newark down the state highway known as the Shore Road.

Some came from sheer curiosity, some because they were searching for relatives. Herman Cluthe's father, a retired manufacturer of surgical instruments, piled his wife and other son into their car, an old Pierce Arrow, and started south. Cluthe's brother had told the mother and father that the *Morro Castle* had burned but that everyone had been saved and that their missing son would come home to Glen Ridge, New Jersey, if they drove down to pick him up. "They stopped to get gas on the way," says Cluthe, "and the gas station attendant told them, 'Good God, you ought to see the beach down around Asbury Park. There are bodies all over the place.'" Trapped in the traffic, moving at no more than ten miles an hour, the senior Cluthes bitterly accepted as fact the assumption that their son was dead. They searched through every morgue and hospital on the shore until they finally found him . . . alive, conscious, burned, suffering from smoke inhalation, but healthy enough to come home with them, wrapped in blankets, in the rumble seat of the old Pierce Arrow.

[7] Told to author.

10

RESCUE AT SEA

Of all the fishing boats on the North Jersey shore, the 60-foot-long *Paramount* was the sturdiest and the fastest, for good reason. She had been a rumrunner, once owned by those prohibition-era gangsters, Dutch Schultz and Vannie Higgins. Then the United States government seized her and put her up for auction. The purchaser was Captain John Bogan, Sr., owner of a fishing pier at Brielle. Daily, in the roughest weather, she carried up to sixty passengers to the reefs offshore, where they could angle for bluefish, small tuna, or codfish. Jimmy Bogan, the captain's son, was the skipper. Young Johnny Bogan,[1] in his mid-twenties, was the mate. But there were infrequent days when the waves were too high and the entrance to Manasquan Inlet too shallow to risk taking the *Paramount* out, and the morning of September 8, 1934, was one of these.

A little before dawn, which came at 5:00 A.M. shore time, Johnny Bogan sat up in his bed, and by habit looked out the window to check the weather. He saw trees swaying in a stiff gale, rain coming down in sheets. The Bogan house in Brielle was just a few blocks from Manasquan Beach. Young Bogan could hear the steady, insistent thunder of waves rolling in on the sandy shore. "It's no day for the *Paramount*," he said to himself. It was half tide at that hour, with probably not more than six feet of water over the bar where the Manasquan River joined the ocean, and the *Paramount* drew five feet when loaded. Young Bogan dropped back to sleep, but not for long. At 6:00 A.M. he was awakened by a hammering on the front door. In his bare feet and pajamas, he padded downstairs to be greeted by a neighbor. "There's a big ship on fire offshore," the neighbor said. "They need help. I heard it on the radio."

Young John dashed in to wake his father and brother, and at the same moment flicked the radio dial to New York radio

[1] All three Bogans still operate the same fishing pier.

station WMCA. "All ships in the area are rushing to the scene," the announcer intoned. "The *Monarch of Bermuda* . . ."

Bogan, Sr., shook his head. "They don't need us," he said. "There are plenty of big ships out there, all the big ships in the world. All they need to do is to lower their boats."

Brother Jimmy agreed with his father. "They've got plenty of help," he said.

"Dad," pleaded young John, "we've got to go. I know they need help."

Finally convinced, John, Sr., and Jimmy dressed. All three Bogans put on their oilskins, walked out into the rain, climbed into their car, and drove to the docks. Help was waiting for them there—six skippers and mates who had also gotten the word: Frank Barry, Jimmy Hughes, William Fuhrman, Knute Lovegren, Charles Gifford, Thomas McDowell, and Clayton Weller. All were experienced seamen, and all were ready to go. Minutes later the *Paramount*'s diesel engine let out an earsplitting roar, the lines were cast off, and the boat headed downriver into waves ten feet high, She bounced like a cork in the nasty chop at the bar and then headed northeastward toward a glow in the distance. "It was all rain squalls and swells," John, Jr., remembers. "We passed people and never even saw them. Then we came up alongside the *Morro Castle*." It was a scene John Bogan, Jr., remembers as terrible in its beauty. The whole ship gave off a red glow. Clouds of smoke swirled off toward the stern. In every porthole the heat had shattered or melted the glass, and tongues of flame licked out. In the water arms waved toward them, mutely pleading for rescue. Coast Guard picket boats, like little minnows, were bobbing across the waves, some piled high with the bodies of the dead as well as the living.

Time stood still for the *Paramount*'s crew as she maneuvered off the *Morro Castle*. One of the first to be rescued was Mrs. James F. Kennedy, the woman in the bathing suit. Wearing a life preserver, she had been pushed overboard by her husband. Mrs. Kennedy could barely tread water; Kennedy was a powerful swimmer. But after an hour in the water he gasped, "I can't go on. Save yourself." She was alone when the *Paramount* came alongside, but she refused the outstretched hands of her rescuers. "Where's my Jim?" she demanded. "Oh, he's O.K.," said one crewman. "He's probably in New York by now." Young John has never forgotten that pathetic moment. " 'No,' " he recalls her saying. " 'I know Jim's drowned.' She swam over to a corpse floating face down and turned it face up to see if it was

her Jim. Not until then would she let us take her on board."
The corpse wasn't her Jim. His body washed ashore at Sea Girt
a few hours later.

When survivors were too weak to reach out their arms but
wore life preservers, the men of the *Paramount* snatched them
aboard with long, hooked steel gaffs and piled them on the slip-
pery deck exactly as if they were fish. Choking, coughing, and
vomiting, they made an indescribable mess of the *Paramount*'s
carefully scrubbed deck. Captain Jimmy Bogan extended his
arms and pulled in a young couple. "Thank God!" cried the girl,
and threw her arms around him. She was Mrs. Paul Lemprecht,
the former Agnes Spies, who had often fished from the *Paramount* with her father and mother. The Lemprechts, married a
little more than a week, had chosen the *Morro Castle* for their
honeymoon trip. Minutes later, in the maelstrom of wind and
water, the boat drew up on a group of six women and a man.
When a crewman reached out for one girl, she said cheerfully:
"Take the others first. I'm all right." It was Agnes Prince, the
reporter. The man with her group, still wearing his white
jacket, was Fireman John Kempf. Mrs. James Hassall, a member
of the Concordia singing group, was rescued—as Bogan now
puts it—"by dumb luck." "We'd cruised twice around the *Morro
Castle*," John Bogan, Jr., says, "and we must have passed by
her twice. The third time, she came up on top of a wave just
as we drew alongside, and we hauled her in. Her watch had
stopped at four A.M., which is probably when she went into the
water, and it was nine A.M. before we got her."

In one cluster of swimmers were three or four young children,
with a man shepherding them. "Get them," he said. "I can stay
afloat." But when the children were aboard and Bogan looked
for him, he had vanished. To this day he does not know whether
the man survived or perished. The strain of leaning overboard
and pulling limp bodies from the water was too much for
Charles Gifford. "Sorry," he finally said, "my back is gone. I can't
do any more." Captain Bogan, Sr., fifty-two years old at the
time, was almost yanked overboard when he reached for one
survivor. It took two crewmen to pull him to safety, and four
to lift in the woman, who was very heavy. Still the frenzy
and the pathos continued. Mrs. Alexander McArthur of Philadelphia seized a rope from the *Paramount* with one hand but
kept a firm hold on her husband's dead body with another.

"We couldn't waste time with the dead," says John Bogan, Jr.
"But it took us at least ten minutes to convince her." Mrs. Mc-

Arthur released her grip and was pulled aboard, weeping, as her husband's corpse floated away. It was a similar, grim story when the *Paramount* came upon the Wacker family—Mr. and Mrs. Herbert Wacker and Doris, their daughter. "Let me go, I've had enough," Herbert Wacker had said an hour earlier, and then dropped his head in the water. Doris Wacker later recalled the numb desperation she felt, the sense of something lost forever when she and her mother realized that to be saved themselves they must abandon a husband and father.

In the middle of this frenzied scene a two-seater Army plane, marked by a star and the words, "U.S. Army," came boring through the storm clouds. It was improbable enough for the men aboard the *Paramount* to see a plane out in such weather, and even more improbable to see a helmeted man leaning from the rear cockpit, waving a red scarf and pointing down toward the sea. Even as he gestured, out from the front cockpit fell planks, each with three smoke bombs attached. They plummeted into the sea and then set up their own small clouds, dwarfed by the massive smoke cloud pouring from the *Morro Castle*. The signal-man was A. Harry Moore, governor of New Jersey, who had been vacationing with his wife at Shadow Lawn, the summer residence of the state's governors, at the National Guard base in Sea Girt. "His signals and the smoke led us to half a dozen people," Bogan recalls, "but by that time we had sixty-seven aboard, survivors and crew, seven more than our ship was licensed to carry under the safety laws. We came up abaft the *Savannah* about that time, just as she let loose with an ear-splitting distress signal. On the bridge Captain Diehl was shouting through a megaphone: "Could you pick up my lifeboat? We have five crew and fifteen to twenty people, and she can't get back to us." On the stern of the fishing boat, John, Jr., held a coil of rope in one hand. He recalls the wind whistling through the rigging, and each wave topped with a comber of flying spray. As the *Paramount* came alongside the *Savannah*'s lifeboat, he tossed the coil of rope out with a semicircular motion, and an oarsman in the lifeboat made it fast.

——. ——-

The waves alone were no longer the sole enemy of those exhausted people still striving to keep alive in the water. The waves wore them out, slowly and subtly, but the flying spray was what killed those with just a spark of life remaining. For when they came up on the crest of each wave, having been pulled below the surface, their impulse was to take a deep breath. And, as they did, they drew in that flying spume, sucked it into their lungs, and it suffocated them.[2]

Aboard the *Paramount,* now headed for shore at 11:00 A.M., skipper Jimmy Bogan had tied down the whistle. To the exhausted crew, it was a sound of triumph. The *Paramount* had achieved more rescues than any lifeboat, picket boat, charter boat, or pleasure boat in the water that morning. There were many men to credit for this, including Bill Fuhrman.[3] He had wakened early and driven to Point Pleasant to buy a Sunday paper. When he got the news, he did not hesitate. He drove to Brielle, joined forces with the Bogans, and put to sea on their boat. To Fuhrman, it was like waking up from a bad dream and discovering that the dream was reality. All of a sudden he was in the middle of an ocean full of people, and in the background a flaming ship pouring out smoke. "It still puts the shivers to me," he says. "The only way I can describe it is to say that it was one big mess: people bleeding, people with cuts and bruises, people with broken bones, people waving for help, and floating all around them the bodies of the drowned."

The simple bravery of the *Paramount*'s crew of owners and volunteers has become a folk tale among New Jersey shore fishermen. A few weeks after the disaster, blushing red with embarrassment, John Bogan was to receive a gold medal from the people of Jersey City, where the Bogans formerly lived. "I accept this," he said huskily, "on behalf of my father, who taught me all I know, and my brother Jimmy, and all the others that helped so much." A direct sort of faith in divine help sustained John Bogan then and sustains him still. He is the sort of Irishman and Catholic who tips his hat as he passes the parish church, and never, as he says, "would take the name of Our Lord in vain."

Of course there were other boats out that wild day, some of them perplexed by the sight of the *Morro Castle,* some diligently engaged in lifesaving. Howard Duncan, in a skiff, engaged in commercial fishing, passed the *Morro Castle* at 4:30 A.M. off Bay Head, and was puzzled to see wisps of smoke pouring from her through rents in the curtain of rain. Bill Hulse [4] also passed her a little south of Bay Head, saw "a lot of smoke," and thought it was out of the ordinary. Both skippers were running ahead of

[2] According to Dr. Gilman, now coroner of Monmouth County, New Jersey.
[3] Now skipper of a charter boat at West Palm Beach Florida.
[4] Both Duncan and Hulse are now dead.

the storm, headed for safety within Manasquan Inlet. They reached shore full of questions, but those questions were promptly answered, and both men volunteered to serve as crew for other boats headed out. These included the *Ogopo,* captained by Charles Miller, the *Diana,* captained by Robert F. Ziegler,[5] the 32-foot *Lila,* captained by Carl Anderson, a boat simply numbered 5346, captained by Holcomb Carleton, and a strange assortment of sailboats and pleasure boats—in all, some forty of them by the end of the morning.

Ziegler, a bluff and laconic man now in his early sixties, remembers it all as a scene of ungodly confusion. He was sleeping snugly, prepared to forget the day's fishing, when the telephone rang. "It was my mate," he recalls, "asking if I wanted to go out to a passenger ship on fire. Of course I didn't hesitate, and we went out from Brielle with my father-in-law, Fred Gunther, Mate Chester Geers, and two or three others. She was well off Spring Lake, just surrounded by a cloud of smoke. A lot of boatmen didn't want to venture out that day, but there was no choice. People were dying in the water. We really picked up only a few of the living: a little boy in a life preserver, and he died on the way in, and a few others. My father-in-law busted three or four ribs trying to haul survivors over the rail. We made three or four circles around the *Morro Castle.* Finally we saw nobody, and we headed for shore again." Captain Anderson of the *Lila,* a less phlegmatic man, exploded when he reached shore. "Not a single lifeboat set off a flare or flashed a light," he said, "though they are required to have both flares and lanterns aboard. Even a lighted match would have shown up from a distance, it was so dark. We could have saved fifty people if someone had only sent up a signal."

▄▄▄ ▄▄▄

A. Harry Moore, a Democratic governor in a normally Republican state, was both a showman and a lover of sensation. A few years later, with dramatic fanfare, he was to announce the sad news that the body of Charles A. Lindbergh's kidnapped baby son had been found. This morning, at Shadow Lawn, he had just come down to breakfast. It was 8:00 A.M. as he dug into his scrambled eggs, felt a pleasant sense of relief at being free of his official duties, and then a slight sense of concern when the private telephone rang. Mrs. Moore [6] answered it and

[5] Ziegler still captains the *Diana.*
[6] Mrs. Moore now lives in seclusion in Jersey City.

came back to say: "Harry, a passenger ship's afire off Sea Girt."

Moore never could resist the dramatic gesture. He picked up the phone and said to the operator, "Get me the adjutant general at Trenton." The adjutant general, William A. Higgins, was at breakfast. "Bill," said Moore, "get hold of Bob Copsey and fly right down here. We've got a ship on fire off Sea Girt and an awful lot of people in the water." Moore did not wait for the National Guard commander to arrive. He summoned his personal pilot, Captain John A. Carr, from the bachelor officers' quarters nearby. Mrs. Moore, who had learned not to argue with her husband, gave him a good-bye kiss as he went out the door to a single-wing, single-engined plane warming up on the parade ground just in front of his summer mansion. The governor donned a pneumatic life preserver, belted himself in the rear cockpit, and the tiny little plane strained against the blast of the wind. Faltering at times, almost touching the ground, the plane battled its way down the parade ground, and—as Mrs. Moore watched—barely cleared the dunes at the ocean end. Then it was gone, into the storm and wrack.

Harry Moore's first view of the *Morro Castle* was of a sullenly smoking ship, anchored a few miles offshore, but as Captain Carr skimmed only seventy-five feet above the water, what he remembered were blank faces peering up at him and arms mutely held toward him in entreaty. As he half-stood in the cockpit, Carr buzzed one rescue boat after another, leading them toward survivors, dipping his wings, with Moore waving the long red scarf he had wound around his neck. Their first mission was the living, but soon they were signaling the location of the dead as well. Whatever the governor's theatrics, he was bound into this intricate rescue mission minutes after his take-off. "I had to go," he said later. "People were dying out there." He was out for an hour, the length of time his plane could fly on its gasoline supply. Bob Copsey, Major Robert L. Copsey,[7] took off with the adjutant general before Moore returned. "All I can remember," he says now, "is fannies—people bottoms up, many of them naked, floating head down, dead, in the waves. We'd nailed a series of smoke bombs to planks, and as we saw bodies we'd light the bombs and drop them overside as a signal to rescue craft. The ocean was alive with boats, but the trouble was they couldn't see over the waves. I guess, before it was all over, we'd located nine bodies, four of them women."

[7] Now a retired brigadier general of the Air Force, living in Colorado Springs, in conversation with the author.

Lillian Davidson still remembers Moore with gratitude. "His plane circled around me three times," she says, "and then I knew that somebody was aware I was alive. I'd been in the water probably five hours—it was a dreadfully lonely, lost feeling— but Governor Moore gave me the assurance I needed to keep going. Within twenty minutes the *Diana* came alongside and hauled me aboard."

The whole experience shook Harry Moore. "Those poor people," he said to Pilot Copsey. "Those poor people." There was one incident he never forgot. As his pilot dipped low, almost to wave level, he looked down into the anguished face of a man paddling feebly, deep in a trough. Leaning out of the cockpit as far as his safety belt would permit, Moore waved and yelled. The rising wind carried his words away, but his signals were unmistakable. Over that face, dulled with exhaustion and blackened with smoke, he saw hope spread. A rescue boat was just twenty feet away, unaware of the man until Captain Carr buzzed the craft and dipped the wings of his plane. Moore saw the boat change course. Minutes later the survivor was picked up. That was the satisfying end of Moore's aerial mission. Captain Carr reached back to touch him and pointed to the gasoline gauge. The needle was trembling at the letter "E," for "Empty." The plane landed, with scarcely more than a teacupful of gas, on the parade ground, and taxied to a stop in front of the governor's mansion.

As commander of the New Jersey Guard and governor of the state, Moore now realized that he must cope with a major disaster. He ordered 250 black quartermaster troops, in late summer training at Sea Girt, to patrol the beaches from Point Pleasant to Belmar. They were to pull in swimmers and to recover bodies. Blankets and Army overcoats from the Guard's warehouse were hurried to the shore; all trucks and ambulances were dispatched; and other troops cleared the low, concrete block commissary building, transforming it into a temporary morgue. When all orders had been given, the exhausted governor suddenly felt ravenously hungry. It was now close to noon, and all he had eaten was one forkful of scrambled eggs.

—·—·— ——·—

Herman Cluthe was almost unconscious when a lifeboat from the *City of Savannah* came alongside and strong arms reached down to pull him aboard. He lay on the bottom of the boat in a foot and a half of water, too numbed to realize more than dimly that he had been rescued. Next to him, he recalls, was a woman whose head had been split open. With his mouth open, gasping for air, he found himself actually drinking her blood. The undermanned lifeboat, helpless in the waves, finally came ashore at Spring Lake. "When one of the aid men worked on me with a pulmotor," he says, "he couldn't understand how so much blood came out of me. But it was blood I had drunk. It wasn't mine."

Young Gouverneur Phelps, by now exhausted from more than three hours' hanging onto one of the *Morro Castle*'s hawsers, had a fish-eye view as the first rescue ships arrived. Number one was the *Luckenbach*, but she was too busy picking up floating passengers to pay attention to him. Number two, and he remembers her best, was the *Monarch of Bermuda*. From his vantage point under the stern, he could see her coming up. "A magnificent sight," he says. "The skipper was out on the flying bridge with a megaphone, bellowing, 'Lower away!' With wonderful military precision all those boats hit the water at the same moment." Years later young Phelps was to dine with Captain Francis in London and to hear the captain's reminiscences of that wild day at sea.

It was not, however, the *Monarch* that rescued him, but a boat from the *City of Savannah*. The waves were so high and the boat so undermanned that it could not tie up to the *Savannah*. A cargo hatch was open at the water line as the lifeboat drew alongside, about ten feet away. A rope sailed out from the freighter, and an oarsman put a hitch around Phelps's chest before shoving him into the water. Phelps remembers being pulled in over rusty, jagged steel plates just as the first mate called out, "Is there a doctor here?" The *Savannah*, a small ship, carried none. "I'm the son of a doctor," said Phelps, "and I know a little about medicine." The mate snorted, "Hell, you're all we've got. Do the best you can. Here's some bandages and brandy, and I'll give you six men to follow your orders." In the engine room Phelps found an old woman lying on a mattress. Her heart was barely beating. He lifted her head and poured brandy down her throat. She turned cold as ice and then died. Later his father told him he had done the wrong thing: The brandy had gone into her lungs and choked her. Still trying to be helpful, Phelps happened on a man, his broken leg bent at a right angle. When he straightened the leg, the man sat up and let go a haymaker, roaring: "Don't ever try that again!"

In Paisley, Scotland, Mrs. Henry George Bartol, the former Helena Phelps, picked up the paper the next morning to find screaming headlines announcing the *Morro Castle* disaster. She knew that her brother, father, and mother were coming home on that ship. She placed a transatlantic phone call to the Phelps apartment on Manhattan's East Side. There was no answer. Then she called one of the New York newspapers. "They're all dead," said a voice on the other end of the phone. Helena Bartol was pregnant. She died of shock at the news, still carrying her baby.

▬·▬· ▬▬·▬

When Robert Smith went overboard at 5:18 A.M. ship's time, he lost his hat. When he came to the surface again, he grabbed a white hat floating beside him. He wanted to be easily identified as part of the staff of the *Morro Castle*. But when he looked at the hat, he shuddered. It said "Surgeon" on it. A minute later his own hat floated by. Holding it tight, he struck out for shore. As he rose on the crest of each wave, he would take a bearing on the shore, for his big worry was that he might be swimming in the wrong direction. The rain actually hurt him as it hit his burned, bare shoulders. The same lifeboat from the *City of Savannah* that had picked up Herman Cluthe also picked him up. He was barely able to keep his head out of the water in the bottom of the boat, and he was in agonizing pain from a constricted bladder. The cold water had chilled him so thoroughly that he could not void his urine.

▬·▬· ▬▬·▬

At about 9:00 A.M. a lifeboat from the *Luckenbach* picked up Mrs. Emil Lampe, but not without difficulty. Two strong black crewmen started to lift her out of the water, but the surge of the waves was so strong that they dropped her off again. The second time, they managed to put a rope around her and dragged her aboard. For her age, she was spry, and also attentive to detail. Few other survivors had enough strength to sit upright and to take a last look at the *Morro Castle*. Mrs. Lampe did. She remembers the awful majesty of the sight: "A ship like a torch, with flames shooting out of every porthole." She also remembers one of the rare moments of humor. "They put me in a bedroom," she says, "and after a while somebody brought me a cup of soup. The young fellow who brought it couldn't stop laughing, and then I realized why. I had no pants on."

In this unutterable confusion husbands were separated from wives, parents from children. Nathene Loveland came aboard the *Savannah*. A cursing sailor, hauling in both the living and the dead, paused long enough to hand her a bottle of applejack and to throw a blanket around her. Warmed by the liquor, ignoring the pain in her knees (they had swollen enormously from the effort she had put into treading water), she insisted on turning over every corpse to make sure that Frank was not among them, and then sent a wire to his brother Gilbert in New York. She was sure that Loveland had been lost. Loveland, meanwhile, had been taken aboard the *Monarch of Bermuda*. He, too, was sure that his wife had perished.

By sheer good luck Mrs. Meissner and her husband were picked up by the same Coast Guard boat and brought aboard the *Savannah*. That she was saved was more than an accident, in her judgment. She was wearing a Virginia fairy stone cross, reputed to bring good fortune. She believed it more than ever after that morning, and when she had recovered she wrote a letter of thanks to the jeweler in Richmond, Virginia, who had sold her the cross.

Bad luck, however, separated the Torborgs. Ruth was picked up by the *Luckenbach*. Young John and his Uncle Herman were pulled into a *Monarch of Bermuda* lifeboat, certain that Ruth had drowned. The separation did, however, give them a first-person view of the skill and precision with which that fine ship was managed. Instead of trying to bring the lifeboat alongside a hatchway in those rolling seas, Captain Francis ordered cables lowered to the water and hooked onto the boat. It was raised to the boat deck and the passengers crawled out without even getting their feet wet.

John Torborg still has the clothes they gave him aboard the *Monarch of Bermuda*, "and, believe it or not," he says, "they still smell of smoke." They took him into the dining room, and on each table was a bottle of brandy. It was the first time he had ever tasted hard liquor. Breakfast that morning was soft scrambled eggs, which didn't appeal too much to fifteen-year-old John. So he breakfasted on brandy and then found his way to a berth, pleasantly tipsy and quite prepared for a long nap.

By midmorning the air was full of planes. Three of them were from the New Jersey Guard, two from the Coast Guard, and another half dozen from New York newspapers. From the cockpit of the New York *Daily News'* single-wing Waco, photographer Charles Hoff snapped one picture after another of the ship enveloped in its mantle of smoke, of passengers waving from the water, and of the entourage of freighters and passenger liners that clustered around the *Morro Castle*. Pilot Aaron

(Duke) Krantz,[8] a World War I military pilot, remembers the scene as totally unbelievable. "To have this happen to a fine ship so close to New York," he says, "seemed impossible, but there was the evidence, right under our wing." Pilot Bill Cleveland, from the New York *Journal,* was certain he could see passengers leaning out of portholes waving for help, though by this hour every living passenger had left the *Morro Castle.* In widely separated staterooms the fire had already consumed the bodies of four unlucky people: Catherine Cochrane; Monroe Berliner, a Philadelphia businessman; Mrs. Margaret Saenz of Havana, and her son Braulio. By this time, such was the intensity of the heat, the body of Captain Wilmott had been reduced to a mass of charred bones.

Wild stories were circulated by some of those flying over the ship. One pilot reported seeing sharks, yet no passenger afloat in the water saw them. The Coast Guard later concluded that the "sharks" were harmless porpoises. Others told of hearing screams for help, yet the roar of the wind and the noise of the airplane motors would have made it impossible to hear them, and those in the water were much too exhausted to scream. Yet the newspaper photos, more than anything else, brought home the magnitude of the catastrophe. No ship disaster in history ever had been covered so thoroughly by the press; but no liner, before or since, ever encountered tragedy so close to New York City.

▄▖▄▖ ▄▄▖▄

In a strange, abstract sense, the burning of the *Morro Castle* helped to bring home the shattering impact of the Depression. Americans had a blind faith in a never-ending cycle of prosperity. The Wall Street crash destroyed that trust. Americans had faith that the machinery their factories built was flawless, and what was the *Morro Castle* but an intricate machine? The fire, that morning of September 8, was another blow at American infallibility, another reminder that even the finest piece of machinery can be destroyed by accident. One of the two safest liners in coastal service had gone up in flames, and the tenet that America built the best ships . . . the best everything . . . had been shattered forever.

[8] Now living in New Jersey.

11

RESCUE ASHORE

Even in 1934 it was still hard for many Americans with salaried jobs or independent incomes to recognize that behind a thin façade of the comfortably well-off there stood an army of the poor. From personal experience, Madelaine Clancy [1] did recognize the grimness of poverty, for she dealt with it daily in her home town, Spring Lake, New Jersey. As secretary of the local Red Cross, she was assistant to the Chief of Police, the director of local welfare. It was her task to distribute clothing to those in need. Then, as now, the mansions of rich Philadelphia families and the pillared resort hotels that lined the seashore left an impression of unruffled opulence. Yet behind them lay the shabby houses of families long out of work, dependent on private charity and government help. Out at sea, like a distant vision of prosperity, the cruise ships sailed serenely by. When she went to bed the night of September 7, Madelaine Clancy had no conception that the paradox of wealth and poverty would be abruptly reversed, that the sea would cast up by the hundreds the well-off made newly poor.

The Clancy home on Fifth Street was a storehouse for public welfare supplies. The government's welfare program was not yet fully organized. "The Red Cross," Madelaine Clancy recalls, "had been given government money to buy surplus commodities. As far as we were concerned, the commodities down here were men's underwear, men's overalls, men's pants, men's work shirts, socks, some women's dresses and stockings, and some children's clothing. There was no place to store all this stuff but the Clancy cellar. My mother didn't welcome it, but there it stayed." Not many hours later, Madelaine Clancy was to wish that the stock of clothing in the cellar were many times larger.

At little after 3:00 A.M., September 8, a thunderous explosion woke both mother and daughter. Though they did not know it,

[1] Miss Clancy is now Welfare Director in Spring Lake.

what they heard was the gunpowder blowing up under the *Morro Castle*'s lifesaving gun. From their bedroom windows, looking out to sea, they could see flames lighting the clouds. That, they felt, was something for the Coast Guard to handle. At 5:45 A.M. shore time, the telephone rang. Miss Clancy sleepily answered it. "Madelaine," said a voice, "this is Lou Norris [2] at the police department. I'm sorry to call you, but something has happened with a ship offshore. People are in the water, swimming this way, and a few already have come in on the beach. Some haven't any clothes at all, and some are in their nightclothes."

"So I said, 'Come on up,' " recalls Miss Clancy, "and I said to Mother, 'I'm going to get up because something is wrong.' I was dressed by the time Lou came. We went down to the cellar, and he took what he thought he needed. He asked if I had anything for women. I said, 'Nothing except what you see here, and I don't feel that fits the bill.' I said, 'I might have three or four dresses of my own, and I might be able to dig up some lingerie.' He said, 'Well, we'll take these for the men and leave the women in blankets for a while.' We had a first-aid building next to police headquarters. I got there about six thirty in the morning, and I didn't go off duty until three A.M. Sunday."

Miss Clancy felt as if she had been transported bodily into a madhouse. Rescue workers were carrying or leading half-blinded members of the crew into the first-aid building. "It struck me as strange at the time that so many crew members came in. We didn't need clothes for them so much. They had their clothes on and their pay in their pockets. A lot of them spoke Spanish, which I understand very little. They were arguing among themselves and blaming somebody. But as the passengers came in, most of whom had swum ashore, I understood all too soon. Those crew members saved their own skins. They weren't worrying about the poor passengers. Even among those who swam in there were cowards. One girl who came in with the crew was pushed away by a crew member with a life preserver and was quite badly hurt when she got into the surf. Oh, that crew should have been murdered!"

—·—· —·—·

Rarely in recent American history has there been such a spontaneous outpouring of human sympathy and human help as on that early morning on the New Jersey shore. Bonfires

[2] Since retired and living in Spring Lake.

flared on the beaches as a signal to the swimmers. Two elderly
aunts of Richard Gibbons,[3] then a reporter for the Asbury Park
Press, lit candles and put them in the windows of their beach-
front home at Point Pleasant. The tiny dots of light, they hoped,
might guide some lost soul to shore. Lifeguards waded into the
boiling surf at Belmar, Spring Lake, and Sea Girt, risking their
own lives in the tumbling water to save the lives of others.
The wind was so high that rescuers could communicate only
in shouts, and even then the words often were blown away.
But above the wind, as 10,000 people lined the beaches, the
cheers of the onlookers could be heard as someone living was
carried ashore, wrapped in a blanket, and lifted into an ambulance. When a body was brought ashore, there was utter
silence. Young Stanley Truax,[4] then a high school student,
remembers going down to the beach just as the first lifeboat
came in. "You could see people trying to get in all along the
beach," he says, "so me and another fellow helped to fish them
out. One of the girls was naked, so I got my trench coat for her
to wear. It took me about four days to find it again. It was
amazing to see how everyone pitched right in to help. People
were running out of their homes to bring dry clothes, or food,
or whatever else they could do." In the mammoth Essex and
Sussex Hotel, kitchen employees turned to and produced mounds
of sandwiches.

The most appreciated bit of help came, perhaps, from a
summer resident named Walter McManus, president of the
Crown Cork and Seal Company. He sent a dozen cases of
whiskey to the first-aid building. Shivering survivors washed it
down with gulps of boiling hot coffee made by local women. William H. Kerr, a New York stockbroker, then appeared with dozens
of cartons of cigarettes. As the day drew on, more than seventy-
five local families volunteered to take survivors into their homes
—those well enough not to need hospital care. A little after
7:00 A.M., as Madelaine Clancy recalls it, the Spring Lake fire
siren let loose with an earsplitting blast. It was an emergency
call for more ambulances. In twenty villages from Long Branch
to Point Pleasant, both inland and along the shore, other sirens
took up the wailing chant. Now everyone on the Jersey coast
knew how grave the emergency was. In all, by 8:30 A.M., some
twenty ambulances were carrying the injured to nearby hospitals. A surprising number of survivors had deep cuts or broken

---

[3] Now editor of the Lakewood, New Jersey, *Times.*
[4] Past captain of the Spring Lake First Aid Squad.

arms or legs. One crewman, never identified, swam in with his left wrist nearly severed by a metal lifeboat cable that broke loose.

Captain Francis O. Ziegler,[5] quartermaster officer at the National Guard encampment, recalls, "I put on my rubber boots at seven A.M. Saturday and didn't take them off again until Sunday night." Ziegler was one of those in charge of Guardsmen assigned to duty on the beaches. He remembers one astonishing incident at Spring Lake beach: "I saw a little boy swimming in with two women hanging to his life belt. Our men waded out to meet him, figuring he'd be exhausted. He just shook us off and sprinted a quarter mile down the beach and back to warm himself up. But that was the exception. We saw a man swimming by himself a hundred or two hundred feet out. He was waving for help. Someone jumped in to save him, and then he went down, and we never found him."

Lou Norris was on the midnight to 8:00 A.M. shift with the Spring Lake Police Department. He remembers the terrific northeast storm that night, "the sort we seem to get in late summer and early fall." Norris, a stocky young towhead in those days, was on the desk at headquarters from midnight to 2:00 A.M., after which he was to go out on motor patrol. The department had a handsome little Model T Ford, but what gave Norris pride was that it also had one of the first two-way radio systems in any New Jersey village. "It was just before two A.M.," he recalls, "when Walter McManus, who lived on the shore, called me at headquarters. He said to me that there seemed to be a big boat on fire just off his house on the oceanfront. He said it was a terrible fire—he could see things or objects falling off, and the ship wreathed in flames. I went to the beach and, sure enough, I saw what he was talking about. At that time our Coast Guard station was in operation at the corner of Worthington Street and Ocean Avenue. I went over and asked them if they were aware of what was going on. They said they were, but they couldn't seem to get any communications."

Norris drove up and down Ocean Avenue all night. Just as it was full daylight, he remembers, the first-aid whistle blew. A night watchman at the Spring Lake Club pavilion had called headquarters to turn in the alarm. "Lo and behold," says Norris, "there was the first boat coming in. One of the men on that boat had his arm almost completely severed, and that was the reason for the call. There were fourteen men in that boat, and one

[5] Now Colonel Francis O. Ziegler, retired and living in Spring Lake.

Cuban woman, Mrs. Capote." A minute later Norris saw another boat coming in four blocks to the south. There was, he thought, nothing in that boat but crew. (Actually, Dr. Cochrane was aboard.)

Chief Engineer Abbott, who by now had abandoned any notion of concealing his rank or identity, was also among those aboard. "He was O.K.," says Norris, "but I couldn't get anything out of him. All he wanted to do was to call the Ward Line. I took him to headquarters in my car, but I never did get anything out of him." Officer Raymond B. Newman, at Norris's suggestion, had already called out all the first-aid units he could contact. In all, between Point Pleasant and Asbury Park, 110 doctors and nurses were on duty by midmorning, under the direction of Dr. Louis F. Albright. McManus, meanwhile, sent his chauffeur in a Cadillac to Sears Roebuck in Asbury Park to buy "all the dungarees, underwear, and shoes you can get in my car." He had a special concern for the *Morro Castle*. He had traveled on it half a dozen times.

Norris, now gray-haired, talks with pride of the skill with which local people, doctors, nurses, and volunteers handled the survivors. People, he recalls, started coming ashore at dawn, and kept coming until about 1:00 P.M. "Everyone cooperated," he says. "Everything worked to perfection. We threw all the wet clothes in a jail cell, and there was no loss of personal property." Rumors of looting infuriate him. "I saw no looting at all," he snaps. The situation bears him out. With thousands of people on the beaches, a looter would have been hard put to make away with jewelry or money.

Madelaine Clancy, meanwhile, had been efficiently backstopped. Katherine F. Duelle, assistant supervisor of Red Cross nursing posts in Monmouth County, had been dispatched to Spring Lake along with five other nurses. In addition, Red Cross nurses summering on the shore showed up to offer their services. At the center of the storm, however, was Miss Clancy, who still remembers the confusion and the poignancy of the day. One little boy, about five years old, kept tugging at her skirt, saying, "Mama," and "Bebe." Somehow she managed to figure it out. His mother and a baby were missing. Another, young Robert Lione, was babbling, "Where my mother, and where my brother Ray?" His mother, Mrs. Anthony Lione, was saved. His brother Ray drowned. "One Latin woman," Miss Clancy says, "—let's describe her as a *mamacita*, a big, fat woman, was screaming blue murder for clothes. I brought her an old dress, but do you think she'd be satisfied? No. She wanted silk stockings too, and I didn't have any."

Clothes for women ran out quickly, but Madelaine Clancy was not about to be frustrated. Seizing a local policeman, she ordered him, "Go down to the stores and buy a couple of dozen dresses and stockings in all sizes. Don't worry about who pays for it. Charge it to Mother." She knew the Red Cross would pay the bill in the end. A little later in the day, compounding her frustration, a contingent of newspaper photographers showed up. "One of them was starting to snap a picture of a nearly nude woman," she said. "I was dog tired, but I knew what to do. As he put his finger on the shutter lever, I lurched into him, stepped hard on his foot, and said, 'Excuse me.' That spoiled the picture, and then I told him to get out of my way, people needed help."

By this time bodies were being collected from points all along the beaches and carried by ambulance to the National Guard encampment. On tables, on cots, and on the floors they were laid out, sheets covering their heads, just their bare feet showing. They had come, piled in stacks, from the front porch of George Scheible's home at Brielle, from the back yard of a local undertaker in Manasquan, and from the beach at Spring Lake. One "corpse" got up and walked away. Edward Kendall, rhythmically swimming toward Spring Lake beach, had been met in the surf by a husky lifeguard. "Stay away from me—I'm all right," he yelled, but the lifeguard grabbed him anyway. In the fifteen-foot waves he was held under water and lost consciousness. A doctor was passing by as he came to atop a pile of bodies. His eyes fluttered. "This man's alive!" said the doctor. A pulmotor crew gave him oxygen, and Kendall dragged himself to his feet.

Dr. James Burrell of Buffalo had jumped from the *Morro Castle* just a second before his wife. He hit the water wearing spectacles, and he came ashore with them still on. His wife drowned. Lou Norris still remembers the Bradys, Mrs. Edward Brady and their daughter Nancy. Recuperating in a Spring Lake home, Nancy told him that while the family was in Havana, she had dreamed the ship would sink. She begged her father to let the family return by seaplane. "Nancy," she quoted him as saying, " don't fret me like that." The Bradys jumped together, but Nancy was separated from her father and mother. After half an hour in the water Brady said to his wife, "I'm going. I can't keep up. I'm not afraid to die, but I hate to leave you."

He pulled a wallet from his hip pocket and handed it to his wife. "Don't worry," he said. "Keep my wallet." With that, he let his head fall forward, and Mrs. Brady knew he was dead. She was reunited with her daughter in Spring Lake.

Inevitably, in the midst of tragedy, there was some comedy. Frank Durand, president of the Spring Lake bank, was the local head of disaster relief. In response to a telephone call from the Ward Line, he persuaded the Jersey Central Railroad to add a special car to one of its trains bound for Jersey City. All of the rescued members of the Ward Line crew were to be locked in this car. In his zeal, Durand and a friend found themselves locked in the same car. No amount of argument would persuade the conductor to release them, and it was midafternoon Saturday before they finally talked their way out to come back on another train. Madelaine Clancy remembers this episode as a light moment in two days of almost unalloyed grief. From late Saturday until late Sunday she was one of two nurses on duty at the temporary morgue at the National Guard encampment. By this time nearly all the dead had been collected. It was, to her, like a vision from the frozen hell of Dante's inferno— fathers in search of their sons, mothers in search of their daughters, brothers and sisters in search of kin. Frozen faces, frozen composure, and then a collapse into soundless weeping as a sheet dragged back revealed the face of someone they had loved.

"There was a man who had sent his son on the cruise as a graduation present," she remembers. "I met him at the door of the morgue, and there was a terrible look on his face. He was weeping. 'I have found my son,' he said. 'At least I know he won't be out there forever in that awful sea.'" Between the smell of death and the awful evidence of death, Miss Clancy was a torn person, who by force of personality retained her composure. She recalls meeting Dr. Albright at one point. "Madelaine," he said, "I'm not sure you ought to be here." "Dr. Albright," she responded, "I'm one woman who can keep her mouth shut and her mind on what she has to do." At which point, she burst into tears.

Captain Ziegler remembers it all as somewhat of an exercise in logistics. "The bodies," he says, "were in pretty good shape. Saturday night they divided the bodies up in groups: men, women, and children. So, if you were coming in to look for a man, you wouldn't have to look at twenty women and children. With all that moving around, a party came in looking for a man with his two sons, and the three of them were next to each other. It was a quiet scene, somber, not hysterical. The priests and ministers from this locality came in, and you could hear the low murmur of prayers. Around noon on Sunday a special train came in. They moved the bodies into the train, and it moved out for Jersey City about seven or eight at night. The bodies were lined, head to foot, in seven box cars. There was a railroad spur that came within fifty feet of the commissary, so moving the bodies wasn't all that hard. It just took a long time. There was a platform level with the freight cars, so all they had to do was to wheel the bodies up the platform and into the cars."

In this fashion, mothers and children, whole families and individuals, finished their trip on the *Morro Castle,* a ship they had boarded with such confidence.

▬▪▬▪ ▬▬▪▬

Once the news was out, the messages flooded into Spring Lake. Lou Norris has preserved some of them. To Senora Capote, rescued and in Fitkin Memorial Hospital: *"Felicitola!"* ("Congratulations!") from the Cuban Consul General in New York. From the chief of police in Erie, Pennsylvania: "Was the H. B. McCauley family aboard?" (It was not.) From Mrs. Anna Stemmerman of Queens, New York: "Wire information about Ann Stemmerman." (She was saved.) From the mother of Gertrude Cohn, New York City: "Wire at once, how are you?" (Exhausted, but saved.) From Queens: "Phone immediately, or wire whether my daughter Doris Landes is safe." (She was.) From Philadelphia: "Are Mr. and Mrs Emanuel Weinberger safe?" (They were. They swam ashore together.) From Wilkes-Barre, Pennsylvania: "Wire immediately the whereabouts of Mrs. James Sheridan." (She survived, but her son was drowned.) To Agnes Prince, the reporter: "Telephone office immediately or write your story, (Signed) Hardy Hill, City Editor." To Ruben Holden (whose father drowned): "Phone me collect. I want to help you." To the Chief of Police: "We have important connections in Cuba and seek information about the Saenz family. Advise us care Royal Bank of Canada, New York." (All Saenzes—mother, two daughters, and son—were either drowned or fatally burned.)

▬▪▬▪ ▬▬▪▬

Norris, among others, was to hear from the thankful saved passengers and their families. It was a tribute to the selflessness

of the people of Spring Lake that impelled Charles and Ann
Menken of Brooklyn, among the rescued, to write him:

> This is to all the good people of Spring Lake who so gal-
> lantly aided in rescue work of the survivors of the *Morro
> Castle*, of whom my wife and myself were one. I have a
> vague idea that after about eight hours in the high seas, we
> were picked up about two miles off Spring Lake by a Coast
> Guard boat. This boat was towed by the *Paramount*.
>
> God bless that crew. From the time we were rescued, we
> received wonderful care. And I felt if it were not for the
> loving care we received at that time, we would not have been
> able to survive the shock of seeing so many drowning people.
> If it is possible, I would like to have the people of Spring
> Lake know of the wonderful humanitarian work of Dr. Rob-
> inson, his family, and Miss Quinn, all of whom live on Lud-
> low Avenue. And if possible, I would like to have you publish
> this letter. At present, we are under the doctor's care, but
> as soon as possible hope to visit Spring Lake and try to show
> my gratitude to all the volunteers who did such wonderful
> work. God bless and keep you all.

Caroline Klintberg, of the Bronx, wrote Norris:

> I do want so much to tell you how grateful I am for your
> kindness on the day of the *Morro Castle* disaster. The news
> of the disaster was kept from my ailing mother until your
> telephone call was received by her, telling her I was safe. She
> was spared the terrible ordeal, the uncertainty of my fate. The
> kindness of the people in Spring Lake helped a great deal to
> lighten our experience, which seemed almost impossible that
> one could go through. My family joins me in thanking you
> for your extreme kindness. Sincerely and gratefully . . .

For Howard Hansen, rescue by the *Paramount* was a home-
coming. At the pier in Brielle he was met by Charles (Bud)
Fitkin of Ocean City, on whose yacht he had at one time served
as captain. After a brief period of first-aid care in Spring Lake,
he was transferred to the Fitkin summer home for a day of rest.
Hansen weighed in with a homely note to Lou Norris: "I was
taken to your station after being rescued. What clothing I had
was taken from me there. If you have my belongings, I'll thank
you kindly if you send them. They consisted of one pair of brown
pajamas, one pair of white pants with white belt, hand-made
with white shell buckle, one white gold Elgin watch with small
knife attached, one black bridge coat." So meticulously had the
rescue parties ashore preserved the possessions of passengers

that he got back all his clothing. His watch was found and returned by Police Chief James Legge of Brielle. In the same fashion, a Spring Lake Police Department memorandum made sure that a diamond ring worn by Mrs. John T. Byrne of Richmond Hill, New York, was returned to her rescued husband after her body was washed ashore.

Pathetic inquiries poured in all through the weekend, to be followed by one that was ludicrous. Mrs. Norma Ama Chenier wrote Norris from Ottawa that the picture of a rescued man in the local *Evening Citizen* resembled her brother, a merchant seaman named Frank E. Ama. Like so many seamen, Ama was a rover. He was not aboard the *Morro Castle*. The father of Raymond Ferner, a wiper, wrote to ask after his son. Young Ferner's body washed ashore at Sea Girt. Nat S. Celi, a waiter, was more fortunate. He survived, and wrote to ask if his pants and the citizenship papers he carried in his wallet had been found. A search uncovered them, and they were returned to him. Dr. Van Zile's body, recovered at Manasquan, yielded a significant bit of evidence. In his hip pocket, police found a blurred letter. It was addressed to his wife and said: "Captain Wilmott died of a heart attack at about 7:45 tonight." [6] That seemed to explode the suspicion that he had been poisoned or drugged. One woman, whose identity has thoughtfully been concealed, besieged the Ward Line and police departments up and down the coast with frantic inquiries about the fate of her husband. "He *told* me," she wrote,[6] "that he was going to take a little vacation on the *Morro Castle,* but I can't find his name either on the list of survivors or the list of the dead." Investigators subsequently learned why. The man had chosen to spend the week in a New York hotel with an attractive blond young woman.

—·—·——·—

The siren woke Mrs. Frederick F. Schock, Jr., in her home just a few blocks from the seashore. Automatically she reached over and turned on the radio. What she heard caused her to forget about breakfast. She threw on some clothes, ran out to her car, and drove to the beach. The Schocks were important contributors to the Monmouth County Red Cross and citizens of significance in Spring Lake. Frederick Schock's father owned the stately Essex and Sussex Hotel and the Monmouth Hotel, luxurious resorts on the shoreline. Mrs. Schock reached the

[6] As reported by Francis W. H. Adams, then Chief Assistant U.S. Attorney in New York.

shore just as the first lifeboats came in. She remembers wishing that her husband could have been there to help. Schock,[7] at this moment, was coming from New York on the "milk train," which was to arrive at Spring Lake at 8:00 A.M.

"When we got to Asbury Park," he remembers, "we started to get news. So I went to the police station before coming home because there was the problem of getting these unfortunate people places to stay." Within half an hour the Schocks had unexpected guests—Dr. Burrell of Buffalo and two secretaries whose names neither of them can remember.

"Our neighbors were wonderfully helpful," Mrs. Schock recalls. "They rushed over with blankets, food, and everything they could think of. Dr. Burrell came ashore with a wad of bills in his pants pocket. Sunday morning, when the sun came out, their chauffeur carefully pinned them all on a clothesline in the back yard and dried them out." Schock, because he felt it his duty, drove the doctor down to the morgue at Sea Girt and waited while Burrell identified the body of his wife. Mrs. Schock put the two secretaries to bed. By Sunday morning they were rested, and they left. "For years after, they sent us Christmas cards."

As the day extended itself, the storm grew in intensity. Madelaine Clancy remembers peals of thunder and the crackling lightning bolts over Spring Lake at about 6:00 P.M. Ambulances were stalled in the torrent; the county chairman of the Red Cross was marooned in his car on a railroad crossing; fortunately not even the trains could run in such a deluge. Miss Clancy has another reason for remembering that storm. She was wearing an expensive knit woolen suit. Every time she went out in the rain on an errand, which was often, the suit would stretch until the hem of the skirt was down around her ankles. Every time she came back into the heat of the first-aid building, it would shrink until it was above her knees—immodestly short for a spinster of that era. Trees were toppling, cars were backed up for miles on the two-lane macadam shore road extending down the coastline from the Pulaski Skyway and Holland Tunnel at Jersey City. The weather, which played such a part in the death of the *Morro Castle*, was orchestrating a grand requiem for all who died that day.

Everyone pitched in to help. The New Jersey American Legion, in convention at Belmar, suspended its sessions and dis-

[7] Now owner of the two hotels.

patched hundreds of its members, in their jaunty blue-and-gold caps, to help direct traffic. By now at least 5000 cars had arrived, and the entire network of shore roads was a shambles. Other Legionnaires went to the beaches to act as stretcher bearers. Over the radio Governor Moore was directing half-hourly appeals: "Don't come down to the Jersey shore. You will only interfere with rescue work, and traffic is tied in knots." The appeals were useless. More cars kept arriving all through the night, and finally 100 state police were brought in to direct traffic. Aid squads from Avon, Bradley Beach, Belmar, Manasquan, Point Pleasant, Neptune, Matawan, Ocean Grove, Eatontown, Dunellen, and Somerville worked on the beaches until their members began to drop from exhaustion, and new squads were moved in. Father Thomas Riley of St. Catharine's Roman Catholic Church in Spring Lake moved from one beach to another, reciting the last rites over huddled bodies—Catholics, Protestants, and Jews alike. Under the lash of the storm, John Bogan recalls, scarcely one word of the ancient Latin rite could be heard. "You had to scream to be heard," Bogan says. Thomas Tighe, who by midday had made his way to the bridge over Shark River Inlet, a few miles north of Spring Lake, remembers that he could scarcely stand against the winds, which had reached a speed of nearly fifty miles an hour. Over the massed people on the beaches, he could see the *Morro Castle* "aflame from stem to stern," trailing a plume of smoke that settled sullenly over the water.

—·— —·—

At Fitkin Memorial Hospital Dr. Gouverneur Morris Phelps, Sr., lurched out of his hospital bed in search of his wife. The husband and wife had been segregated by sex in well-separated wards. Still half-blinded from smoke, Dr. Phelps peered into one ward, then another, until he located Mrs. Phelps. He promptly crawled into bed with her as a nurse protested, "You can't do that!" Phelps replied: "Yes, I can. I'm a doctor, and I'm here to stay." Choruses of nurses: "But, Doctor! . . ." and he stayed. His wife fell asleep in his arms.

Frank Dittman, Jr., still carrying the little boy he had taken in charge, was hauled aboard the *Paramount*. Desperately, he put the boy across his knees to give him respiration. The boy lived then but died later. Dittman, even after a grueling swim, was able to hop out on the pier at Brielle. Scarcely more than a boy himself, he remembers saying, "Take good care of that boy." Whirled to Fitkin Memorial Hospital and thrust into bed, he was greeted by a nurse with a pint of brandy, saying, "Son, this is for you. Have the whole thing." By the time his father, stepfather, brother, and sister arrived midway through Saturday evening, he was hilariously drunk. He had company. Martha Bradbury, a survivor, a nurse at Presbyterian Hospital in New York, remembers hearing shocked murmurs from nurses at Fitkin: "They shouldn't give young girls so much to drink." Dittman went home the next day. Within the week he was the proud recipient of a letter of commendation from "Uncle Horace" Taft, headmaster of the Taft School, advising him he had acted in accord with the highest traditions of that institution, and within two weeks, blushing and embarrassed, he stood up at a formal dinner to receive a medal from the American Legion post in his home, Whitestone, Queens, presented by Supreme Court Justice Charles S. Colden.

Thomas Cannon, Jr., was the only survivor on the fishing boat that brought him into Brielle. He was dehydrated from overexposure, but for reasons he cannot understand, the nurses at Fitkin Hospital would not give him any water. That night he lost his sight; the next day he was unable to walk. He was in the hospital five days. Though the doctors did not want him to go, he signed himself out. Cannon's own doctor gave him only six months to live because of his almost-severed spinal cord. "I made up my mind I'd prove him wrong," he says. "I exercised, carefully, and eventually the spinal cord healed. And now here I am, in my late sixties, and I'm in fine shape."

Lillian Davidson, taken to Point Pleasant Hospital, remembered her duties as a nurse. Feebly, she told a doctor there, "Please call Presbyterian Hospital and tell them I won't be on duty at one P.M." Presbyterian Hospital forgave her absence. A week later, when she had recovered sufficiently, an ambulance from that hospital came down to pick her up with her friend and fellow-nurse Martha Bradbury, and transferred them both to Harkness Pavilion in New York. It took weeks before their burns healed and they could go back to duty.

As for the people in Spring Lake who had done so much to alleviate the shock of the *Morro Castle* disaster, Lou Norris describes it: "We all went to bed Sunday night and we slept right through all day Monday."

12

LAST OF A GREAT SHIP

Pilot Apprentice Bill Warner [1] had never known that the sturdy old pilot boat *New York* could travel so fast. After all, she had been in service for thirty-seven years, a coal-burner in the age of oil-fueled ships, with an old-fashioned engine that rarely had been called upon to produce a top speed of 12 knots. Warner, standing on the bridge with Captain Gus Swainson, kept a tight grip on the railing as the *New York* lurched southward. Every few hundred feet her lee rail dipped far under the green water until it seemed she might capsize. But each time she shuddered back. At 8:50 A.M. ship's time she burst out of a rain squall into sight of the dying *Morro Castle*. The liner glowed cherry red like a blacksmith's forge. Strips of flaming paint were flying astern, and a sullen cloud of smoke trailed on the water. On the forepeak Swainson could see a huddled group of fourteen men—Acting Captain Warms and a remnant of the ship's personnel. "It was a terrible and beautiful sight," he says, "though I realize that's not a nice thing to say."

Apprentice Si Haraldsen [2] felt physically sick. As an apprentice rowing the pilot boat's 30-foot yawl, he had carried many a senior pilot to the side of the *Morro Castle*. He knew most of the officers and a few members of the crew aboard her, and counted them as friends. From his viewpoint at sea level, coming alongside the towering steel well of the *Morro Castle*, watching the pilot step aboard, she had seemed to him to be a happy and impressive ship, respectable evidence of the solid quality of the U.S. Merchant Marine. Now he was staring at a floating ruin. He turned to Apprentice Bill Baeszler,[3] who was to man the yawl with him, and said, "I can't believe it. I can't believe it."

[1] Now Chief Pilot of the Hudson River Pilots' Association.
[2] Now a retired pilot.
[3] Also now a retired pilot.

117

Gus Swainson wasted no time in musing. "Baeszler and Haraldsen, get ready to lower the yawl," he snapped. "I'll go with you, and we'll get under the bow. Warner, take the wheel." The yawl, built like a lifeboat but designed for greater speed, hit the waves with a splash, with Baeszler and Haraldsen each pulling an oar. It was a job for strong young men like these, for each oar was 18 feet long and weighed 20 pounds. Simply lifting the oars out of the water after each stroke represented a major effort. "But we were tough young bucks in our twenties," says Haraldsen, "and we'd been yawling in worse storms than this one."

Down into the trough of the waves and then up on their crests, the yawl sped 600 feet toward the bow of the *Morro Castle*. Bracing his legs, rolling with the motion of the boat, Swainson cupped his hands and shouted to Warms as the yawl came directly under the bow: "You want to be taken off?" He had to bellow, for the rising wind blew the words from his mouth. Warms shouted back: "No."

"Do you want a tow?" called Swainson. "We'll tow you, and it won't cost a thing." The offer was wildly irrational. No boat weighing 400 tons, like the *New York*, could pull a 12,000-ton ocean liner through such a storm. Warms, dulled by almost thirty straight hours on duty and a surfeit of disaster, was equally irrational. "Can you tow us?" he shouted through his megaphone. "What kind of line you got?"

"Eight inch," Swainson called back.

George Alagna, standing alongside Warms, has never forgotten his next words. "You heard that, fellows," he said. "He said it won't cost us anything for a tow. You know, after they land us in harbor, these fellows forget things like that." Warms at that moment was talking like a "company man," whose prime responsibility was to his employer. For, under maritime law, a ship taken in tow by any commercial vessel can be claimed as salvage for all or most of her value. In his exhaustion, either Warms did not know the truth or he refused to accept it: His ship was a total loss.

Aboard the cutter *Tampa*, Commander Earl G. Rose kept binoculars clapped to his eyes as his battleship-gray ship drove steadily through the storm. Between rain clouds he finally saw a pillar of smoke on the horizon. Exactly at 9:00 A.M. the *Tampa* took a long swing around the burning ship. Like a fish, she darted between anchored rescue liners and smaller craft before rounding into the east-northeast just 600 feet off the

Morro Castle's bow. By now, as Bill Warner recalls, the yawl had made three trips to the pilot boat for water, coffee, and sandwiches, which were hauled up to the liner's foredeck in a tin pail. Swainson, bobbing far below, looked up at Warms.

"Go over and ask him what he's going to do," Warms called down. He knew that a government vessel could not claim his ship as salvage. With Baeszler and Haraldsen still manning the oars, the yawl skittered over to the *Tampa*. By now the wind was at 34 miles an hour, approaching gale force. With one hand clapped on his gold-braided cap to keep it from being blown off, the other clutching a megaphone, Commander Rose yelled: "We'll take her in tow. We've got a twelve-inch hawser. We'll try to pull her into quiet water behind Sandy Hook, and then the New York City fireboats can put some water on her."

The wind was playing an unholy, screeching tune in the rigging of the *Morro Castle* as Swainson came back with the message. "Our rudder's jammed," Warms called down. "You'd better go aft and put a line on to steer us." As the yawl came even with the stern, Bill Warner grabbed a trailing line and swarmed up the side of the ship to D Deck. Waves of heat buffeted him, and he gagged on acrid smoke, but he threw down a light line. This was attached to the *New York*'s towing hawser. Two other apprentices, who also made the climb, helped him haul in the eight-inch rope and make it fast. As Warner and his companions slid back into the yawl, the *New York*'s engines began to turn, pulling the rope taut, holding the liner steady against waves and wind. Standing once more on the deck of the pilot boat, Warner heard a new sound from the *Morro Castle*— a loud *wham!* as superheated rivets burst loose from the ship's plating. Every porthole glowed the same shade of red.

—·—·——·—

For most people ashore, the New York and Asbury Park radio stations were the sole source of information about the disasters. WOR in New York went on the air at 5:45 A.M. shore time; WMCA at 6:00 A.M., and WCAP in Asbury at the same moment. That early in the morning the newspaper extras had not yet started to roll from the presses, and the newsboys were not yet crying their wares down quiet city streets. A few, a very few, people took a vicarious part in the last agony of the *Morro Castle*. These were the amateur radio operators, the "hams," who made a hobby of talking and listening to the ships at sea. Among them was Geoffrey T. Azoy,[4] a vice president of the

[4] Now retired and living in Rumson, New Jersey.

Chemical Bank of New York. He was sleeping poorly in his apartment in East Orange, New Jersey.

"Well, if I can't sleep," he said to himself, "I might as well listen." He rolled out of bed and flipped on the wireless receiver. On the ship-to-shore frequency of 600 meters he could receive any signal within 2000 miles. It was then about 4:30 A.M. shore time; 3:30 A.M. ship's time. He heard Operator Rogers aboard the *Morro Castle* send the numerals "73," which means, "Best wishes, and I am closing down."

Then silence, and he knew what that meant. An emergency. There was only more silence as Azoy strained to hear further signals. Tuckerton was silent, the winds lashing and rain weep-around its 200-foot skeleton towers of steel. There was only silence from WNY, the New York station of the Radiomarine Corporation, from the Mackay Radio station at Sayville on the remote Long Island beaches, and from WIM, perched on a Cape Cod sandbar at Chatham, Massachusetts. Then, just minutes later, there was a babble of dots and dashes as wireless transmitters on one ship after another chimed in with its position. Finally the U.S. Navy station in New York took firm charge, monitoring the channel, permitting only rescue ships to transmit. Red-eyed, in rumpled pajamas, Azoy stuck by his set until the *Tampa* finally took the *Morro Castle* in tow. When he finally tuned out during the afternoon, he went back to his bed and slept more soundly than he ever had in his life.

––·– ––·–

A little after 9:00 A.M. the ocean liners and freighters began to leave the scene, bound for New York with survivors. Duke Krantz, flying low over the scene in the *Daily News* plane, re-called it as a somberly impressive procession. First there was the trim *Monarch of Bermuda*, appropriately the leader; next, the tubby *President Cleveland* with the "$" (for Dollar Line) prominent on her single stack; then the *Andrea Luckenbach*, oddly squared off above decks by her record load of sawed lumber, and finally the wallowing, utilitarian, rust-streaked *City of Savannah*. They departed when they had taken aboard all possible survivors, excluding only the *President Cleveland*, which had none at all. Captain Francis of the *Monarch* did not leave until he had seventy-one persons, twelve of them in critical condition, and had radioed the Coast Guard that he could carry no more. It was 1:15 P.M. shore time when tugs warped his ship into Pier 95 Hudson River, on 55th Street, Manhattan. He had purposely reduced his speed so as not to buffet the sick, injured, and sleeping tucked into every spare bunk aboard.

The *President Cleveland,* with Captain Carey exuding bonhomie on the bridge, came in a little later at a pier in Jersey City, across the Hudson from lower Manhattan. Like the old salt he was, he spun a good seafaring tale. When he received the SOS, said Carey, "I ordered full speed ahead. And I didn't know the old *Cleveland* had so much jump in her. In fact, we didn't get a chance to boat any survivors. Other boats beat ours every time. And we were all concerned with keeping a proper distance between the rescue boats. We couldn't have them colliding and killing more people." It was an apt if disingenuous explanation for his inaction when confronted with a human tragedy.

"We stood by," continued the captain, "until there was nothing more to stand by for. Then we steamed on toward New York." The captain, who said all this during an interview with the New York *Journal-American,* plunged into an even more romantic interlude. "It was strange and it was horrible," he said, "particularly since we had lain in the same berth with her in Havana last Wednesday. We remembered how she looked then —how she swarmed with people, alive, happy. We left Havana just two and a half hours before she did. She saluted us then with a whistle blast. Next afternoon she overtook and passed us, and saluted again. Then she passed on over the horizon. For her, the last horizon."

The salt-streaked old *Savannah,* in her dull, red paint, came during the afternoon to her pier on the Hudson near 42nd Street with sixty-five passengers aboard. The *Andrea Luckenbach,* with sixty-two aboard, had docked a little earlier, at a pier in Brooklyn. A special train from Spring Lake had dropped off sixty-eight crew members in Jersey City, and nine passengers came across the river to Manhattan on a puffing Jersey Central ferryboat.

These were people who had come back from the dead, too shaken to recognize the miracle of continued life. As a young reporter for the New York *Daily News,* I traveled that day from pier to pier, interviewing the survivors. Everywhere the scene was the same—ambulances from a dozen Manhattan hospitals lined up in ranks outside, more than two hundred policemen, kinfolk with stricken faces looking for family members, half-blinded passengers with smoke-swollen eyes lockstepping off the gangplanks, hands on one another's shoulders, strangers joined at this moment in a mute communion of shock and

misery. Frank Loveland's brother Gilbert was astonished to dis-
cover that Frank and Nathene didn't realize that they had both
been on the *Savannah* all the time: they were too exhausted
and shaken. They were whisked away so fast—one to a hotel,
another to a hospital—that hours passed before they were
reunited at Flower Hospital. Frank Loveland himself remembers
his rage and futility when he was stopped at the hospital ad-
missions desk: "They spent hours, it seems to me, making sure
I could pay my bill." In those days there was no Blue Cross,
and hospitals felt they had to be careful. In fact, the Lovelands
lost all their clothes, and replacing them involved a heavy
financial burden.

Robert Meissner and his wife, stunned and smoke-blinded,
came down the gangplank of the *Savannah* arm in arm, feeling
their way. Meissner was wearing the same fedora he had
jammed on his head before jumping overboard, but by now it
had shrunk. It was like a vise. "Damn thing!" he snorted, rip-
ping it off. But he held onto it, and for years after it was a
Meissner family souvenir. Getting off the pier was slow work.
Flashlights blinked and reporters halted them for questions as
they slowly made their way downstairs to ground level and
started out toward West Street in search of a taxi. Both were
too blind, too exhausted, and too shaken to wonder why nobody
from their family was there to meet them.

At that moment their son Kenneth was weeping with ex-
asperation, and their daughter, Eunice Meissner Bennett, was
stunned and tearless. They had driven from Brooklyn together
to the Ward Line offices and pier at the foot of Wall Street.
During the whole distance of the trip, they were listening to
the car radio, where announcers babbled rumors, reports, and
horror stories about the disaster. When they burst into the
waiting room, they found it jammed with weeping people.

"Do you know anything about my father and mother?" young
Meissner asked one bemused Ward Line office employee.

"Sorry," was the answer. "We don't know anything yet." Tall,
brown-haired Henry E. Cabaud, executive vice president of the
Atlantic, Gulf and West Indies Line, came out of his office for
a few brief moments to report that rescue ships were on the
way into port. But still there was no list of survivors.

Young Meissner was in a frenzy, but a patrolman took pity
on him. "The *Monarch of Bermuda* is coming in with survivors
right now," he said. "Why not drive over there and see if your
father and mother are aboard?" By luck, Meissner found a park-

ing place, and by luck he was able to get aboard the ship and find a purser, holding a list of those the *Monarch* had rescued.

Meissner's heart sank when he looked at it. He found the names of Mr. and Mrs. Lampe and of George Ridderhoff, all family freinds and members of the Concordia Society. He did not find the names of his father and mother. But when he drove back to the Ward Line pier, luck was still with him. The same patrolman had another thought. "Why not go up to the Savannah Line pier?" he said. "We've had a call to send radio cars up there."

Shooting through traffic lights and dodging trucks, young Meissner got to the Savannah Line pier. The whole area was cordoned off, and Meissner's car was the last permitted through the lines. Just as he reached the pier, he saw his mother and father wandering up West Street.

"Dad! Mother!" he called, and led them to the car. Back they went to the foot of Wall Street to pick up Eunice and her husband, Naval Ensign Bradley Bennett. All Eunice Bennett could think to say, after embracing her parents, was to ask her father: "How did you ever manage to keep your hat?"

The news of the *Morro Castle* spread its web far through many families that day. At Point Pleasant Beach, New Jersey, Mrs. George Durland got up at 7:30 A.M. and turned on the radio. What she heard was the litany of names of those missing and those rescued from the *Morro Castle*. Among the names of the missing were those of her mother's brother and sister-in-law, the Meissners. Between the rain clouds offshore, she could see a duller and more persistent cloud, the smoke from the *Morro Castle*. It was half an hour later when her mother, Mrs. George Einsetler, came into the kitchen and said, "Well, what would everybody like for breakfast?" It took Mrs. Durland a few minutes, but finally she broke the news. A sturdy woman, her mother accepted it in silence. She had her own way of coping. Silently she cooked breakfast. Next she put together a casserole for lunch. All morning long, as the radio talked about nothing but the *Morro Castle,* she continued to cook, to sweep, and to clean the cottage. It was midafternoon before the phone rang and the voice of Kenneth Meissner said, "They're both safe." Mrs. Einsetler then said only two words: "Thank God." The whole family piled into a car and took off for Brooklyn.

━·━· ━━·━

It was a morning when the city of New York lost its coldness. Normally surly taxi drivers, carrying home drenched survivors, burst through red lights with impunity and flatly refused to accept either fares or tips. Policemen at the piers, faced with beseeching relatives, shed their gruffness and did their best to mitigate the tragedy. Ambulance drivers from ten different hospitals, more accustomed to dealing with traffic accidents and shootings, moved gently and deliberately as they loaded survivors into their vans. New York was too big to come to a halt because a ship had been destroyed, but in every cranny of its life there was a shocked awareness of this particular happening. It was a time when most New York newspapers were brash and aggressive, but this brashness was muted in the face of so shattering an event. Reporters did not press for answers to their questions; photographers snapped pictures without demanding that survivors stop and pose.

The least human response, perhaps because the news was so numbing, came from the officers and employees of the Atlantic, Gulf and West Indies Company. Sylvester Murphy,[5] then working for the associated Clyde Mallory Lines, was summoned at 4:00 A.M. from his home in Teaneck, New Jersey. He arrived amid a scene of confusion. Ward Line and AGWI staff members were huddled in little clusters, talking somberly; Henry Cabaud was locked in his office, talking long distance to his superiors. Like all the others, Murphy was completely dumbfounded by the news.

To him, the double tragedy seemed impossible—Captain Wilmott dead and the ship afire. "It might have happened to the Ward liner *Mohawk*," Murphy thought, "for she was an old ship. But not the *Morro Castle*. Never the *Morro Castle*." What the newspapers later reported may have suggested heartlessness, but it was something quite different: an inability to face up to the facts.

The first relatives began to flood in about 7:00 A.M., surging through the barnlike waiting room in search of information. Some women were screaming; some sat immobile. A few fainted and were revived in the company's inner offices. It was a moment when Henry Cabaud should have taken charge of the situation, but it commanded him instead. He could bring himself to issue only one statement, in midmorning. "It does not appear," he said, "that there are many dead." Then he locked himself up again. His numbed response was to cause trouble for Henry Cabaud later. In the public outcry over the disaster, he was accused of iciness and indifference, and this in turn

[5] Now retired.

made him a prime target when the federal government began a predictable series of investigations.

There were long, aching hours of waiting, broken now and then by a rush to the bulletin board when a new list of survivors was posted. For dark-haired Muriel Rubine, it was a particular ordeal. Her fiancé, Dr. S. Joseph Bregstein, was not listed among the saved. They were to be married the first of October, a little more than two weeks away. Then in late morning came the news. "He's safe!" cried Muriel, and burst into tears.

Mrs. W. J. Landes, unaware of the disaster, had come early to meet her sixteen-year-old daughter Doris. In her hand she clutched a letter. It had come from Havana in midweek, and in it Doris had written: "I have never been so happy in my life." The cruise had been a birthday present for Doris, who had never been away from home alone before. She had celebrated her birthday on the boat, on the day that Captain Wilmott died. She, too, was saved.

Mrs. Juana Vallejo kept her eyes on the Ward Line employees, waiting for word of her daughter, Julia. All that she could think of was that Julia had gone to Europe the summer before and nothing had happened to her. Now, on a routine coastwise cruise, she might have perished. But she didn't. Julia was brought safely ashore.

Almost timidly Louis Cohn asked a clerk in Cabaud's office: "Have you heard anything of my sister, Gertrude Cohn?" The clerk shook his head. Cohn turned away, trembling. Yet by the end of the day he was reunited with Gertrude.

In a modest white house in semisuburban Hollis, Queens, Captain Wilmott's stepdaughter, Mrs. Robert Reed, had received the news of the captain's death at 1:00 A.M. Somehow, in all the confusion attendant on his death, Ward Line officials had delayed four hours and fifteen minutes in passing the word to his family. Matilda Wilmott, married less than a year, collapsed. The next morning her collapse was compounded by the news that the *Morro Castle* was afire. The reunion with her husband was to have been brief, just three hours before he had to travel back to Manhattan and take his ship out again. Pearl Reed's son, Bobbie, just three years old, broke into her conversation with reporters. "Captain Bob is a real hero," he said. "Captain Bob's ship has burned up." "Hush," said Mrs. Reed. "Please don't talk about it, Bobbie."

Back at the Ward Line pier, Mr. and Mrs. Charles Widder sat with bowed heads. They were waiting for news of their daughter Selma, who had been on her honeymoon with her husband, Charles Filtzer. Selma did survive, but as a widow. Filtzer drowned.

All day long a brother and sister huddled in a corner waiting for news. Ruth Griesmer, sixteen, was crying. Her brother Donald, seventeen, was resolute. Ward Line employees offered them sandwiches and coffee, but they refused. Relatives of others aboard the *Morro Castle* urged them to take a nap. Donald Griesmer shook his head sternly. "We won't eat or sleep until we know."

They were waiting for news of their mother and father, Mr. and Mrs. Fred Griesmer, and their sixty-five-year-old grandmother, Mrs. Augusta Griesmer. Now and then there were cries of "Thank God!" as the name of a survivor was called. The names of the Griesmers never were called. Finally Ruth and Donald went forlornly home to Brooklyn. It was late that night when relatives called with condolences. All three Griesmers had died, and the children were orphaned.

It was almost an equal tragedy for Henry Jacoby, Jr., whose father—a brewmaster for Piel's Brewery in Brooklyn—was one of the most loyal members of the Concordia Society. His mother came home safely, though in shock; his father drowned.

But for the family of Roger V. Toole, it was a moment of happiness. Roger's grandfather was superintendent of police at the Ward Line pier. All through the hours he put the thought of Roger out of his mind. He knew he was aboard the *Morro Castle* as a crewman; he could scarcely forbear remembering that another grandson, Dan, was to be married in a few days, and that Roger had promised to be his best man. About 4:00 P.M. a grin split Chief Toole's face. Roger, in wrinkled clothes, with his hair hanging dankly, walked into the waiting room, stuck out his hand, and said, "Hello, Grandpa." The wedding went off as scheduled.

There was a sardonic interlude at 2:00 P.M. Passengers began arriving to board the Ward liner *Iroquois*, put into service as a substitute for the *Morro Castle* on the Havana run. Some fifty persons had canceled, but two hundred still went aboard. Among them was a newlywed couple, Mr. and Mrs. Robert Suvriano. Wedding guests, ignoring those who grieved, showered the couple with rice as they went aboard. At 4:00 P.M. the whistle of the *Iroquois* broke the tension. It was "business as usual" for the Ward Line on this day of tragedy.

It was a helter-skelter day, with the four rescue ships docking all over the watery expanse of New York harbor. Ruth Torborg, who came in aboard the *Savannah*, remembers thinking that forever after she would be living on borrowed time. The experience left her with no fear of travel. She has regularly traveled abroad by plane. When friends ask her if she isn't frightened, her answer is: "Why should I be frightened about a plane getting in trouble? I was aboard a boat once, and it blew up."

John Torborg, separated from his sister, was happily tipsy aboard the *Monarch of Bermuda*. What he gleaned from the experience was the helpfulness of everyone that day. His Uncle Herman, who had lost his wallet and identification papers, was able to cash a blank check with the ship's doctor. The check was never deposited, so he wrote the doctor later to ask why. "I've framed it," was the reply.

Now, as the puffing tugs took the *Monarch* in tow at Quarantine, everyone began to go blind from smoke except young John. He was the first one in line, coming off the gangplank, with a dozen people behind him hanging on to each other. He signaled a cab and loaded aboard a few passengers—Patrolman Price, George Ridderhoff, and his Uncle Herman. One by one they were dropped off, and then young John went to his own home. The cabdriver wouldn't take a cent. Finally John threw down the ten dollars his Uncle Herman had cashed and said, "Take it. I'm going in the house." The whole family was there except for his father. Torborg, Sr., had driven frantically all over Manhattan until he finally located Ruth aboard the *Savannah*. His cabbie also refused to take a cent, but Torborg, Sr., forced a twenty-dollar bill on him.

Eleanor Friend, cool as always, took a cab from the *Savannah* pier to the Ward Line pier, phoned her mother to say concisely, "I've been in an accident," and waited placidly until members of the family arrived. The only discomfort she felt was from an earache caused by the salt water; the only regret was that she had abandoned a case of rum intended for a friend at the Museum of Natural History.

For some of those saved, talking was a catharsis, a way of wiping out the memory of the fire, putting it into perspective. It was here that impressions collided most sharply. Were the crew members cowards? Some insisted they were. Were they heroes? Others were vehement in supporting this appraisal.

White-haired Sarah Kirby, a seagoing veteran, at sixty-eight completing her last trip aboard the *Morro Castle*, remembered the fire as a horror. But to her it was ennobled by the courage of the bellboys (whom she called "the buttons," for their brass buttons) and the stewards ("the white jackets"). From her vantage of old age, they all looked like little boys and behaved like men. Cursing and straining, they threw big, muscular men back from the rail so that women could jump first. Sarah Kirby did not live many more years, but her memory of the *Morro Castle*'s crew in that moment of crisis was a memory of brave men, some of whom died to assure that the passengers got off the ship.

Dr. and Mrs. Phelps had a different memory, one of cowardice. The lifeboat carrying Chief Engineer Abbott passed within a few feet of them and made no effort to pick them up. Mrs. Phelps, looking across the crest of the waves, could see Abbott in the bow, fully dressed, even to his black bow tie. She wasn't worried about reaching shore; she was enraged because so many other passengers, weakened by smoke inhalation, foundering in the waves, were cold-bloodedly left to save themselves.

Yet Bishop and Mrs. Hulse recalled the behavior of the crew as "magnificent." Marguerite Gilligan, who swam ashore, said, "The officers were wonderful and helped us keep our heads. The crew fought the fire to the very last moment."

Kathleen Canavan bitterly remembered being awakened by one of the stewards, fully clothed and wearing a life belt— evidence, to her, that the crew was preparing to leave before the passengers were awakened. Charlotte and Ethel Behr were equally bitter at this apparent evidence of "crew first, passengers last." William H. Weil, who had a right to be angry, for his wife was drowned, instead took a more considered attitude. In view of the darkness, the smoke, and the frantic passengers, he felt the crew did its best. As he tied a bowknot in the life preserver worn by his wife, a sailor pulled it loose and tied three heavy knots so that the preserver could not come loose. It was still holding Mrs. Weil afloat when her body washed ashore.

Perhaps the most kindly comment came from the oldest couple aboard, Katie Dulk and her twin brother, John, aged seventy-two. It took them six hours to swim ashore, and both were totally exhausted. All Katie had to say, when she and her brother came back to New York the next day by special train, was, "The crew was very kind and very helpful."

To this day, the impression exists that the members of the *Morro Castle* crew were cowards to a man, determined to save only their own skins. There were some, notably the members of the engine room crew, who wasted no time in boarding the lifeboats and rowing for shore. But then, these men were not trained to deal with passengers. Their job was to keep the engines running. The stewards, the bellboys, in most cases all who worked in the public sections of the ship, seem to have done their best at a moment of total confusion, with no leadership at all from the officers. The acts of heroism on that dark and stormy night cancel out by far what few acts of cowardice took place.

13

ADRIFT

By Saturday morning, between eight thirty and nine, William F. Warms felt himself the mere hulk of a man, as gutted by shock and exhaustion as his ship had been gutted by fire. The cutter *Tampa* was standing by to rescue him. Two seagoing tugs, the *Willett* and the *Moran,* were rolling alongside. All their skippers felt was concern for a ship in distress, but to Warms they represented the worst alternative that a skipper could face—the threat of salvage and a huge bill for the Ward Line. He was grasping at straws at this moment. Anything would do but to call on these tugs. "Dad," says his son Donald,[1] "was a company man. He was not about to do anything that would cost the company money."

Balancing on feet scorched from the heat of the deck, with black rings of exhaustion around his eyes, Warms reached his own judgment. "Go into the carpenter shop and bring back a hacksaw," he ordered one of the mates, who took off on the double for the forecastle. From this distance in time, it seems a mystery that Warms would rely on what few tools his carpenter shop could offer. These were meant for small repairs, not for major ones. He had to release the anchor in order to be taken in tow, and he could do so only by cutting through two inches of forged steel, the thickness of each link of the anchor chain. Commander Rose had offered him superior equipment and fresh men, but in this moment he chose to use his own exhausted personnel and a two-foot hacksaw that was pitifully inadequate. As one man after another took turns sawing painfully on the chain, deepening the cut a trivial distance, Chief Operator Rogers turned to his assistant, Alagna, and said, "It's a damn shame we have to use these five-and-ten-cent methods."

But it was a five-and-ten-cent time in the United States. The hit song of 1934 was "Brother, Can You Spare a Dime?" The

[1] In conversation with the author.

130

fear of every man with a job was that he might lose it. William F. Warms would not have been out of tune with the times if he chose to do everything in a manner that his company would approve. A job paying $185 a month at that period of the Depression was not one to be carelessly sacrificed. Every junior officer on his ship had a master's license, meaning that any one of them could be promoted to take his place as chief officer or captain. Warms had a wife, a son, and a pleasant little house in Greens Farms, New Jersey. He had been trained never to take a chance, and would not now.

At about 9:30 A.M. ship's time, Assistant Chief Bos'n's Mate George Hyde, of the Coast Guard, swarmed up a hawser with a light line wrapped around his waist. Below him, a Coast Guard lifeboat with six youngsters at the oars battled against the waves. The light line was attached, at the other end, to the *Tampa*'s twelve-inch towing line. Hyde stayed only a minute. The oarsmen below were obviously exhausted; he had to get back to the *Tampa* before they collapsed. He left behind him a new dilemma. For Warms and his men had to haul in not only the light line but the immense weight of the hawser attached to it some 600 feet away. A Coast Guard powerboat from Sandy Hook helped by dragging some of the hawser through the seas to minimize the dead weight. Finally, reeling from the effort, the *Morro Castle*'s crewmen made the line fast.

It was at about that moment, for some reason never thoroughly explained, that George Rogers decided to go into the forecastle. He said it was to find a pair of shoes. He said he had kicked off his own shoes, expecting to go overboard to rescue a drowning woman. Those on the forecastle who still live do not remember either that he was prepared to undertake a rescue or that he had lost his shoes at this particular moment. Rogers was a mass of blubber; he weighed about 250 pounds and was totally unathletic. In George Alagna's memory, he never left the ship except to trundle himself to the nearest grog shop, at either end of a voyage, to buy himself a bottle and to drink himself into insensibility. He did, however, disappear from the forepeak, and he came back with a black Cuban canary in a cage. That canary was later to appear with him in a vaudeville act on the stage of the Rialto, a Broadway theater. What "in person" appearances are to TV today, "in person" appearances were to the dying art of vaudeville in the early 1930s. Talking pictures killed them off a very few years later.

Now, at approximately noon, the anchor chain dropped overboard with a rattle and the crew began to leave the *Morro Castle,* dropping down the ropes into the Coast Guard powerboat from Sandy Hook. George Alagna, recognizing that he had a salable news story, made his own pilgrimage into the forecastle a few minutes earlier, and came back with half a dozen brown paper sandwich bags stuffed inside his shirt. He felt in his uniform jacket for a pencil, was pleased to find it there, and prepared—in due time—to write his own account of the *Morro Castle* disaster. He remembers looking over the edge and seeing the limp bodies of six men and women flung carelessly in the bottom of the Coast Guard boat. With an involuntary shudder, he lowered himself hand over hand, feeling his black oxfords sink into their yielding flesh.

Chief Radio Operator Rogers, his thick arm muscles straining, slid almost all the way down and then tumbled into the arms of a Coast Guardsman. Robert Beresford, the young Yale graduate, thinks he was next to the last to go overboard. He remembers hearing Warms call out, "I will stay here."

"No," said the bos'n's mate in charge of the lifeboat. "It is the skipper's orders that you abandon ship." Painfully burned, with his broken knuckles aching, Warms came down the rope and dropped into the boat. It is a Warms family tradition that the captain was ordered off at the point of a .45 pistol, but no record exists to confirm this.

At 12 noon ship's time the *Tampa*'s propeller began to move, the hawser appeared from the depths of the sea like a prehistoric monster, the line tightened, and the cutter slowly picked up speed. On the *New York,* Captain Swainson was guiding his cockleshell of a boat out into the wind, painfully slowly, acting as a rudder. The stricken *Morro* was resisting. The wind, blowing against her starboard side, was seeking to push her toward the shore. It was an impossible task, and confirmation came at 1:00 P.M. With a sharp, screeching sound the *New York*'s towing line burned through and fell in snakelike coils behind her. Now it was all up to the *Tampa,* laboring forward, pulling the ship's full weight in a 40-mile gale. A dungeon fog, as mariners call it, blanketed the sea, and with it was mixed the smoke still billowing from the *Morro Castle.* Aboard the *New York,* now freed to make her way back to port, Bill Walsh felt a sense of rage and frustration. He could foresee what must inevitably happen to the *Morro Castle.*

Still the wind increased in power. Lifeboats had long since taken shelter in their harbors. At 2:30 P.M. the order came from

Commander Harry S. Yeandle, in charge of rescue operations:
"All powerboats return to port." Now the sea was clear except
for the *Tampa,* the tugs, and the *New York,* the latter boat
laboring ahead at a speed no greater than one mile per hour.
Fog signals were blasting at sea and ashore. A laconic mate
on the *Tampa* threw aboard a weighted sounding line that
measured the depth of the water, and slowly counted the
fathoms as they grew steadily less. Commander Rose realized
what this meant: Dragged by the dead weight of the *Morro
Castle,* he and his tow would eventually be driven onto the
beach. It was a nightmare moment for the skipper. Duty required him to keep towing the ship; common sense told him the
result would be disaster, unless . . .

The "unless" was the increasing probability that the towing
hawser would snap under the strain. At 3:20 P.M. Rose was
quite certain that would be the next disaster. "It appears the tow-
line is going," he radioed to Coast Guard headquarters on
Staten Island.

At 4:15 P.M. an offer of help came from the most improbable
source, the mammoth battleship *Arizona,* on her way toward the
Brooklyn Navy Yard. Rose realized that in such shallow waters
and in such a storm the big battleship would only get herself in
trouble. He radioed his thanks but declined assistance. Nor
could he use the tugs, though they continued to stand by. There
was no way to get another towing line aboard. By 5:00 P.M. the
weird procession was three or four miles off Long Branch, New
Jersey, a short distance to the north of Asbury Park. "Derelict
becoming unmanageable," Rose curtly advised New York. Cursing Coast Guardsmen [2] urged the cutter on: "Keep going, you
bastard! Keep going!" But it was no use. The *Morro Castle* had
taken charge. The *Tampa* simply could not pull the liner's bow
into the wind. Slowly, over the next hour, Rose increased the
speed of his engines from 60 revolutions per minute. As he did
so, the towing hawser stretched out and became thinner under
the double strain of the pull from the *Tampa* and the dead
weight of the *Morro Castle.*

"We'll make one last try," he said to the quartermaster standing beside her on the bridge. "Give her maximum power, 110
rpm's. If that doesn't work, we'll have to cut the hawser."

Down in the engine room of the *Tampa* the signal bell
sounded for "full speed ahead." Stubborn in death, the *Morro*

[2] According to George Alagna.

continued to float broadside to the wind. At 6:12 P.M. with a *crack!* the hawser snapped. It sprang back and wound itself around the *Tampa*'s propeller shaft. Now the *Tampa* itself was in peril, like the *Morro Castle* drifting toward the beach, certain to become a derelict, with the lives of her crew in the balance.

"Let go the anchor!" roared Rose. The *Tampa* came to a stop at the edge of shoal water, just seven fathoms. The humming engine fell silent. Men were lowered over the side, secured by ropes, battling to free the propeller. It was touch and go. At 6:23 Rose was so skeptical of success that he megaphoned to the *Willett,* "Stand by to take us in tow." Just two minutes later the hawser was cut, the propeller was freed, and a bos'n's mate reported, "She's all clear now, sir." The next few minutes were agonizing. Slowly the engine turned. The propeller had not been damaged. Just at this moment the lookout took his binoculars from his eyes and reported, "The *Morro* seems to be grounded, sir."

Rose had no time to reflect on the sad ending of the *Morro Castle*'s story. He had to bring his own ship safely into port, and that would be no easy job. Even at full speed he could make scarcely more than a mile an hour. By 8:00 P.M. he was pushing into blinding rain and mountainous seas. The wind had reached a hurricane force of 65 to 70 miles an hour. Out to sea and out of sight, the pilot boat *New York* was undergoing her worst ordeal, battling through a storm she had never been built to withstand.

——·———·—

In the red brick Convention Hall at Asbury Park, radio announcer Tom Burley was reading off the news bulletins over the transmitter of Radio Station WCAP. "The *Morro Castle*," he said, "is adrift and heading for the shore." He glanced at the clock. It was 7:34 P.M. shore time. He glanced out the window of his balcony office and gulped.

"My God!" he said into the microphone. "She's coming in right here!"

Out of the murk and the lashing rain, the massive bulk of the *Morro Castle* loomed up, headed straight for Convention Hall. She towered over the building, implacably moving shoreward. Burley, for one panicky moment, wondered whether he should flee. Then neatly, precisely, the *Morro Castle* edged her nose in alongside a rock jetty. As if tugs were pushing her, she moved sidewise until her massive steel plates blocked off Burley's view of the sea, then gently slid up on a sandbar and stopped just 200 feet from shore.[3]

Reporter Thomas Tighe witnessed the scene from a point on the shore only a few blocks away. "She came toward shore," he wrote for his newspaper, "with fire belching from every port-hole. With rain beating down in torrents and a northeast gale blowing, she was a ghost coming out of the night. Fire and smoke drove in sheets over Convention Hall as she came to rest."

[3] As he later told Thomas Tighe.

14

CARNIVAL!

"Asbury Park needs a shipwreck," said the heading of an editorial in the Asbury Park *Daily Spray* late in the summer of 1884. "We need a first-class shipwreck," wrote editor William K. (Billy) Devereaux. "Why? To make Asbury Park a famous winter resort. She should strike head-on, and we could accommodate her all winter. A pontoon or suspension bridge could be built from the pier so the ship could be used as a casino. Atlantic City would then yield place to Asbury as a peerless winter resort. We need a shipwreck."

Just fifty years later Asbury Park at last had its shipwreck, one that followed almost exactly the specifications laid down by Billy Devereaux. The *Morro Castle* had struck almost head-on, so close that a pedestrian bridge could have connected her to the shore. Wrecked and gutted, pouring out flames and smoke, she could scarcely have served as a gambling casino, but she was certifiably a tourist attraction. That Saturday night she provided a private spectacle for the townsfolk of the north Jersey shore. Drenched by rain and buffeted by wind, they stood for hours staring at her.

Howard J. Rowland, a young Asbury Park fireman,[1] had gone on duty at six that morning, patrolling the beach to watch for survivors and bodies. At six that night he drove to the temporary morgue at Sea Girt to see if he could help. Coming back, he heard on his car radio that the ship was drifting toward Asbury Park. To Rowland, it was a nightmare experience. With red lights blinking and horn blasting, he forced his way through crowds to a parking place alongside Convention Hall. Just as he stepped out of his car, the *Morro Castle* loomed up in front of him. Every porthole, every segment of the ship, was illuminated by the fierce glow of the fire. He remembers people shouting, "Let's swim out and see how she is!" Rowland, using the

[1] Still an Asbury Park fireman at age sixty-two.

authority of his fireman's uniform, gruffly ordered at least a dozen of them back. By 8:00 P.M. he was helping police and other firemen to rope off the boardwalk. "She'll explode when the fire reaches her oil tanks," one officer explained. "We've got to keep these people a safe distance back." Red-eyed, exhausted, Rowland stayed on duty all that night. He went home for two hours' sleep and was back on duty again, none too early, by 8:00 A.M. Sunday.

For by 7:00 A.M., with the storm ended and the sun shining, the sightseers began to pour in—crowds such as Atlantic City never had known. It was a mass movement of the curious and the ghoulish, all anxious to associate themselves with one of America's greatest marine disasters. And it could be viewed so comfortably from the beach and the boardwalk! Methodist Bishop Francis Asbury, for whom the city was named, would have been appalled by the carnival atmosphere, but in fact Asbury Park had long since left behind the sober policies of its churchgoing founders. South from the Convention Hall, along and beyond the boardwalk, were all the trappings of a typical seaside resort: shops selling souvenirs and saltwater taffy, Ferris wheels and shooting galleries, movie theaters and "rides" almost matching those at Coney Island. One by one, during the day, they reopened for the best day of business in the city's history. At a time when the Depression had colored life a dull gray, at last something out of the ordinary had happened.

It was an occasion not easily forgotten, and I was part of it. It was my day off, and interested in seeing the ship about which I had been writing, I joined the mob. Early Sunday I hopped into my Dodge coupe and started for Asbury Park, only to become a part of the worst traffic jam in East Coast history. At the Manhattan entrance to the Holland Tunnel cars waited for hours to cross the Hudson River. Horns honked, engines stalled, and sweating policemen threw up their hands in despair along the bridges of the Pulaski Skyway, spanning the Jersey Meadows. It was noon before I reached Asbury Park, and another hour before police found me a parking place half a mile from the beach. Into the brilliant sky a black plume of smoke poured upward. That was the *Morro Castle*, consuming herself.

Police Chief Alfred N. Giles, as exhausted as his fifty-nine men, established an innovation that day, the first one-way streets in the United States. Families opened their yards to parking, at a twenty-five-cent fee. Few people in Asbury Park failed to profit from the disaster on their doorstep, many of them the same people who had been manning the beaches, exhausting themselves in rescue work without thought of recompense. Fifty American Legionnaires and fifty helmeted soldiers from Fort Monmouth and Fort Hancock helped to direct the traffic. By late afternoon street hawkers appeared with the first souvenir photos of the *Morro Castle*. At fifty cents to a dollar apiece, they were a sellout within minutes.

It seemed to me almost as if these sightseers were gloating. Every time flames spouted from the ship, the crowd let out a roar. Planes buzzed overhead, and a flotilla of small boats lay offshore, their rails lined with spectators. Now and then smoke poured from the funnels, almost as if the *Morro Castle* were getting under way. On the balconies of the luxurious Berkeley-Carteret Hotel, across the street from Convention Hall, other spectators were massed solidly. The hotel management suddenly found every room booked.

There was something faintly ghoulish about this preoccupation with disaster. At one point, a man [2] said to his wife and young daughter: "There's a lot of excitement out there. I bet they've found a body." He lifted the rope and jumped onto the beach. "I want to see it! I want to see!" wailed his daughter. Young men swam out and ripped sheets of paint from the liner's blistered sides, exposing the red lead primer coat beneath.

Others were more purposeful. James Kontajones, a member of the city engineer's department, had served on the *Morro Castle*. He rowed out in a small boat at 9:00 A.M. and shinnied up a line hanging from the stern. From the shore, Coast Guardsmen of the Deal station shot out another line from a Lyle gun on the beach. Once Kontajones had made this fast, a breeches buoy was rigged, connecting the ship with the ground floor of Convention Hall. Next he made fast two lines from the tugs *Willett* and *Rescue*. The puffing little ships pulled these taut, and now authorities could be sure that the *Morro Castle* would drift no closer to the beach.

Even at this moment there was a graceless incident. Frank B. Conover, the local representative of the companies that insured the *Morro Castle*, insisted on being first to board the breeches buoy. Carl Bischoff, the city manager, was equally determined to be first. "We have riparian rights," he insisted. In the shouting match that followed, someone threatened Conover with arrest for disorderly conduct. He stood firm. He was the first aboard. Bischoff came later, followed by city firemen, but

[2] Reported in the Asbury Park *Press*.

none of them stayed more than a few minutes. The steel frame-work of the ship was blistering hot. Gas fumes choked those who had come without masks. Finally two hoses were brought out. "We can't flood out that fire," said Chief James Taggart. "All we can do is to cool her down so we can make an inspection."

When Howard Rowland went aboard in late afternoon, he thought, "She looks like a ghost ship." As he sprayed water on the steel plates, he could hear rivets pop as they suddenly contracted, and then whiz by "like machine gun bullets."

Rowland remembers the *Morro Castle* as the mere skeleton of a ship. His clothes steamed from the heat as he made his way from deck to deck. Staterooms had vanished. A few sparse bits of wood remained on the sizzling decks. On the port side three ruined lifeboats hung in their davits, one hanging straight down from the stern. From C Deck upward, there was enough breeze to part the smoke. Below, the ship was a mass of smoke and gas. City Manager Bischoff made perhaps the most touching dis-covery. On the stern of B and C decks there were rows of men's shoes and women's slippers, women's rings, compacts, and vanity cases—even a few girdles. People had taken them off, at the last minute, before they jumped. Glass and lead, melted by the heat, had hardened again in fantastic patterns on some of the bare girders. And in the wreckage of a passageway there were the charred bones of ten-year-old Braulio Saenz, one of those who never had a chance to escape.

Money dominated the day. City Manager Bischoff posted a sign at Convention Hall. For twenty-five cents, "benefit of the survivors," sightseers could go out on the seaward side of the hall for a closer look at the ship. Insurance representative Conover charged newspapermen five dollars to use the breeches buoy and five dollars for gas masks, which actually belonged to the Asbury Park Fire Department. It was a painful experience for Larry Froeber, a photographer for the New York *Daily News*. He burned both hands when he touched the metal railings along a staircase and had to be taken to Fitkin Memorial Hospital.

In Manhattan that morning parishioners were leaving churches. It was at last a sunny, mild day with only a few lingering clouds in the sky. Crassness might dominate the scene as Asbury Park, but sober meditation was the theme of many clergymen. At Central Presbyterian Church the Reverend Dr. Ernest Findlay Scott of Union Theological Seminary said: "What could be the reason? How could such a dreadful thing have happened? We can explain nothing, yet we know that over all the mysteries of life is His life and wisdom." At Broadway Temple Methodist Church Pastor Christian F. Reisner surveyed his congregation somberly: "Such accidents arouse questions with some people about the goodness of God. They forget about the countless other evidences of His care. Only a fool explains such catastrophes as sent to punish man." Under the arches of the Romanesque Episcopal Church of St. Bartholomew, parishioners knelt in prayer. Theirs was a minority voice, measured against the pandemonium at Asbury Park, but in a handful of other churches, less gentle voices were raised.

Dr. Ralph W. Sockman, speaking at Christ Methodist Church, put his finger on a central problem. "Nothing," he said, "can be discovered to explain a situation in which officers and crew left passengers to drown while they sailed away to safety. Investigators should inquire whether the business policy followed by the steamship lines might not be responsible for the inefficiency, demoralization, and cowardice aboard the ship." At the Brick Presbyterian Church Dr. James McCullough Farr blamed the tragedy on the spirit of the age, with its demands for speed, luxury, and excitement. His comments could have been made with equal justice about the *Titanic*.

"Ocean voyages," he said, "are too often irresponsible joyrides for those who embark on them, and the steamship companies in their intense competition for business must cater to public tastes. The luxuries, the overelaborate decorations, the hangings and upholsteries are both incongruous and perilous." Even sharper words came from the Reverend Dr. John W. Bradbury in his sermon at the Wadsworth Avenue Baptist Church. "It seems," he said, "that people on the sea leave all moral law behind them. Drinking and gambling are carried on until five o'clock in the morning. There are no hours for bars on board ship."

＝･＝･＝＝･＝

William F. Warms and thirteen of his men finally stepped on dry land at noon Sunday. They were still dazed, still exhausted, and some of them were burned. Chief Operator Rogers was complaining of pain every time he took a breath. "My lungs must be burned," he insisted. Acting Chief Officer Freeman and Acting Second Officer Hackney ached in every joint. Among the others was a helter-skelter cross section of crew—Radio Operator Alagna, Bow Watchman Beresford, Fireman Harry K. Steuber, Printer Otto Dunnheupt, Bellboy John Howell, and Junior

Engineer Martin Melbard among them. The cutter *Tampa* had made such a slow progress up the coast that her skipper, Commander Rose, anchored inside the Sandy Hook peninsula late at night and waited until morning to move slowly on to his pier on Staten Island. Then, to the frustration of Alagna and the others, he had to wait until ten thirty and a rising tide to move into his berth, reaching it at eleven thirty in the morning.

That was not the end of the delay. United States Attorney Martin Conboy had to go aboard with a group of his assistants to conduct a cursory questioning of Skipper Warms. Blue-jacketed Customs and Immigration men had to check through the survivors. Finally, exactly at twelve, after officers of the Steamboat Inspection Service had ordered them all to appear the next day at a hearing, they filed or were carried off the boat. Mrs. Rogers flung her arms around her husband, who lay on a stretcher. Mrs. Warms embraced her husband. Young Donald, awed by the panoply of brass, stood quietly to one side, storing away memories of the event. The tugboat *Eugene P. Messeck* landed them all at the Ward Line pier at 1:15 P.M. It had been a brief reunion. Waiting ashore were attorneys from the firm of Burlingham, Veeder, Clark and Hupper. "Dad—" said Donald Warms, but before he could finish a sentence his father and all the others were hustled into cabs and taken to the firm's law offices. Alagna remembers only the one sentence, repeated often to him as he told his story: "The company will take care of you if you take care of the company." Then he was turned loose, with an admonition to appear at the United States Customs House the next morning.

George Alagna was clutching half a dozen paper bags, scrawled with his penciled notes. He realized the importance of what he had seen, and he was anxious to make it public. His first thought was to go to *The New York Times*. But because he was dressed in wrinkled pants and a Coast Guard blue turtleneck shirt, he was ashamed to walk into that austere institution, though it was his favorite newspaper. Instead, he walked crosstown to the New York *Journal*, a Hearst newspaper, much closer by. Feeling frightfully self-conscious—he remembers his embarrassment—he asked to see an editor. After the receptionist looked at his notes, he was snatched into an elevator. Rushed upstairs, he was seated beside a cigar-smoking reporter who deftly transcribed his notes. It was not until he left, with several hundred dollars' cash in his pants pocket, that he learned the identity of his questioner. It was Damon Runyon, a legend in

New York journalism. The next morning the first edition of the *Journal* was on the streets with a scoop.

Donald Warms felt as if he were in the middle of the typhoon. First his father was standing alongside him, then he had vanished to the lawyers' offices. Next he was back again, at 3:30 P.M., only to tell reporters that "I'll tell my whole story tomorrow morning." He wore a blue wool seaman's jersey, on the front of which the Ward Line insignia was buttoned, and a pair of white duck trousers tucked into turned-down seamen's boots. A reporter asked him: "Where did the fire actually start?" Donald remembers that his father compressed his lips, shook his head, and did not answer. Chauncey Clark, one of the lawyers for the Ward Line, was asked: "What is the reason for not permitting him to talk?" "He'll tell all he has to say tomorrow morning," the lawyer snapped back. With that, Warms was hustled off to a hospital to rest. Young Donald, Mrs. Warms, and her sister-in-law, Mrs. Dorothy McBride, were taken to a hotel to spend the night. It had been quite a day for an eleven-year-old, and it was to be a sleepless night.

There were other, grimmer sidelights to that Sunday. Forty-seven of the *Morro Castle* dead had been taken to the Jersey City morgue, where they lay sheeted on marble slabs. Mrs. Samuel Petty, whose husband was a dining room steward, came in during midmorning in search of her husband. One by one, sheets were pulled back and faces exposed. "No," repeated Mrs. Petty. "No," and then suddenly, "Oh, my God, that's Sam!" An attendant hastily pulled the sheet back over her husband's face. "Don't do that," said Mrs. Petty, weeping. "I want to see Sam again." She looked at him a moment and murmured, "Hasn't he got pretty hair? Let me have a lock of it." The attendant scurried to find a pair of scissors, snipped off a lock of black hair, and Mrs. Petty kissed it before she put it in her purse.

In a Brooklyn funeral parlor Selma Filtzer sat with her head bowed, surrounded by friends, as Rabbi Arthur H. Neulander recited the prayers for the dead over the coffin of her husband, Charles Filtzer. Orthodox Jewish canons required that he be buried before sundown of the day after his death, and that requirement was being fulfilled. Just eight days earlier Rabbi Neulander had read the marriage service over Selma and Charles. They jumped hand in hand from the *Morro Castle*, but a great wave swept Charles away from his wife. She had become a widow by the time she saw him again.

—·—·—·—

Monday, September 10, there were an estimated 150,000 sightseers in Asbury Park. That night, as the city council held a special meeting to discuss what to do about the *Morro Castle,* a lonely woman in black stood apart from the crowds on the beach, staring at the ship. A pencil of light from a spotlight mounted on Convention Hall roved from stem to stern, outlining the stark ruin of the liner. The woman was Matilda Howell Wilmott, come to see her husband's funeral pyre. In the wreckage of his cabin, still too hot for firemen to enter, the flames were consuming his bones.

The mood of the council meeting was one of high excitement, as reporter Richard Gibbons remembers it. "I move we buy or rent that liner," said Alderman Louis Croce. Bluff Tom Burley, the city's public relations man, had a better idea. "You don't have to buy or rent that ship," he said. "There she is in our front yard. Just raise a city flag on her and make your claim." City Manager Bischoff carried the thought a step further: "We could run out a gangplank and then people could go aboard her." The report of the council meeting, published in the newspapers, produced an angry outcry. Said Councilman Max Silverstein: "It's a shocking, revolting, base, and vicious attempt to exploit a horrifying misfortune." Whether the council did or did not vote to lay claim to the *Morro Castle* cannot be established from the records. On September 13 its members issued a statement denying the whole thing.

The night of the tenth, the night of the council meeting, a reporter said to a woman, "Have you been here long?" "Yeah," she said. "I been sitting here for hours." "Aren't you tired?" "Yeah, but I ain't going to see anything like this again for a long time." She left a bit early, nevertheless. At one thirty the morning of September 11 the hulk of the *Morro Castle* rumbled, her plates bulged outward, and she spewed smoke, embers, and steel into the starlit sky.

A little earlier that night, a city fireman was completing his watch over the *Morro Castle.* Beside him was a telephone, connected to a station aboard ship. He knew that nobody was aboard. Firemen, insurance men, Captain William A. Hall of the Ward Line, and representatives of the Steamboat Inspection Service had cleared the ship at dusk. Suddenly the telephone rang. "My God!" he said. "There must be somebody still alive out there!" Carrying flashlights, other firemen rode out on the breeches buoy. They found two frightened teenagers from Locust Valley, Long Island, Bobby Menzinger [3] and Bill Scott. "We sort of thought it would be fun to go aboard when nobody was around," Menzinger recalls. "I picked up the phone just to see what would happen, but when somebody said, 'Hello,' I put down the receiver again in a hurry." Menzinger and Scott were held in custody at fire headquarters while someone put in call to their fathers. The parents arrived, late at night and infuriated. "They really gave us hell," says Menzinger. "I remember that better than I remember swimming out and boarding the ship."

—·—· —·—·—

By now public clamor was at a peak. Members of Congress, as well as newspapers and kinfolk of those who perished, were demanding action. Representative William I. Sirovich introduced a resolution calling for an investigation into the ship safety laws, and it was approved by a voice vote. In the Senate, Senator Royal S. Copeland of New York ordered the staff of his Commerce Committee to prepare for hearings on the steamboat inspection code. That Monday or the next day the case of Nathene and Frank Loveland was formally presented to Secretary of Commerce Daniel Roper—the only one carried to Cabinet level.

Their friend, Assistant Secretary of State Francis B. Sayre, forwarded a letter from a mutual acquaintance in Boston. In deference to the Lovelands' dislike of publicity, he referred to them only as "N." and "I." The letter was bitter: "The crowd was left to its own devices, and without leadership the individuals ran back and forth crying, praying, and looking for relatives. She jumped; he was caught on a flagpole. The smoke was so thick, the night so dark, and the noise so great that neither saw or heard the other. Chief Steward Speierman stood at the rail ready to be the first over. In the confusion, neither N. nor I. had taken their life preservers.

"I. called out: 'Aren't there any men who will give their life preservers to women?' He was ignored. N. approached two men in the water who did have life preservers. She only wanted to rest and tread water, but they pushed her off." The letter was urgently forwarded by Secretary Roper to Dickerson Hoover.

The letter gave the whole investigating process a powerful push, but what really assured maximum action occurred on

[3] Now a contractor in Syosset, Long Island.

Thursday, September 13. White House reporters filed into the study at the Franklin D. Roosevelt home in Hyde Park, New York, where the President held a press conference. Roosevelt was a seafaring man. He was an excellent yachtsman, and he had been Undersecretary of the Navy during World War I. A reporter asked him for comment. Modern ships, he said coolly, are overelaborate and overdecorated. They should be built with few, if any, wooden decorations, and those decorations should be commercially treated to resist fire.

—·—· —·—·—

The saved as well as the curious came back to Asbury Park: Ruth Fabel, Elsie Suhr, Ruth and John Torborg, Herman Cluthe, and Robert Smith among others. It was not a question of curiosity or sensation-seeking in their case. They had jumped from the decks of the *Morro Castle* in darkness, they had survived, and now in a sense they were expressing a personal thanksgiving as they looked at the ruins of a ship they last knew as a cheerful place to spend a holiday. Says Ruth Torborg: "It didn't bother me at all. I was sad for those who had died, of course, but I felt a sense of deliverance. How close we all were to death! How fortunate we were to have been saved!"

On Sunday all the surviving members of the Concordia Singing Society had been reminded of that good fortune. There had been a memorial service at St. John's Lutheran Church, in the heart of East New York. Pastor F. W. Otten read off the names, solid German names, to a sobbing congregation—thirty-two names in all . . . Sophie Altenburg . . . Augusta Griesmer . . . Henry Jacoby . . . Anna Kuhn . . . Mary E. Price . . . Louise Voigt . . . Clara Weil, among them. These were the names of friends and neighbors, solid German-Americans, nearly all of them. Gone now. To be buried, most of them, in Cypress Hills Cemetery, where a memorial plaque now marks their common fate. That was the heart of the *Morro Castle* disaster, not those who died, but those who lived to remember. "We were about one third of the passengers," reflects Mrs. Emil Lampe, "and we contributed about one third of the dead."

15

SCAPEGOATS

For William F. Warms, Monday, September 10, was simply another nightmare day. Accustomed to the comfortable, unvarying routine of shipboard life, he found himself caught up in a frantic pattern of movement. He had been questioned again and again by Ward Line lawyers, granted brief visits with his wife, stuffed with sedatives, and hurried in and out of hospitals. Now, at nine forty-five in the morning, he was walking up the steps of the baroque old Customs House overlooking Battery Park, pursued by newspaper photographers and besieged by newspaper reporters demanding answers that his lawyers had ordered him not to give. He was about to testify before a hearing called by the Steamboat Inspection Service. He was still thoroughly weary, still hard put to remember exactly how it all had happened. There were deep circles under his eyes, and dark patches that revealed his exhaustion.

The inspectors were waiting for him behind a low table—Dickerson Hoover and three members of the local Steamboat Inspection office, all men he knew from their past visits to the *Morro Castle*. Flanking Hoover were Captain Karl Neilson, hull inspector; James Smith, boiler inspector, and John L. Crane, supervising inspector for the New York district. It was a bit different from the old days when these men would come aboard the ship, walk through it with him, ask a few questions, and then depart to certify her seaworthy. Sometimes they stayed for lunch, with Captain Wilmott affably presiding. A wallowing old freighter might require a lengthy check-out, but nobody in the Steamboat Inspection Service really worried about the *Morro Castle*. After all, she had been built to the Navy's tight specifications for a troop-carrying ship, including even the steel-and-concrete foundations on which guns could be mounted, she was about the most modern liner afloat, and she was insured for five million dollars by Lloyds of London, whose requirements were exacting.

This Monday the inspectors were all business. As if to underline the seriousness of the occasion, Warms found himself sitting beside Martin Conboy, United States Attorney for the Southern District of New York. Standing against the wall were two of Conboy's assistants, Francis W. H. Adams and Joseph R. Pendergast.[1] On the table in front of him was perhaps the most frightening object, a radio microphone. Station WMCA had persuaded Hoover to authorize the first broadcast ever of a federal hearing.

The words came slowly as Warms thought back over the events leading up to the fire. Wilmott had been an old friend. They had served together on many Ward Line ships, but over the preceding year tension had intruded on their relationship. Wilmott had developed high blood pressure. He had become increasingly nervous and excitable. More and more Warms had had to spend time calming him. Thursday evening, the night before the fire, had been particularly tense. Wilmott had complained of indigestion, often the warning sign of a heart attack. He had slept badly that night, but on Friday he had been on the bridge again, professing to feel better.

Warms continued his review of events. The weather was heavy—gusts of rain and banks of fog, through which the *Morro Castle* plunged northward. Warms had the ship on his mind, but he also was worried about the captain. Just before 7:30 P.M., in mist so dense that visibility was nil, Warms recorded the *Morro Castle*'s bearings and went below to report them to Wilmott. The captain was lying on his bed, reading. "How do you feel?" the chief officer asked him. "All right," Wilmott said. "I'm going to get some sleep now." Just a moment after Warms closed the door, on the way back to the bridge, the captain felt another cramp, phoned down to Surgeon Van Zile for an enema bag, and at about 7:40 P.M., it was delivered by a steward. In the wheelhouse Chief Officer Freeman was on duty, peering into the wrack. "I think we better slow down," Freeman said. "Yes," said Warms, "slow down and blow the whistle."

"Will you tell the old man?" asked Freeman. "Yes," said Warms, "I will go." Steadying himself against the roll of the ship, Warms climbed down from the wheelhouse and knocked

[1] Now president of the National Trust for Historic Preservation.

on Wilmott's door. He stood waiting a moment, blue-coated shoulders hunched against the rain, but there was no answer. "Bob," he called, and knocked again. Still no answer. He turned the knob and walked in. The captain was not at his desk, not on his bed. For one appalled second Warms stood stock-still, and then turned toward the open bathroom door. Wilmott, his clothes in disarray, lay half-in, half-out of the bathtub, face down. He was obviously dead. Warms was not a man given to emotion. "A cold fish," was how several of his officers described him. "We had been like pals, brothers, roommates for years," he choked out at the hearing. Then, to the astonishment of officers and crewmen in the hearing room, he burst into tears, weeping for two minutes before he could control himself and go on.

He seemed numb, speaking in a monotone, when he resumed his testimony.[2] Captain Neilson asked him: "How did you get along with the captain?" He answered: "We had our little spats, but they all blew over when he smoked a cigar."

Q   Were all watches set at the time of the death?

A   Yes. There were two watchmen on A and B decks. They reported every hour. They reported last at 2:00 A.M.

Warms had not been satisfied to accept the "all quiet" report these two watchmen had sent in by telephone. "I'm going to take a turn around and see for myself," he told Officer Hackney. His junior looked at him with concern. He was, in Hackney's judgment, about to pass out from exhaustion. "You'd better rest," said Hackney. "You've been up a day and a half." Warms sat down for a second, but only for a second. Then he was off, leaning against the wind, to circle A and B decks, with an occasional glance inside to assure himself that everything was shipshape. It was a decision that helped to exonerate him later of a charge that he had been negligent. Only forty-five minutes and a few seconds later the fire broke out.

Warms could not exactly pinpoint what happened next. He was certain he could smell smoke coming from the ventilators in No. 1 and No. 2 holds as he stepped out on the bridge. Because of the odor of rawhides in the holds, Captain Wilmott had ordered the smoke detector system vented outside the wheelhouse. A watchman had reported smoke coming from the fiddley, a space above the engine room, but by now the dining saloon watchman reported that it was billowing out of the

[2] According to Norma Abrams, then and now a reporter for the New York *Daily News*.

writing room. Of all the frustrations Captain Warms was to face that night, this was the worst. He could not leave the bridge, for by now he was the lone officer there. Hackney, Freeman, Hanson—all were below, either looking for the fire or fighting it. Only seconds later, or so it seemed to him, his fears were confirmed. Dark-haired Hackney, panting for breath, dove in the wheelhouse door.

"It's bad," he gasped. "It's coming out of a locker in the writing room. There was fire on the ceiling, too, but I put that out with an extinguisher. All of a sudden the locker just blew out. It's burning as if gasoline or kerosene or something else is feeding it." A few seconds before 3:00 A.M., Warms made his decision. "Get all the passengers out," he ordered. "Use the fire hose." The fire, it appeared from reports reaching him, was coming out "as if somebody had lighted gunpowder." One-two, he pushed the button that set alarms clanging all over the ship and then sounded the double blast, meaning "Fire!" on the *Morro Castle*'s whistle.

Now came the moment for which newspaper reporters had been waiting. Warms was asked: "What started the fire?"

A I have two answers. One, it was incendiary.

Q Why?

A I think somebody put something in that writing room locker. There might have been gasoline or kerosene. Or else somebody threw a cigarette in there.

Within an hour the presses of the New York *Evening Post*, New York *Sun,* New York *Journal* and *World Telegram* were rolling with the heavy black headline: "Sabotage!" On a ship so riddled with mistrust, so rent by suspicion, plying to a port where every day brought new rumors of revolution, the idea seemed as sensible to the public as it did to Warms. On an earlier cruise, he recalled, there had been a fire in No. 5 hold. "I think," he said, "somebody set that fire. There was cardboard in that hold, and I found a piece of charred newspaper. I reported to Captain Wilmott, and he said, 'Perhaps somebody threw a cigarette in there.' I said, 'Captain, the way it happened, and the place where the fire was located, a cigarette couldn't have done it. Somebody had to throw a piece of paper in there.' "

Arson was a handy solution to the mystery, and it was accepted unanimously by the other ship's officers. Young Hackney, at thirty-two already a fifteen-year veteran of the sea, said firmly: "I believe the fire was set."

Q   What makes you believe that the fire had been set?

A   The way it burned so fiercely all of a sudden. If it was like a cigarette fire, it would start on the outside and burn a rug or a chair.

Q   You say it burned so suddenly and spread so rapidly; how would you explain it?

A   The fire must have been inside and burned away before it broke through.

Q   Would you explain it that the fire had been in there for some time?

A   It must have been.

Acting Chief Officer Ivan Freeman was even more positive. "The only conclusion I can come to," he said, "is that it was deliberately set by someone who saturated oil all around to feed it. God knows what the motive was."

Q   Had you any labor troubles?

A   Not directly. There was some trouble in Havana, but there is always trouble there.

Q   How do you think it was started?

A   Someone watched his opportunity when the watchman had gone by.

Howard Hansen, looking back on the fire, says, simply: "It was set." That also is the verdict of Cruise Director Smith. Yet Sirl Boggetti, whose father as chief steward knew the ship well, is convinced that the cause was spontaneous combustion. That, in fact, was the suspicion of the Steamboat Inspectors as they plodded forward with their hearings. It was not an easy atmosphere for fact-finding. On Wednesday, September 12, District Attorney Conboy summoned a grand jury to hear the same witnesses in secret. Two days later, dissatisfied with progress, he caused a second grand jury to be called in. Passengers, officers, and crew shuttled frantically from the Customs House to the gray granite United States Post Office building opposite City Hall, where the federal courts and the offices of the United States Attorney were located.

That first day there were more moments of emotion. Warms had stolidly denied any delay in sending the SOS, had insisted that every action he took was taken in time. It was more than he could stand, however, when he was asked what he had done after ordering boats lowered to deck level, hoses played on the fire, and the SOS sent out. That memory reduced him to tears once again. "I climbed down and tried to get the captain's body out of his cabin," he said. "The door was jammed. I smashed my fist against it, and that was when I must have broken my knuckles. I couldn't get it. I couldn't. The fire was out of control. The chart house was one fire. The plates were buckling under my feet." Again the tears came, and again the hearing room feel silent until he recovered himself.

What of the fire doors? What of the automatic trip wires that were supposed to function when the heat reached a certain intensity? Dickerson Hoover again and again came back to this point. "I ordered them closed," Warms insisted, "but I don't know if they were." Said Hackney: "If they had been closed, the passengers would have been locked in." Much later in the hearing the truth came out. The trip wires had been removed by order of Henry Cabaud and replaced by latches that had to be opened manually. Nobody thought to operate them. In fact, if they had been operated, the fire still would have spread. Above the wood-paneled ceilings there was a six-inch opening, interlaced with wooden studding that attached the ceilings to the steel bulkheads. The fire had a free run through this hidden space, and the fire doors would not have stopped it. More than that, the bulkheads were so hot that every bit of studding material had to burst into flame.

There was a terrible innocence to these hearings, and a terrible sense of confusion. The inspectors, distant in time and space, were trying to establish why men in the grip of a totally unexpected event acted so unexpectedly. The newspapers, engaged in a bitter competition for sales, were egging on the inspectors. Clarence Hackney, for one, must have felt as if he were attending the Mad Hatter's tea party in *Alice in Wonderland*. He did say to Howard Hansen, "They sure do ask a lot of questions." One of these questions, addressed to Warms, was: "Why didn't you beach the boat?" To a mariner, the idea of running aground a great liner in lashing surf was completely irrational. Warms, a less than forceful man, at this moment did react. "Men on the boat," he said, "asked me why I didn't beach her. From my experience on the Jersey coast, nobody would have been taken off alive if I'd beached her." There had been much talk from survivors about the fact that the few lifeboats lowered from the ship did not pick up people in the water. Warms, honestly struggling to remember, could only say: "All the men went to their boat stations when I pulled the whistle. They were orderly. Very orderly. When they dropped the boats in the water, I shouted, 'Stay around.' They stayed around. Then some went for shore. I shouted and waved my flashlight, but there was no response from them."

To Clarence Hackney, disaster was inevitable from the beginning. Everyone, as he remembered, was fighting the fire. Everyone was calling the passengers. Boats were dropping helter-skelter. One of them, No. 9, simply upended on its davits and could not be lowered. Passengers, screaming, refused the directions of crewmen. "The fire," he said simply, "took control even before the engines were shut down."

Q   Did the boats lay aside for more people to get in them?

A   They couldn't. The wind seized them.

Q   How do you think the fire started?

A   I don't know. But it burned so fiercely I think it might have been set afire.

And then a significant point:

Q   Was there a smell of kerosene or gasoline?

A   I only smelled smoke, burning wood.

The same testimony came from Second Steward Pond. Doris Wacker and Paul Arneth, the first two passengers to see the fire, made no mention of any odor. All this, to Dickerson Hoover, suggested that the fire could not have been set. Several times in his questioning he mentioned the possibility of spontaneous combustion, either from an unknown cause or from a short circuit in the mass of electrical cables that ran through the back of the locker.

▬·▬· ▬▬·▬

John A. Kempf had been a New York City fireman for twelve years, anonymous in his work, never singled out for special attention. Now, sitting in front of the WMCA microphone, with reporters scribbling down his words and photographers' lights flashing in his face, he was a prized witness, and his testimony reflected this. He was, after all, the only professional fireman aboard the Morro Castle, and he had plenty to say about the incompetence of the crew. They did not, he remarked, even know how to unroll a fire hose, and when they finally turned on the water, they didn't know enough to direct the water at the base of the flames. Kempf didn't realize that he was not working with crewmen; he was working with passengers Phelps and Kendall. Together, they played the hose on the door of an elevator, from which smoke was pouring. "It was no use," he said. "We couldn't get to the bottom of the fire. Besides, air was coming in through broken windows and through the ventilators." For a few hours at least, until other testimony blacked him out, he was a star in the newspaper headlines. For, when asked when he first smelled smoke, he said: "About 12:45 A.M." That was two hours before anyone else did. And although a stewardess, Mrs. Harriet B. Brown, gave almost the same testimony, no one else did. He became, for a brief period, the best-known fireman in New York City.

All this, apparently, went to John Kempf's head, and raised some questions. He had been floating in a circle of six women when the *Paramount* picked him up. "I hope," he said, "the red-headed girl and all the other girls and those I met on shipboard will remember me and the pleasant times we had and send me some postcards." With that, he put his lips against a microphone. A member of the board of inquiry pulled it away from him. However, another witness, unidentified in the records of the hearing or in newspapers, went him one better. "How'm I doin', Mom?" he cried when he took the witness chair.

—·—· —·—·

Ivan Freeman, as exhausted as his skipper, had to force himself to keep awake through hours of questioning. He, too, was convinced that no fire could have burned out of control so quickly unless there had been incendiarism.

Q   How do you account for the rapidity with which the fire swept through the ship?

A   There are two theories. One, it may have been caused by a cigarette, but I cannot see how a cigarette could have made such headway in such a short space of time. The only conclusion is, then, that it must have been deliberately set. Unless there was some oil or something saturated and thrown around, it could not have spread so quickly.

Q   How could that have happened?

A   Well, consider the circumstances. The usual entertainment had been shut off after the death of the captain. The weather outside was dismal and the only thing people could do was to go to bed. A few people were around having a good time. If the fire had started from a cigarette, ordinarily someone beside the watchman would have seen it and put it out.

The watchman made his last rounds at two o'clock, and that gave from two to three o'clock—a full hour—for someone to saturate everything with kerosene and to have everything in readiness for a fire without detection.

Q   What motive could there be for such a thing?

A   I don't know. In all fairness, I don't know of any animosity or grudge against the captain. I eliminate lightning as a cause, because I passed two open gas tanks on the top deck, and I know one was empty and there was no fire in the other. The planting of a time bomb in Havana is also unlikely, as I don't see how it would escape discovery within forty-eight hours. A cigarette fire would have burned itself out, and it would have been a slow, smoking fire. Eliminating these things, it brings us down to one thing—someone, no matter what their reason or motive, must have started the fire.

Q   How do you think he started that fire?

A   He would have watched his opportunity after the watchman had passed. He would have had forty-five minutes at least in which to work.

In charge of so complex an investigation, one with no precedent, Dickerson Hoover was understandably bemused, and visibly so. Questions that need not have been asked were asked. Questions that should have been asked were not. And one such question was: Why, with passengers strolling through the lounge, the smoking room, and the open passage alongside the writing room, did no one report seeing anyone in the writing room during that forty-five minutes of grace for an alleged act of sabotage?

The most pitiable figure of the entire investigation was now to take the stand on Tuesday morning, September 11. Eben S. Abbott did not look pitiable. Dressed in a dark suit with a white shirt and a figured tie, the chief engineer of the *Morro Castle* stood handsome and erect as he took the oath in a strong voice. His own testimony belied this impression, and the jeopardy in which he stood was attested when two company lawyers stepped forward with him.

Abbott had gone to bed at 10:00 P.M. after a long visit with Captain Warms. "The best of luck," he said as he departed. "We'll make it, old boy," was Warms's reply. It was a little before 3:00 A.M. when the alarm wakened him. Deliberately he put on his white dress uniform and his gold-braid officer's cap because, he said later, he thought it would impress the passengers and calm them. He "took a walk" on A, B, and C decks, met First Assistant Bujia, and told him to keep the men in the engine room: "Don't let a soul leave until they have to." He told Bujia to shut off the fuel system and then started toward the bridge, choking and gagging from smoke. "I don't think we can run much longer," he gasped as he tumbled into the wheelhouse to confront Warms. There were gaps in his testimony then, gaps filled in by Warms and Alagna, the second radio operator describing him as a man in a panic.

Q When you went to No. 1 boat, what did you learn?

A Well, the crew was standing ready. (Abbott began to fidget.)

Q What boat did you go in?

A I went in No. 1 boat.

Q What time did you leave the ship?

A About forty-five minutes after the fire.

Q Well, now you stated previously that the fire started at three o'clock, and you say you left at three forty-five. Why did you leave?

Eben Abbott fell silent. Dickerson Hoover leaned over the table and said sternly: "Didn't you know there was work to be done on that boat?"

"The captain," said Abbott in a faltering voice, "told me to take that boat."

Q Who else was in that boat with you?

A The quartermaster, Dr. Cochrane, and a lady passenger. There were thirty-two in all. Two passengers and all the rest crew.

Q You commanded the lifeboat?

A I started to, but I was so knocked out by the smoke that I couldn't start the motor.

Q And all the rest were crew? What I want to know is why No. 1 took off with only two passengers aboard.

A On the deck there were no passengers. A Deck was deserted.

Q How many did the boat carry?

A Fifty-eight.

Q   What efforts were made to pick up passengers in the vicinity?

A   I do not know.

That was the end of Eben S. Abbott as an officer to be trusted. He had stridden to the witness stand; he shuffled away, head hanging, in a silent room.

Young Arthur Stamper, with dark glasses and a bandaged right eye, was the antithesis of his chief. Methodically and carefully, the third assistant engineer had shut off the engines, put full pressure on the water lines. "I was the last engineer to leave the engine room, me and a junior. All my men left before I did. I waited to make sure they did. I hollered to see if anybody was there, and there was no answer." Where Stamper's senior had left the ship in a panic, Stamper stayed. Though he could barely see, he made his way to the stern through the shaft tunnel, and even then his thought was for the passengers. He could hear them screaming on C Deck. With another man, he went up through the smoke to bring forty or fifty of them down to D Deck, still free of fire and comparatively free of smoke. There was a murmur of approval as he left the witness stand.

It was now time for this dismaying inquiry to produce a hero, and an unlikely-looking one he was. On Thursday morning Chief Radio Operator George W. Rogers, a hulking six feet two inches and a blubbery 250 pounds in weight, took the stand to recall what happened in the radio room. Through countless newspaper interviews he had already established himself as a pillar of strength, and in his pocket was a contract to appear on the stage of the Rialto Theater, with the canary he rescued, to tell his story. Rogers was asleep, or at least in his bunk, when Operator Maki awoke him. He dressed, went to the radio room, and adjusted the transmitter to distress frequency. "George," he said he'd told Alagna, "go to the bridge and see what orders the mate has to give." He then explained, "I referred to Mr. Warms as mate because I always knew him as mate." Calmly, Rogers ordered Operator Maki to stay in the radio room, to soak a towel in the wash˙basin so he could breathe through it. Then, when Alagna didn't come back, he sent Maki to find him. Maki never returned. He was later picked up in the water.

Q   What happened then?

A   Alagna returned and said, "Chief, get out of here. The whole place is afire outside, and you're only going to get caught like a rat in a trap if you don't get out of here." I said, "What about the distress message?" I can't pass on his veracity, but what he said was, "They're running around on the bridge, and I can't get any cooperation."

Q   Did you question him?

A   No. The emergency was too great for questioning anybody. At that moment I heard the *Andrea Luckenbach* calling the shore station at Tuckerton asking for information about a large liner burning off the coast. I heard the answer that they had no information, so I thought it would be advisable to come on the air during the silent period, when all ships stand by for emergency messages. I did it on my own initiative.

Alagna was standing by his chief and remembers the whole incident. Rogers, ignoring the smoke, sent his "CQ," at 3:15 A.M. Ignoring a warning from Tuckerton to be silent, he sent a "CQ-QRX-KGOV," warning of an emergency, at 3:18 A.M. Just then the lights went out. The emergency power system failed. Still calm, Rogers reached over and switched on a second emergency system, operated from batteries. Whatever deficiencies the *Morro Castle* may have had in its fire detecting system, it had none in its radio room. On orders from Rogers, Alagna went back to the bridge. "See if they want to send a distress signal," Rogers said.

In a room so thick with smoke that he had to shine a flashlight within six inches of the transmitter key to see it, Rogers suddenly realized his feet were blistering. He put his hand down, and the floor was hot to his touch. The bulkheads were becoming discolored from the fire. Flame was blowing in through the open portholes. At 3:22 A.M. ship's time Alagna appeared, blinded, in the doorway. "Okay, chief," he said. "Send the SOS. We're twenty miles south of Scotland Light." Rogers was almost unconscious when he tapped out the call. Halfway through, there was an explosion in a corner where the batteries were housed. A second later the generator stopped. Walking on blistered feet but with total sureness, Rogers found a loose wire, shaped it around a lug, and the emergency generator started again. Boiling acid from the batteries was spilling across the floor. He just managed to tap out, "Can't hold out much longer," when there was a final explosion, and the transmitter went dead.

In his deep voice Rogers said, "I lay there across the table and said to myself, 'If I'm supposed to be dying, it doesn't hurt very much. I'm just getting sleepy.'" Still, automatically, he refused to leave. He ordered Alagna back to the bridge for any last orders. Then, a few minutes later, when Alagna reappeared, both men left the radio shack and made their way down to the forepeak of the ship. What happened until everyone but Warms left the ship had already been told by other witnesses, but there was more to Rogers' story. He was asked: "Did you have any trouble with radio operators?" With seeming reluctance, he said, "Might I not be asked that question?" Then he promptly answered it:

Captain Wilmott had told him that Alagna was untrustworthy, that the radio compass was to be locked so that Alagna could not get at it, that he was afraid that Alagna would vengefully damage the equipment, and that he was to be fired when the ship reached New York. That was not all. Maki was a trouble-maker, failed to carry out orders, and was hated by the ship's officers, particularly the purser. The inspectors began to see a new side of Rogers. He was a hero, maybe, but he did not mind telling tales about his men. Reporter Norma Abrams, perhaps with a woman's intuition, wrote a news story in which she sardonically noted that all this part of Rogers' testimony involved quotations from a man who was dead, a man who could no longer say whether the story was true.

16

HERO AND VILLAIN

George Alagna was a hot-tempered young man, and he was tired of answering questions about the *Morro Castle* disaster. First he had written his own story for the newspapers. Next he had been questioned endlessly by attorneys for the Ward Line. Soon he was to appear before the Steamboat Inspection Service hearing, and now he was being questioned by Joseph R. Pendergast, a persistent young assistant in the United States Attorney's office. He had been one of the bravest men aboard the ship, running to the bridge again and back again through smoke and flame until he had finally wrung permission from Warms for the sending of an SOS. Yet all the credit for heroism had gone to Chief Operator Rogers, who stood by his wireless key to the last possible second. As for Alagna, he knew that the Ward Line considered him a troublemaker, and the questions posed by Pendergast touched on this point again and again. Alagna finally exploded.

"I'm not going to answer any more questions," he said. But he did. He was called before the grand jury, where he had to reply or face a term in jail for contempt. Until he left the grand jury, it seemed to Alagna that he had shriven himself. As he walked into the corridor, a hand fell on his shoulder. "You are under arrest as a material witness," said a tall United States marshal. It was a hot day, and Alagna was in his shirt-sleeves. Handcuffs clicked on, cameras snapped, and the next morning his picture was on all the front pages. The term "material witness" was one that Alagna did not understand, but the newspapers did, and said so. It meant either that he was under suspicion and might flee the jurisdiction of the court, or that he was holding back testimony of immense value. Bail had been set at $1000. It could have been a million dollars so far as penniless Alagna was concerned. It was raised, a day later, to

$3000, but this time his friends in the radio operators' union put up the money.

That same day he found out why he had been arrested. Chief Operator Rogers had called him a "vengeful man." He was suddenly a prime suspect. It was small consolation when Conboy dropped the charge a few days later, and when Rogers belatedly described him as "a man that I was proud to have as my first assistant." Alagna had never trusted Rogers anyway. On September 21, when he appeared before the Steamboat Inspectors, he discovered that others aboard the *Morro Castle* also suspected Rogers. Rogers was a loner. He stayed aloof from the crew, and they resented him. He rarely went ashore at Havana. Instead, he stayed in his bunk and slept most of the time.

Alagna already had told most of his story to the newspapers, but still some of the drama lingered. More than any other witness, he was able to bring into context the panic, the confusion, and the numbed helplessness of Captain Warms. On the first of his five trips to the bridge, Warms simply ignored him. In the smoke and the darkness, he suspected, Warms did not even know who he was.

Q   How did you try to make him understand?

A   On my second trip I put on my radio operator's cap and stood between him and the flames so he could recognize me.

Q   What did he do?

A   He just pushed me aside and murmured, "It's out of my hands."

Q   When did you finally get his attention?

A   On the fifth and last trip. I pleaded with him for several minutes. I kept telling him, "We've got to send an SOS." But he kept running over to the port side to take another look at the fire. I couldn't understand why he didn't look at the starboard side, where the people were jumping over and there was so much to be done. I followed him around and finally got him to understand that the radio room was taking fire, and Rogers being overcome with smoke, and it would soon be impossible to send a message.

Q   What happened then?

A   It seemed to me finally as if inspiration came to him and he asked if we could still send a message. I told him that was what I had been trying to tell him all along. Then he said, "All right, send the SOS." I asked him our location, and he said, "About twenty miles south of Scotland Light."

Q   Had you tried other means to get him to listen?

A   Yes, at one point—because I knew how close he was to Captain Wilmott—I said, "Captain, what about Wilmott's body? Can't we put it in one of the lifeboats?"

Clarence Hackney brusquely intervened. "The living," he said, "are more important than the dead."

"Sometimes that's the case," Alagna reflected, "but in this case I am sure that if the dead captain were live, this fire would have been handled differently."

The testimony was damning to Warms, but even more damaging to Chief Engineer Abbott. Alagna still remembers telling the inspectors: "Abbott was on the wing of the bridge away from the fire, looking and wringing his hands and saying in a crying sort of voice over and over, 'What are we going to do? What are we going to do?' It struck me very much because I knew Chief Engineer Abbott had no business on the bridge, and it impressed me that he should be dressed up in full uniform as if he were going to the Captain's Dinner."

Finally, Alagna said, the SOS was sent; and, as Alagna and Rogers stumbled forward, they saw Warms leap over the rail from the bridge and scuttle down a ladder to the forecastle head. It was a moment of anguish for Alagna. He felt abandoned. "You're a yellow rat!" he screamed, but if Warms heard the cry, he ignored it. When the two operators reached his side, the captain was still staring at the fire, muttering, "I must be dreaming," or saying again, "It's out of our hands." This was the most coherent testimony the inspectors had heard, and it vindicated Alagna. "He seemed a very intelligent witness," said Hoover, "and he gives a very plain picture of the captain being in a state of mental paralysis."

On October 16, after fifty-seven witnesses had been heard and fifteen thick volumes of testimony compiled, Inspectors Neilson and Smith issued their report, damning enough to serve as a criminal indictment. William Warms was stunned when he read it through, able only to say to his wife, "They're taking away my master's license." Five officers in all were temporarily suspended: Warms, Hackney, Hanson, Abbott, and Bujia. The report itself, in clipped official words, summed up the whole disastrous affair, a mélange of incompetence, delay, confusion, panic, and carelessness.

There was, it said, no organized effort by the officers to fight and control the fire, to close the fire screen doors, to shut off the ventilating system. No effort to organize the crew and meet the emergency. The crew itself made no effort to take its regular fire stations. "The Master, Captain Warms, did not leave the bridge to make any personal investigation as to the extent of the fire. It appears that the vessel continued at full speed into a twenty-mile breeze for some distance after the fire had been reported. It was not until the fire was out of control that the course was changed and the vessel slowed down.

"At this time the gyro pilot, the telemotor gear, the electric lights, and all communication systems between the bridge and the engine room failed, and no efforts were made to use the emergency steering gear or the emergency lighting set."

This was damaging comment, but worse strictures were to come: "Had the vessel been stopped immediately after the fire had been discovered in the superstructure, which would have tended to prevent the rapid spread of the fire, and the call for assistance not delayed, it is apparent that rescue vessels would have been in the vicinity of the stricken liner much earlier, and no doubt would have been instrumental in saving a greater number of lives."

The board of inquiry, said the report, visited the *Morro Castle* on September 18. The inspection showed that no fire doors had been used to check the fire, that a number of hydrants were not used, and that at least five hydrants had steel caps screwed over them—including one on the port side of B Deck which covered the writing room. There followed another, more serious accusation:

"It is apparent that no successful effort was made on the part of any of the officers or crew to lead these people up to the boat deck by way of the crew's service stairways, nor to lead them up outside.

"Thus they were cut off from the lifeboats by the flames, and their only means of escape was to lower themselves into the water by means of ropes or by jumping overboard from the stern of the vessel." As for the six lifeboats that did hit the water, the first of them, No. 10, was lowered by panicky seamen without any orders from any officer. These boats, with a total carrying capacity of 408 persons, had only 85 persons aboard, the majority of them crew. "No successful effort was made by any of these boats to go under the stern of the burning vessel and render assistance to the large number of passengers gathered there. . . . No effort was made on the part of officers to keep these boats in close proximity to the burning vessel."

It was a summary that a prosecutor could not have bettered. Said the inspectors:

"The fire and boat drills on this vessel were carried out in perfunctory manner and a great number of the crew were not familiar with their stations in case of fire or abandoning ship. When the alarm was rung and an actual emergency existed, there was a complete breakdown of discipline on the ship.

"The engine and fireroom watch stayed at their posts until driven out through the emergency exits. It is apparent that the same cannot be said of the chief engineer, who never appeared in the engine room during the fire to inform himself . . . and the first assistant engineer paid but a brief visit to the engine room and was apparently the first member of the standby crew of the engine department to make his exit."

———· ——·—

The United States Attorney's office, weighing the criminal aspects of the case, was more deliberate in its investigation. A score of FBI agents, directed by Frank Kilmartin, chief of the New York office, fanned out to interview every survivor. A spry young man named Francis W. H. Adams was in charge of the case as chief assistant United States Attorney, with Assistant United States Attorney Joseph R. Pendergast as his associate. Francis Adams, in his seventies, is still practicing law on Park Avenue. He has forgotten very little about the *Morro Castle* case.

"It took weeks," he said, "for FBI agents to put together the mosaic, but then we could virtually tell minute by minute what happened. The investigation was so thorough that when one man would report having been awakened by another man crying, 'The ship's on fire,' we could find that man and confirm it. As to Warms, I think there were some extenuating circumstances. From our interview we learned that Wilmott ran the ship completely. Warms did what he was told.

"The case hinged on the element of time. If the personnel did not have time to act, if the fire was out of control almost immediately, then no negligence could be proved. Nor could it be proved if the interval between discovery of the fire and the moment it went out of control was so short a reasonable human being could do nothing. We did not find such proof. It was natural for Warms to think he might reach an anchorage inside Sandy Hook, for he was less than twenty miles from Scotland Light. One disastrous coincidence followed another. He didn't really have a competent crew, so the fire gained headway until it was uncontrollable. He was steaming into the wind with all exhausts and venting systems wide open and in full force, spreading the flames. I still feel a trained crew could have controlled that fire, and that the ship could have been maneuvered to confine it to a limited area."

On December 3, 1934, after interviewing nearly a hundred witnesses, a grand jury of the Southern District of New York handed down indictments against Warms, Abbott, Cabaud, and the Atlantic, Gulf and West Indies Steamship Company. At his home in Green Farms, New Jersey, Warms answered the telephone late in the day. A reporter from the Asbury Park *Press* was calling. "The grand jury has indicted you," he said. "The charges are misconduct, inattention to duties, negligence, fraud, connivance, and violation of law, causing the destruction of the steam vessel *Morro Castle*."

Outwardly, Warms was calm, according to his son Donald. Inwardly, he was shaken. A statement of censure and suspension pronounced by the Steamboat Inspection Service damaged his reputation, but eventually he could hope to go back to sea again. A criminal indictment, with its threat of a prison sentence, would ruin him forever. And this indictment was unpleasantly specific. It spelled out the requirements of the maritime law:

Station bills must be prepared, assigning crew members to their posts in case of fire or other disaster. There must be a muster (duty) list. Stewards must be specially assigned to warn passengers and to see that they had life jackets, were assembled at boat stations, and that order was kept in passage and stairways. An equal number of sailors was required on each tour of duty, day or night. Motorboats were to be operated five or more minutes a week, the crew drilled on the handling of oars, and the lifeboats swung out once a week.

Quite contrary to these regulations, said the indictment, the station bills failed to cover the whole crew. There were no prearranged alarm signals. Fire and boat drills were not listed in the ship's logbook. Chief Engineer Abbott failed to assign fire stations to the engine room department. Warms failed to control the vessel so as to localize the fire, to issue distress signals to other ships, or to lower lifeboats on time. Abbott failed to take charge of the engine department. He told the fire fighters to report to him at the chief engineer's office, but never went there himself. Members of the crew were without discipline or training. Many did not know their stations or duties. "In the panic and confusion," concluded this section of the indictment, "passengers were left to help and save themselves."

Warms, an uncomplicated man, was now faced with a complex and agonizing ordeal. He must justify his actions during a crisis few skippers ever had to face. If he failed and the jury found him guilty, he might be sent to prison for as long as ten years. He was to be defended by one of the most eminent law firms in New York—Burlingham, Clark, Veeder and Hupper— but he knew it would be an uphill fight. Few juries in United States Court ever reject the findings of an indictment, and this one had been prepared with the most painstaking care.

━·━·━━·━

Dickerson Hoover,[1] as he later remembered, had summed up the lessons of the *Morro Castle* disaster six years before it happened.

In 1928 Hoover headed an investigation into the sinking of the Lamport and Holt liner *Vestris*, which capsized at sea with the loss of 110 lives because her cargo was improperly stowed. "The thing that stands out most prominently in this disaster," he wrote, "and the lesson first to be learned, is that we must stress *men* more than *things*.

"In this modern age we are prone to direct our efforts as far as possible toward the invention of mechanical devices that will make things safer, and this is true not only on ships but also on shore.

"As a result of it, I fear that we have unconsciously become the slaves of those things that we have invented to help us, forgetting that no matter how excellent a device there may be, there must be competent men to handle it, and this competency in men must be stressed at sea more than in any other place."

━·━·━━·━

The *Morro Castle*, dead and gutted on a sandbank at Asbury Park, still possessed a certain malign power over people and events. By October 12, 1934, she had begun to stink. The odor of burned hides was a miasmic cloud over the boardwalk. Autumn visitors were complaining, and local residents were annoyed. On that day, the city distributed the profits from its twenty-five-cent fee for viewing the ship from Convention Hall. Exactly $7750 was divided among the West Side Mission, the St. Vincent de Paul Society, the Salvation Army, the Ladies Hebrew Relief Society, the National Urban League, the New Jer-

[1] In conversation with Norma Abrams of the New York *Daily News*.

sey First Aid Society, the West Side Community Center, the Searle Home for the Aged, and the Milk Fund. But to the embarrassment of the City Council, the American Red Cross refused to take even one penny. By now Asbury Park had begun to wish heartily that somebody would tow the ship away.

A little more than one month later, the *Morro Castle* confirmed her reputation for malignity. Captain Harry N. Cole II, commanding the salvage operation, was seized by a heart attack. He fell dead and tumbled from an upper deck to the bottom hatch, where his body was found. It cheered nobody in Asbury Park, and astonished many, when the cheerful salvage workers lit up a Christmas tree on the bow the evening of December 24. Asbury Park didn't even want to remember that the *Morro Castle* was on its doorstep. There was relief, on March 14, 1935, when tugs finally wrenched her from the sandbank and towed her to a temporary anchorage in Gravesend Bay, Brooklyn. President Roosevelt had asked the Navy Department whether she might be rebuilt as a troop transport. Secretary Claude Swanson replied that the ship was a total loss and should be sold for junk. The remains of this five-million-dollar investment in national pride were auctioned off as junk on March 27, 1935, to the Union Shipbuilding Company of Baltimore. On March 29 tugs strained at the hulk, and the *Morro Castle* was towed from Gravesend Bay. The same day, George Alagna attempted suicide in his Jackson Heights apartment. Life had dealt badly with Alagna. Hearings, trials, and all the testimony had made him a dubious figure. "You're a nice fellow," prospective employers kept telling him, "but there just isn't anything open." Alagna knew he had reached a dead end. Fortunately for his future, which has been a happy one, neighbors smelled gas. They found him on the kitchen floor, with three hissing jets open on the stove and with two suicide notes nearby. He recovered, finally found a job, and on July 11 married Ethel May Carty, of Asbury Park, whose sister he had met at the *Morro Castle* hearings.

For those who had followed the career of the ship itself, there was to be one final reminder. On June 28 the hulk caught fire in the Baltimore shipyard where it was being scrapped. Bilge oil in the hulk was ignited by a workman's blowtorch. A fireboat and three land companies of firemen rushed to the scene and put out the flames. Even at the moment of dismemberment, the *Morro Castle* still was able to produce one blazing reminder of that September night off the New Jersey shore. There was a tiny news item in the *Herald Tribune*, but it was a mere footnote to an event best forgotten, so far as the offices of the Atlantic, Gulf and West Indies Steamship Company were concerned. Insurance companies had already paid them $4,186,000 —$263,000 above the book value of the *Morro Castle* as a functioning ship. They in turn magnanimously paid survivors, and the heirs of those who perished, an average of $894 each. Under an obscure provision of the Maritime Law, a fire at sea was defined as an act of God.

It was autumn 1935 before the processes of justice got around to William Warms. Day after day he sat in District Court while a procession of witnesses repeated their familiar testimony of cowardice, incompetence, and confusion. Day after day he listened as the officers he had commanded so briefly told what they were doing at the moment of the fire. Newspapers barely mentioned the testimony. By now it was stale copy, and there were more exciting current events. He was, it seemed, existing in a vacuum, and he was not alone. Chief Operator Rogers had disappeared from sight. Neither side called him as a witness.

There were enough others to damn all the defendants, particularly since the jury—as Warms put it—consisted of "landlubbers, with not a seafaring man among them." The Ward Line, whose role in the disaster already was in question, lost the last shreds of its reputation with the testimony of Angelo Vlaco, its hiring master.

"When the steamer arrives," he said in a broken Greek accent, "I go aboard. I see the chief officer, and the chief officer, he tells me what men he wants. If he wants an AB [able-bodied seaman] or a quartermaster or a deck boy, whatever it is."

Q   Can you read the lifeboat ticket?

A   I know it says lifeboat ticket and the number of the ticket, and that is all I know. I don't read very much, but I could read "lifeboat" very easy.

Q   What do you usually read on the able seaman's certificate?

A   AB ticket, that's all, also the American seaman's passport.

Q   Could you read the whole of the certificates?

A   No, not at all.

Joe Pendergast was questioning Vlaco. He remembers the hush that fell over the courtroom. For Vlaco, the Ward Line's agent, was responsible for hiring the most competent possible crew, and how could a man who scarcely read or spoke English distinguish between a competent man and an incompetent man?

On went the procession of witnesses—dry and conscientious Purser Tolman, a "company man" par excellence, whose first thought was for the ship's records (he carried them ashore in a bag) but who never relinquished his life preserver; James A. Flynn, the philosophy teacher, who was one of the first to smell and see the fire; Radio Operator Silverman and Chief Mate Frank Magruder of the rescue ship *Luckenbach*, and then Quartermaster Hoffman, red-haired, freckle-faced, and thoroughly matter-of-fact. Numbed William Warms did not realize it, but more than any other witness "Red" Hoffman demolished the charge that Warms had been inattentive to duty.

He heard the shout, "Fire in the lounge," just as a button on the fire detector board flashed red and clouds of smoke poured into the chart room. It was a clear sequence of events, as Hoffman saw it. "Warms ran in, grabbed the telephone, talked to the engine room, and then rang the 'stand by' signal. He told Welch to shake the crew out, and then he was out on the port wing, bawling orders. He commanded, 'Left wheel,' 'Hard left,' and just at that moment the gyrocompass burned out. I says, 'Captain, she won't steer,' and a minute later, between orders, he says to me, 'You better leave.'" Faithful Hoffman relived that moment for the jury. "No," he had told Warms, "I'll stick with you." Said Warms, coughing and gagging, "You go. There's nothing more you can do." Hoffman got into Lifeboat No. 6 and took one of the heavy oars. The lightly loaded boat was a mere chip of wood in the towering seas. The wind seized them, and they were drifting toward shore through a corridor of upraised arms, passengers mutely pleading to be taken aboard, but there were not enough oarsmen to stop the boat.

Night Watchman Tannenbaum, even long after the event, was still dazed. "The members of the crew were shaken out of their sleep in the middle of the night by the cry of fire. The chances are they didn't believe it. I didn't, either, until I saw the whole writing room and the corridor in flames." To this confusion was added the unquestioned fact that the crew had been trained improperly in the handling of lifeboat drills. Cadet Tripp, one of the most precise witnesses before the jury, was asked: "How did you spend your time during lifeboat drills?" "Just standing nearby my lifeboat," he said. Waiter Joseph Bertocci, preparing for drill, was told by an officer: "If any passengers inquire what's going on, just explain to them that it's a fire and boat drill, and if they care to, they can go." Compounding this slackness was the fact that only a few members knew how to operate the fire doors. Milton Stephenson, an assistant steward, saw these doors closed and reopened only once. "The carpenter," he remembered, "came up and closed and opened them in succession, but he didn't spend any time explaining to me how to do it."

Would it have mattered anyway? There were fire doors between the lounge and the writing room, and also at the fore and aft ends of the mezzanine. Steward Campbell and the two night watchmen could have closed all three of them: They did know how, but in the emergency their only thought was to give the alarm and to try to put out the fire. Chief John Kenlon, a bluff veteran of the New York Fire Department, was certain that closing the doors would have done no good. "Closing those doors," he said, "would not have affected the spread of the fire. Those steel bulkheads were superheated to fifteen hundred degrees Fahrenheit, and it was through the bulkheads that the fire spread."

What doomed the *Morro Castle* was the combination of this intense heat plus the elegant paneling installed to give the passengers a sense of luxury, a reassuring sense of being in a hotel onshore.

A little aghast, the jury listened as Harold F. Norton, in the matter-of-fact way of a technician, explained how this paneling was installed. Norton was a naval architect for the builders of the ship, the Newport News Corporation. On the ceilings, wood frames had been fastened to wooden furring pieces bolted to the beams and dropping one to two inches below them. Still lower, seven to eight inches below the deck, were plywood panels, in effect creating a hollow ceiling. On the bulkheads it was the same, with a twelve-inch hollow space. The result was a continuous area full of inflammable wood through which the flames could race. Closing the fire doors would shut off this hollow space, but it could not shut off the movement of heats that reddened the steel frame of the ship.

Q   Then the plywood used in the construction of the *Morro Castle*, which your company put in there, was not fireproof?

A   That is correct. It was used because it was fairly light.

On went the procession of witnesses, day after day, adding bits and pieces to the story, all too often contradicting each other. Chief Engineer Abbott took the stand as a defense witness and stubbornly stuck to his story. "I did all I could before I was ordered off," was his refrain, and government counsel could not shake him. Finally came Warms, telling for the last time how it all happened. Tears welled into his eyes. "I was standing in smoke in the wheelhouse, and the decks were buckling, they were red hot, they scorched my feet. I had to leave. I'd done everything I could." He wiped his eyes with a handkerchief and then went on with his recital, by now familiar. There was no cross-examination. Chauncey Clark said quietly, "The defense rests." Judge Murray Hulbert's charge to the jury was brief. He raised all the familiar questions about carelessness, inattention to duty, and incompetence in lifesaving. The jury retired. On January 25, 1936, the trial at last was over. The next morning, pursued by reporters and photographers, half running down the hall, Warms, Abbott, and Cabaud came back into the courtroom to wait for the verdict. It was not long in coming.

"We, the jury," said Foreman William Allen, "find the defendant Warms guilty . . . the defendant Abbott guilty . . . the defendant Cabaud and the Atlantic, Gulf and West Indies Steamship Company guilty." Judge Hulbert slammed down his gavel. "The defendants," he said, "are released in their own recognizance for sentencing January 28." On that later day, before a crowded courtroom, he tersely pronounced sentence: Abbott was sentenced to four years in federal prison, Warms to two years. Cabaud was fined $5000 and given a one-year sentence for "willful" negligence. It may have seemed unequal justice, but by the philosophy of the times Henry Cabaud had been punished enough. "After all, he was a man of standing in the community," muses ex-Prosecutor Adams, "and there was punishment enough for him in the mere fact of conviction." The steamship company was fined $10,000, the maximum permitted by law.

Warms and Abbott went back to their homes on bail, stunned by the injustice of fate. Now the case was up to the lawyers. It moved to the United States Court of Appeals, and on April 7, 1937, fate proved to have its just side. Justices Learned and Augustus Hand, with Justice Martin T. Manton dissenting, reversed the convictions of Warms and Abbott, but left standing Cabaud's $5000 fine. In 4471 printed pages all the testimony before the District Court was made a matter of record. The decision was a vindication for Warms, a lukewarm vindication for Abbott, and an indictment of the Morro Castle's dead captain.

"The responsibility of Warms as master was a new one," said the decision. "That situation required the management of passengers in a terrible emergency. He maintained the best traditions of the sea by staying on his vessel until the bridge had burnt under him, and then until no one else remained on board.

"He has been charged with failure as mate to conduct proper fire and boat drills, but Captain Wilmott was in general charge of these drills before Warms joined the ship, and after the advent of the latter he continued his former practice. The instruction of passengers in the use of life preservers he left to the stewards. Wilmott controlled the drilling of the lifeboat crews in the use of oars. He apparently exercised control at all times." It was as Warms had testified: The master gave the orders. "I assigned nobody to anything."

On the record, said the judges, Abbott also did eveything required of him: "The men in the engine room did their work properly. He made sure the water pressure was maintained, and it failed only when more hydrants were opened than the system would stand. Even after the engine room force left, the steam pump was left running. His other acts on the ship during the fire seem largely futile." There was a note of skepticism in what they had to say about Abbott after he abandoned ship in Lifeboat No. 1. He could and should have saved passengers, they commented. He claimed there was not enough power in the oars to bring the boat up to the stern of the ship, but if the lifeboat motor had been operated there would have been no difficulty in reaching the ship. With apparent reluctance, the decision concluded, "There appears to be insufficient proof of support of a criminal negligence conviction over his conduct in the boat."

The trials were over at last. Warms went back to sea as master of a Ward Line freighter. Even then, bad luck traveled with him. A year later he ran his ship aground on the Mexican coast. Nobody would give Eben Abbott a new berth. His reputation had been blighted. He went into retirement and died a few years later. Only his home town paper noted his passing.

It seemed that the *Morro Castle* could finally be forgotten, but the case was dying a harder death than the ship, by now scrapped, melted down, and converted into steel that may well have found a new home in a Japanese battleship. That was where most American scrap steel wound up in the middle 1930s. In 1938 an explosion in an annex to the Bayonne, New Jersey, police headquarters brought the *Morro Castle* disaster back to life.

17

THE TRIALS OF
GEORGE WHITE ROGERS

If ever a town was starved for a hero, it was Bayonne, New Jersey, a place where nothing ever seemed to happen. Just five blocks wide, on a peninsula jutting into Newark
Bay, it has changed very little since the autumn of 1934, when
the City Council awarded George White Rogers a $200 gold
medal, and the Veteran Wireless Operators' Association named
him the maritime hero of 1934. George Rogers bought himself a
jaunty red pickup truck and settled down to a modest living as
a radio repairman, but not for long. A mysterious fire gutted his
little radio shop in 1935. Early in 1936 he applied to the Bayonne
Police Department for a job. He was appointed a patrolman,
assistant to Vincent J. Doyle, lieutenant in charge of the first
two-way police radio system in the United States.

Doyle is now dead, but his widow has every reason to remember George Rogers. On March 4, 1938, her husband—everyone called him "Bud"—came home for lunch. Before he left
the red brick police headquarters on C Street, Rogers had
stopped by his desk to say, "There's a package here for you."
Doyle, busy typing a report, said, "Leave it there." "But don't
you want to open it?" "After lunch," said Doyle. When he came
back to headquarters to finish his report, Rogers interrupted
him again. "Hey," he said. "Don't you want to take care of that
package?" Doyle finished the last lines of his report, typed his
signature, and walked outside to the police motorcycle garage,
over which the radio repair room was located. He picked the
package from a table in the hallway. It was wrapped in brown
paper, tied with a white string, and marked in printed letters
with the name, "Lt. Doyle." He carried it to the second floor,
with Rogers following behind him, and unwrapped it. A typewritten note fell out:

"Lieutenant Doyle, This is a fish-tank heater. Please install the switch in the line cord and see if the unit will work. It should get slightly warm." It was a gray tube five inches long and three inches in diameter, with a half-inch opening in the center. A length of cord that ended in a socket plug hung from one end. "George," asked Doyle, "what do you make of this?" "Oh," said Rogers, "it's one of those things you use to heat a tropical fish aquarium to the proper temperature."

"Well," said Doyle, "let's see how it works." He looked up from his work table, only to see Rogers walking toward the staircase, making the remark: "Bud, I'm going to mail a letter."

The nearest socket was some distance from the work table. Doyle, holding the tube in his left hand and resting it against his knee, leaned out and inserted the plug. In the headquarters building there was an earsplitting blast. Detective Captain Thomas J. McGrath and two other officers dashed out of the building. Looking up, they could see that the windows had been blown out above the garage. In the radio room they found Doyle moaning on the floor. Blood spurted from his mangled left hand. Three of his fingers had been blown off. The bone of his left thigh protruded through blood-soaked clothing. Still, Doyle was lucky. If he had not leaned forward so far to insert the plug, he probably would have been blown to bits.

He was on the operating table when Mrs. Doyle arrived at Bayonne Hospital. "I'm afraid he's going to die," a nurse told her. A determined little woman, Mrs. Doyle insisted on seeing him. Smoking a cigarette, he calmly reassured his wife. "Bud," she asked, "you aren't going to die and leave me?" "No," he said, "I'll be all right. I just want to find out who had it in for me. I don't know a soul that hated me enough to want to kill me." Early that evening Rogers paid a call at the hospital. There were tears in his eyes as he put his arm around Mrs. Doyle. "God is good," he said. "Nothing is going to happen." Doyle survived, minus three fingers, with a hole in his thigh.

At police headquarters the investigators were busy. In the radio room they found a shred of cord dangling from the socket Doyle had used. From the floor they recovered tiny fragments of gray metal, a piece of scorched wrapping paper bearing Doyle's name in penciled letters, and the typewritten note. New York police examined the fragments and determined that the "fish tank heater" had contained TNT. The wrapping paper was a brand stocked in the police department's supply room. The type-writer used to write the note was Doyle's own typewriter in the headquarters building. Finally Captain McGrath checked the department's time sheets and found that Rogers was officially off duty at the time of the explosion. Paint in Rogers' home matched the paint used on the bomb, and a waterproof cement in his home matched the coating of the bomb. Under the floorboards in his bedroom, police found a piece of tubing that duplicated the "fish tank heater."

It was all circumstantial evidence and took time to accumulate, but what clinched the case was an examination of Rogers' record.[1] At the age of thirteen, an orphan, he was placed on probation in Oakland, California, for stealing a wireless receiving set. The children's home to which he was sent described him as a petty thief, a liar, and a pervert. In 1915 he was committed to another home, where he made a sexual attack on a younger boy. Two years later he became a wireless operator on a steamship, joined the Navy, and was discharged nine months later for a physical disability. The dismal litany went on. He stole radio tubes, was present at a mysterious fire, was accused in other radio thefts, and finally settled down to steady work as a wireless operator. Even after he joined the *Morro Castle*, he could not resist a bent for the conspiratorial. He had by now moved to Bayonne. A friend, Preston Dillenbeck, was attending school to become a radio operator.

After Rogers became a patrolman, he showed his badge to Dillenbeck and said he was going to have it chrome plated. "Why not have it gold plated?" Dillenbeck asked wryly. "I'll be having a gold one soon," Rogers said, "because I'm a very ingenious young man."[2] Had Lieutenant Doyle died, he would have succeeded to his job.

Veteran and retired members of the Bayonne Police Department remembered Rogers' obsession with the *Morro Castle* fire. He compared it to the Black Tom munitions explosions in nearby Perth Amboy, New Jersey, during World War I. In each case, he claimed, an incendiary pencil was used, set to go off hours after it was activated.

A few weeks after the explosion Rogers was indicted. Lieutenant Doyle, still in bandages, sat grimly in the courtroom. One day, as Rogers was led in, he leaned over and said to Doyle, "Hello, Bud. How're things going?" Mrs. Doyle remembers how her husband gritted his teeth and flinched away from Rogers. On December 30, 1938, Rogers was convicted of attempted

[1] Assembled at the New Jersey State Prison in Trenton.
[2] According to Mrs. Doyle.

murder and sentenced to twelve to twenty years in the New Jersey penitentiary. The judge accepted the prosecutor's thesis that Rogers was an egomaniac who found it impossible to serve in a subordinate position, a man who envied Doyle his rank and job and meant to obtain them for himself. The judge called him "diabolical . . . a fiend."

Rogers gone was not Rogers out of mind. Crippled Doyle set himself to amassing proof that the chief radio operator had set the *Morro Castle* fire. During the next fifteen years he devoted all his spare time to writing survivors, checking police files, and amassing so much data that he wrote two hundred typed pages intended to prove his thesis. "I am convinced," he told George Alagna in 1947, "that George Rogers set fire to the *Morro Castle*. Thousands of people share a like opinion. . . . During the questioning at police headquarters he explained rather thoroughly to our Lieutenant of Detectives just how the *Morro Castle* fire was set. He explained that an incendiary fountain pen was placed in the pocket of a jacket which hung in a closet in a writing room on the ship, and spontaneous combustion did the rest. He had already described to me in detail exactly how an incendiary pen was constructed."

Three years and ten months after he walked into the New Jersey State Prison at Trenton, George Rogers walked out again, paroled to join the armed services. None of them would have him, but he still had friends who believed in him, among them J. B. Duffy, superintendent of the Radiomarine Corporation. He went to sea again. According to Doyle, he was returned from Australia in irons and ordered by the Coast Guard never to serve again on an American ship. The Coast Guard has no record of such an order. He was questioned but released by the Jersey City Police Department in connection with the theft of equipment from a war plant where he worked. The FBI suspected him of poisoning a water cooler in a Brooklyn defense plant where he later worked. Finally he came back again to Bayonne, where he bought and sold surplus radio equipment and repaired radio sets.

"And he is making money," Doyle told Alagna. "I had a report last week that he was flashing hundred-dollar bills in a store where he buys his usual *Doc Savage* and *Gruesome Tales* or occasionally *Superman*."

Doyle was correct. Rogers had suddenly come into money. He had become a close friend of William Hummel, eighty-three, a printer for the Bayonne *Times*, and Hummel's spinster daughter,

Edith, fifty-eight. They lived only a few houses from each other. When the Hummels' television set needed repairing, it was Rogers who did the work. In 1953 the Hummels decided to sell their house and move to Florida. First they planned to visit a nephew, William Wimmer, who lived in Bloomington, New York. They never arrived, but it was Rogers who first raised questions. "There's a mystery here," he told a friend. "The Hummels left last week to visit relatives. They're supposed to be in Bloomington and they haven't arrived. Nobody has inquired. I wonder why." Five days later the relatives did inquire. On July 2 police broke into the Hummel house and found them both bludgeoned to death. Suspicion of Rogers was immediate. He had driven Hummel to the bank. Hummel had drawn out $2000, all of it in $100 bills. Just the day after, Rogers bought raido equipment for $300 and paid for it with three $100 bills.

From Hummel's own handwritten records, it was established that he had loaned Rogers $7500. Apparently he also loaned him the $2000 he drew from the bank. He wrote Rogers a letter but never mailed it. "I'm just worried sick," he wrote, "over the thought I did not get the return of that money. It is making me a nervous wreck and disturbing my sleep. Perhaps my nephew, William Wimmer, should look after my interests . . . I feel I should let someone know who can look after Edith's interests." That, the police concluded, was enough to trigger the murder. Rogers was a short-tempered man. Once, when his wife went on a trip, he asked her to take their little dog along. When she refused, he roared, "You'll be sorry." She returned to find the dog dead of poison. Everything about the case was circumstantial, but it was enough to bring Rogers to trial on a charge of murder in the first degree. On September 25, 1954, he was convicted, with a recommendation of life imprisonment. His lawyers did not call a single witness.

On January 10, 1958, George Rogers died of a stroke in the New Jersey State Prison. His criminal record, kept on file there, revealed him as a sodomist, a man present at several suspicious fires. One of his hobbies was chemistry—in particular, explosives and incendiary compounds.

▄▄▄▄ ▄▄▄▄

The *Morro Castle* was nearly twenty-four years in the past, and not one newspaper made the connection between the fire that destroyed it and the possibility that George Rogers had started that fire. Only Lieutenant Doyle, brooding over the injustice of fate, was determined to prove his case. One day he was visited by a young writer named Thomas Gallagher, compiling the history of the *Morro Castle*. It was Gallagher who first sensed the possibility that Rogers had set the fire, based on the information compiled by Doyle. Subsequently he talked to Rogers at the state prison and asked him: "Did you start the *Morro Castle* fire?" Rogers did not deny it; he simply evaded an answer. His death left the case unsolved.

Did he start the fire? The only verdict has to be the Scotch verdict, "Not proven."

Rogers was a compulsive talker and a braggart. He was also a psychopath, very probably a pyromaniac. On his record, he was capable of starting the fire. But when? And how?

George Alagna, who perhaps knew him best, remembers Rogers as a recluse who divided his time almost totally between his bunk and the radio room, not even bothering to go ashore in Havana. He remembers, also, that radio operators were forbidden to go into the public rooms on the ship. Even in early morning, on the *Morro Castle*'s last cruise, those rooms were occupied by a certain number of convivial passengers. None of them ever remembered seeing him, nor did the watchmen on their half-hourly rounds. It would have taken a remarkably ingenious, remarkably lucky man to dart into the writing room, open the locker, insert an incendiary device, and disappear without being noticed. Neither Maki nor Alagna, the other two radio operators, noted his absence from their bunkroom at any time he was off duty on the final trip.

However, on occasion, it was his job to repair the loudspeakers on deck, just eighty feet forward of the writing room. Could he, perhaps, have sneaked in during one of these visits? Again, if he did, nobody saw him, and anybody who saw the hulking six-foot-two-inch Rogers would not be likely to forget him. And if he set the fire, what was his motive?

Doyle, according to his wife, told of a mysterious visit he had received from an unnamed passenger. Captain Wilmott, according to this passenger, told him that Rogers was "a vengeful man," and that he intended to have him fired when the ship reached port. Those were the same words Rogers used in reference to George Alagna, and they were corroborated by Captain Warms. Would Warms have lied, and why? What had Rogers done to infuriate the captain? Why did the captain not communicate his suspicions to Warms or to any other officer aboard? And why would Rogers set a fire in which he nearly was burned to death? Why did he stick by his transmitter instead of fleeing to safety?

Arson is one of the most baffling crimes. Arsonists almost always stay around to see the ugly results of their work. However, arsonists rarely are burned in the fires they set. What motivates them is a matter on which even psychiatrists cannot agree.

Fires aboard ship often are mystifying. There are dozens of them a year around the world, even in these times of modern fire-fighting equipment and sophisticated warning devices. Mystery leads to suspicion, and suspicion often leads to the firm conviction that some one criminal was to blame. That was the case with the *Morro Castle*. No fire, said all the ship's officers, could ever burn with such speed unless it was set. None of them, however, had ever experienced a fire of such lethal dimensions.

There were calmer voices expressing a more rational view— Chief Steward Bogert, who suspected the spontaneous combustion of newly cleaned blankets, stored in the writing room locker; the federal prosecutors, whose whole investigation was directed toward the same theory—either that or a short circuit in the tangled mass of wires that ran exposed through the back of the locker, setting one blanket to smoldering and gradually igniting them all. The locker did not, according to the testimony, become "a mass of flames" until its doors were opened and fresh air swept in. Its contents could have been smoldering for hours.

The theory of arson on the *Morro Castle* is such as to boggle the imagination. If all the speculation is put together, it suggests that the criminal first poisoned the captain so he would have a heart attack and then selected the writing room because it had no fire alarm. The distinguished maritime writer, William McFee,[3] came up with a more rational suggestion. Back of the locker, he pointed out, was the ship's one working funnel, carrying away the hot fumes from six engines. Suppose, said McFee, that the funnel had been overheated, that the steel around the funnel had been heating for hours, spreading out through the bulkheads and the steel decks, until at one moment the whole amidships section of the ship burst into flames? From the evidence, the fire was not only in the locker. It burst out almost simultaneously along the ceilings and walls of the writing room, and in little more than half an hour had consumed the whole ship.

[3] In *The Aspirin Age*, Simon & Schuster, 1949.

These are theories, and only theories. An incendiary device is far more romantic than a malfunction in the ship's funnel or spontaneous combustion in a pile of stored blankets.

"An act of God," the insurance companies called it, and that indefinite description best fits the *Morro Castle* disaster. Very possibly, if Captain Wilmott had lived, the fire could have been contained or its effects at least minimized. He was a man accustomed to emergencies, who directed every action of his crew. He might have organized the fire fighting efficiently enough to stop the spread of the flames. He might have directed the evacuation of the passengers more effectively, getting them to their lifeboat stations before the flames got there. He could have ordered the use of the crews' passageways, protected from fire by steel sheathing. Instead, the command was in the hands of William Warms, a man who followed orders and had never been required to make decisions on his own—an exhausted man, shattered by the tragedy of death, exhausted from long hours on duty, required to face an unprecedented emergency of staggering dimensions.

The questions never end. If Wilmott was poisoned, or given a violent emetic, as Officer Howard Hansen thinks, who did the poisoning? It could not have been Rogers, for he had no access to the ship's kitchen and was seen asleep in his bunk when a steward delivered Captain Wilmott his dinner on a tray. Who else aboard hated him this much?

Or was it a conspiracy, Rogers and an unnamed crony working together? If so, how could the conspirators be sure that Warms could not command his crew efficiently? He had never been tested in such an emergency, and Rogers barely knew the man. It is, like all other theories connected with the disaster, totally unprovable. The best answer maritime experts can give is that it was an act of God: The confusion, the panic, and the inefficiency that followed the fire were also, in their own fatal way, another act of God.

18

THE LAST WORD

Theodore E. Ferris never recovered from the shock of the *Morro Castle* disaster. In his offices downtown, he could hear the hoarse bellow of the *Morro Castle* as she cast off for the trip to Cuba once a week, and betweentimes the slightly higher blast of the whistle on the *Oriente,* her sister. Now the *Morro Castle*'s whistle was silent, and the *Oriente*'s whistle was an unhappy reminder that he had, somehow, failed. Something of Theodore Ferris had gone with the *Morro Castle.* At lunch with a friend [1] one day, he said: "I put everything I had into that ship. She had every known scheme of fire prevention and was adequately compartmented. A good, strong ship, broad of beam, and with everything modern. That took something out of me. Her total loss staggered me. I somehow felt as if I were to blame for the casualties. Maybe it was my fault. . . ."

Nor did William Francis Gibbs ever forget. He was the only American naval architect whose eminence rivaled Ferris's. Each man had completed designs for the superliner to be called the *United States.* Ferris was favored to win the competition, but what happened to the *Morro Castle* put him out of the running. Gibbs won, and the ship he built had the most modern fire-retarding materials and the most complete fire-extinguishing-detecting systems. Only the piano was built of wood, and that only because the noted piano-maker Theodore Steinway established that he could not build one of metal.

The Senate Commerce Committee, under Senator Royal S. Copeland of New York, drew up a 586-page report, calling for asbestos paneling, a minimum amount of wood, and a vastly enlarged sprinkler system. The House Commerce Committee abolished the antique regulation limiting a shipowner's liability in case of fire. Ten principal lessons learned from the fire have been incorporated into merchant marine safety regulations.

[1] Durward H. Primrose, editor of *Marine Journal.*

Interior walls must now be fire-retardant. Automatic fire alarms must be installed everywhere on a ship. Fire doors must be capable of being closed by remote control. Staircases must be totally enclosed and fitted with self-closing doors. Self-closing, smoke-stopping doors must divide all long corridors. Emergency generators must be carried aboard. Crews must be thoroughly trained in fire fighting. What to do in case of fire must be clearly spelled out for passengers and crew. All escape routes must be clearly indicated.

What helped feed the fire on the *Morro Castle* was layer after layer of paint on the superstructure of the ship. It can't happen that way again. Said a Coast Guard officer: "If we find a ship with too many layers of paint on her bulkheads, we make them scrape it off and paint it over just once." The fiery lessons taught by the *Morro Castle* ushered in a new era of safety on passenger liners flying the U.S. flag.

Not only the *Morro Castle* but the whole Atlantic, Gulf and West Indies line has vanished. The sturdy *Oriente,* as the *Thomas H. Barry,* carried troops throughout the Second World War, and then was broken into scrap. The liners *Monterey* and *Mexico* were sold to a Turkish line and may still be plying the Mediterranean. All other ships were sold to the highest bidder. On October 6, 1953, the stockholders of AGWI met in the public library at Eliot, Maine, to dissolve the company. It was hardly a disaster for them. They whacked up $7,749,000 in cash and securities.

There are still a few reminders. A dispatch to *The New York Times* ten years ago reported that the *Morro*'s whistle now calls workers to their jobs at a factory in a remote part of Pennsylvania. In the New York lobby of the American Institute of Marine Underwriters, a heavy ship's bell hangs from the wall. Beneath it is a plaque:

> S.S. *Morro Castle.* New York and Cuba Mail Steamship Co. Ward Line, charterers and operators. 11,500 gross tons, length 508 feet, breadth 70 feet, depth 39 feet. Built Newport News, Va., 1930. On a voyage from Havana to New York with 318 passengers and 231 crew, mail and general cargo. Caught fire at sea September 8, 1934, off the New Jersey coast. Drifted ashore at Asbury Park. Burned until Sept. 15, 1934. Loss of life, 94 passengers, 30 crew members. Hull and machinery a total loss to underwriters of $4,215,888. Cargo and indemnified losses were in excess of $1,500,000. Name

plate given by Kenneth Stephens in Memory of Chauncey E. Clark.[2]

Most of the time the bell is silent. Once in a long time some prankish young underwriter may swing the clapper, and a solemn clang rings out in the quiet offices. It is the last and most lasting artifact of a ship and an era.

[2] These figures cannot be verified, since the donor of the plaque is dead and did not preserve his records.

DECK PLANS OF THE LINER "MORRO CASTLE"

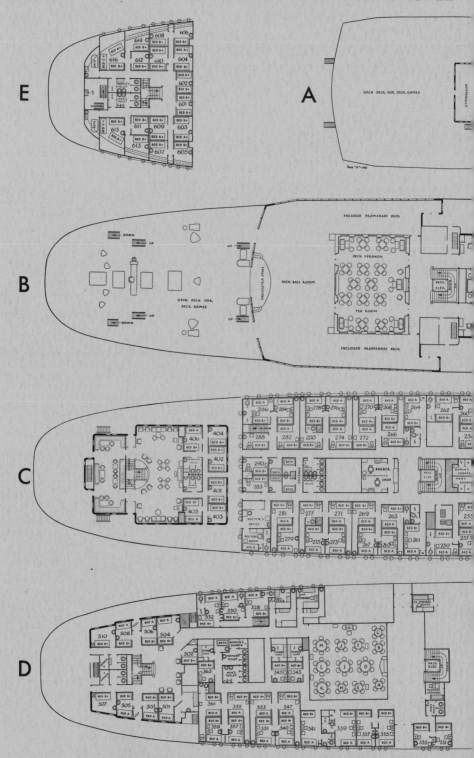